P9-CSB-337

Game Bird Carving

New Revised Edition

Game
Bird
Carving

Bruce Burk

Winchester Press

An Imprint of NEW CENTURY PUBLISHERS, INC.

All photographs, drawings, and carvings by the author.

Copyright © 1972 by Bruce Burk
Revised Edition © 1982 by Bruce Burk

All rights reserved. No part of this book may be used or
reproduced in any manner whatsoever without prior
written permission from the publisher except in the case of
brief quotations embodied in critical reviews and articles.
All inquiries should be addressed to New Century
Publishers, Inc., 220 Old New Brunswick Road, Piscataway,
New Jersey 08854.

Printing code
  23 24 25 26
Library of Congress Catalog Card Number: 82-62347

ISBN 0-8329-3591-3
Printed in the United States

Dedicated to

Wendell Gilley
Arnold Melbye
Lem and Steve Ward

Acknowledgments

I must first express my gratitude to my very good friend Wendell Gilley of Southwest Harbor, Maine, whose persuasion, and help, encouraged me to attempt this book on bird carving. His generosity, with not only his time but also his possessions, is impossible to repay.

I am also deeply indebted to those carvers, collectors, and other people interested in birds who, by their conversations and letters, have encouraged and aided me in this undertaking.

I wish to thank, as well, Jim Robertson of Woodland Hills, California, who gave me invaluable assistance in planning this book; Milt Weiler of Garden City, New York, who made helpful suggestions about the carving of working decoys; and Dr. Paul Johnsgard of Lincoln, Nebraska, who shared his extensive experience as a bird photographer.

My most sincere appreciation to Dr. Ken Stager and Jim Northern of the Los Angeles County Museum for their patience in supplying answers to my layman's questions and for permitting me unlimited use of the museum's large collection of skins and mounts.

The game bird dimensions presented in Chapter 11 are the result of a great deal of cooperation and effort given by Dr. Paul Johnsgard; Dave Hagerbaumer, Independence, Oregon; John Carter, Salem, Oregon; Gilbert Maggioni and Grainger McKoy, Beaufort, South Carolina; Wendell Gilley; Glen Smart, Bowie, Maryland; Tom Carlock, Fair Haven, New Jersey; Bruce Buckley, Costa Mesa, California; and others. These men deserve the credit for any benefits that this data may give to the carver. All shortcomings and errors are the sole responsibility of the author.

I would like to thank my two friends and hunting companions, Gene Mellon, Sherman Oaks, California, and Bill Bartha, Rosamond, California, for often and generously allowing me the lion's share of the bag so that I could obtain specimens needed for game bird carvings.

My thanks also to Frank Schultz, Saugus, California, who made all of the original black and white prints used in this book. His patience, cooperation, and excellent work are deeply appreciated.

Last, but by no means last in importance, I wish to thank my long-time secretary, Mrs. Virginia Garhardt, Hermosa Beach, California, for editing and proofreading the text of this book.

I would also like to give my sincere thanks for the kind and generous words I have received during the past nine years from many happy readers and users of the first edition of this book. Their thoughtfulness is deeply appreciated. Their suggestions and comments have been most helpful in planning this revised edition.

I would especially like to thank Ed and Esther Burns of St. Michaels, Maryland, for their suggestions and their answers to many questions I had about upgrading and updating *Game Bird Carving*.

B.B.
Grass Valley, California
April, 1982

CONTENTS

Introduction

Of today's many creative hobbies, wood carving, realistic bird carving particularly, is one of the most fascinating and rewarding. Not only does the carver express himself in three dimensions by sculpturing the wood to the naturally graceful lines of the bird, he also finds great challenge and satisfaction in attempting to duplicate with paint and brush the complexity and elusive coloring of the bird's plumage. Also, this absorbing and satisfying hobby almost immediately leads to additional interests and activities.

Once the beginner starts carving birds, he actually sees these wonderful creatures for the first time. He finds it impossible not to observe in great detail every bird he chances upon. By firsthand observation and by study, he starts learning more and more about their habits and soon acquires a true appreciation of their incredible beauty, their tremendous power and endurance, their marvelous adaptability on the ground, in the air, and, in the case of waterfowl, on and under the water. With this knowledge, it is almost impossible not to become interested in the conservation of wildlife and preservation of habitats.

Quite often the carver, after the experience gained from painting bird carvings, tries his hand at canvas painting and opens the door to another exciting and rewarding pastime.

In many cases, he becomes interested in amateur photography, if only to take pictures of his carvings. This interest easily leads to photographing actual birds, the results of which are invaluable to the carver for detail and natural shape, to say nothing of the enjoyment he experiences in perfecting his photographic skills.

A smaller number of bird carvers will discover at least one more fringe interest: preservation of specimens, or taxidermy. When most game birds are prepared for the table, the plumage is discarded; with little effort, this beauty can be saved for many years and can provide invaluable first-hand information.

The popularity of bird carving as a hobby or craft has increased tremendously during the past few years. This surge, without a doubt, has been largely due to publications such as Wendell Gilley's book, *The Art of Bird Carving*, Hal Sorenson's quarterly magazine and annual, *Decoy Collector's Guide*, the National Woodcarvers Association's bimonthly, *Chip Chats*, Byron and Maureen Cheever's quarterly, *North American Decoys*, William Tawes' book, *Creative Bird Carving*, and others. The revival of competitive decoy and bird carving contests and the widespread interest in antique decoy collecting have also contributed greatly.

Since 1965, when the first national bird carving exhibit was originated by Dr. Dan Gibson of Chestertown, Maryland, rapid strides have been made in realistic bird carving techniques. Earlier techniques produced carvings that were generally stiff and hard in appearance and lacked the texture and detail so necessary for imparting the feeling of softness and realism. Painting, in most cases, was amateurish and failed to capture the delicate details of the bird's plumage. As a result of the Chestertown exhibits and their informal competition, carvers of this era were exposed to, and inspired by, the work of others. They started improving their techniques and began originating new ones. Many other national and regional exhibits and contests were organized and held at regular intervals. These shows have been largely responsible for the continual improvement in the state of the art. What began as a craft for utilitarian purposes had blossomed into a full-fledged American art form. Its practical ancestry in the carving of decoys, however, was still very much evident.

In the early 1970's, the individual feathering technique, in which numerous individual feathers are painstakingly shaped and detailed and assembled accurately in their proper sequence and position, was developed. By use of these individual feathers, lifelike representation of the actual bird, which previously had been almost unobtainable with carved feathers, became a reality. The feeling of motion was greatly enhanced by the use of thin, but strong, and completely separated flight and tail feathers. Some of these carvings were breathtaking in form, daring in position, and exquisite in detail — masterpieces that had to be seen to be fully appreciated.

During this period, carvers also began to complement their carvings with more elaborate and beautiful bases, usually embellished with handmade, realistic plant and animal life to reflect the natural habitat of the bird being depicted. Realistic bird carving as a respected art had finally come into its own, and any connection to its decoy parentage had been completely severed. Unfortunately, many shows and exhibits are still decoy-oriented, although some of the better ones are now putting more and more emphasis and prize money on fine, decorative pieces.

There are many publications available today that provide a wealth of information for the bird carver. However, one of the great obstacles the carver of realistic birds still faces is the difficulty of obtaining accurate, detailed structural information on the particular bird he is attempting to depict. The scarcity of published data primarily prompted the writing of this book. Hopefully, the information assembled here will benefit both the rank amateur and the professional bird-carver.

A secondary motivation is to pass on to the amateur carver some of the ways a good carving can be produced. However, no claim is made that the various procedures described here are the best ways to ge+ the job done. I am sure that by the time this book is published, I myself will have discarded some of these methods for better ones. A successful carver should always be on the lookout for newer, better techniques and should never give up trying to improve his work.

The ultimate purpose of this book is to help the carver-artist to plan and to produce realistic carvings, as much like the birds they represent as possible. I share with many carvers and collectors the opinion that for man to attempt interpretations and changes in the already graceful forms and exquisite coloring of birds is trying to improve upon perfection itself.

A firm believer in the old adage regarding pictures versus words, I have used graphics as the primary means of conveying information. The drawings included of the various birds and the photographs of the carvings should be considered only as aids; the birds themselves and actual bird photographs are what the carver should strive to duplicate. In this way the beginner will develop his own style, and the mistakes he makes will be his own, not a copy of someone else's.

I sincerely believe that hard work, study, and most important, *stick-to-it-iveness* can replace so-called inherent talent, if such an attribute exists in man. The only way the novice can learn bird carving is by doing — not just once or twice, but again and again — each time trying to improve the imperfections of the preceding carving. If this procedure is conscientiously followed, the aspiring bird-carver who feels he was endowed with little or no natural carving ability will soon hear his friends saying, "I sure wish I had your talent!"

Game Bird Carving

PART I

Getting Started

This book explains the techniques of realistic game bird carving. The methods and information covered here aim at helping the carver produce carvings that look as much like the birds they are supposed to represent as possible – not only in shape but also in detail and color.

Depending on the degree of realism desired, the bird carving can be as simple or as complex as the individual carver wishes. Bird carving is an ideal hobby because the beginner can experience a great deal of satisfaction from the results of his very first effort; and regardless of the number of carvings he does or the degree of perfection he attains, he will thrill to the challenge each new project presents: coming just a little closer to duplicating the beauty and perfection of nature.

Although a large portion of this book covers information the author hopes will help the serious carver to achieve advanced amateur or professional status, Part I is devoted to the beginner who has never attempted carving or painting. In order to give him a chance to make a start without reading endless pages and without becoming involved in making drawings and getting into other more complicated details, several carving projects, complete with drawings and instructions, have been included in Chapter 1. As soon as the beginner has developed some confidence in his carving ability, he should either start making his own drawings or at least introduce some changes to drawings not his own. This is the only way he can project originality into his carvings and develop his own style. Much more on this important subject will be covered in Part II.

1

Carving for Beginners

Bird carving is not nearly as difficult as most people anticipate. However, the one and only way the aspiring bird-carver can find this out is to take a block of wood and a knife and start to carve. The most important thing is to start – *now*!

CARVING WOODS

Basswood, or linden, is probably the most popular and the best wood today for realistic bird carving. The hardness of this wood varies considerably, and it is important to select the softest pieces available. Basswood, especially in thicker pieces, is often difficult to obtain, but depending on the carver's location, white pine, sugar pine, or white cedar can usually be obtained and substituted with good results. Unfortunately, good-quality seasoned wood of these species is becoming scarcer and prices have increased accordingly.

Jelutong, a wood imported from Malaysia, is now being substituted by some patternmakers for sugar pine. Jelutong is a light-colored wood, stable (if properly cured), medium-grained, free from pitch, and easily worked. Compared to basswood, it has a somewhat coarser grain and is not quite as strong. However, it is more easily carved, sands cleaner, receives burning detail better, and probably has a more consistent quality than basswood. Jelutong has defects called latex pockets, which resemble blades of marsh grass about ¼ to ⅜ inches wide and approximately ¹⁄₃₂ inch thick growing through the tree. These bladelike pieces of latex can be removed easily from the wood and the remaining holes filled with little trouble.

Spare no effort in selecting good, dry wood, free from pitch and checks and reasonably straight-grained and clear. When weighed against the many hours spent on a carving, the small amount of money saved by buying inferior wood is a very poor economy.

CARVING TOOLS

A fine workshop with a large collection of chisels, gouges, drawknives, spokeshaves, rifflers, a band saw, and other power tools may be desirable, but it is certainly not necessary for the beginner to have all of this equipment or to spend much money in order to get started. An abundance of fine, expensive tools are very impressive to admire and to show to friends, but they will not produce beautiful carvings by themselves. Fancy tools can only supplement, not replace, ingenuity, ambition, perseverance, practice, study, and hard work. There is no question that a well-balanced collection of hand and power tools will aid the beginner in his first attempts at carving. However, there is a very strong tendency during these days of affluence for the rankest amateur to be convinced that he must have the very best, the most professional equipment, before he can even think of starting out. As a result of this attitude, the beginner who is short of cash may not try to start out at all; or if the money is available, he will very likely end up with equipment that later proves to have very little practical use. Begin with simple tools and, as your interest and skill progress, add to your collection accordingly, taking the time to find the tools that most closely meet your personal requirements.

Actually, the first few carvings shown here can be accomplished with nothing more than a sharp knife, a piece of sandpaper, and some glue, although it is not suggested that the beginner start out with just these bare necessities. A list of tools has been included here as a guide; other tools will be mentioned in subsequent parts of this book as the aspiring carver progresses into more advanced carvings. Some of the tools suggested now may not be of the very best quality, but they will get the job done until the beginner's interest and ability develop to the point where he is sure that he wants to invest in more expensive tools. He should then buy the very best quality tools that he can afford.

In addition to the equipment listed below, a workbench or a fairly sturdy table upon which to work is most desirable. It need not be anywhere near as elaborate as the one shown (Fig. 1-3), but it should have some storage space for tools. An attached vise, either a woodworker's or metalworker's, is almost a necessity.

Practical Tools for the Beginner

Knife, either pocket or replaceable blade (Fig. 1-1)
Coping saw and fine blades
Set of inexpensive carving chisels, to be replaced eventually with better-quality chisels (Fig. 1-2)
Hand drill with a few assorted drills
Drawknife (6- to 10-inch blade)
Rasps (Stanley Surform half-round and round)
C-clamp, 6-inch approximately (if vise is not available)
Whetstone
Garnet paper (0, 2/0, 3/0, 4/0, and 6/0)
Sanding block
Glue (Willhold, Elmer's, etc.)
Tube or can of Plastic Wood (or a similar product)
(It is assumed that the beginner already has the commonly used home-maintenance tools such as a hammer, screwdriver, pliers, handsaw, etc.)

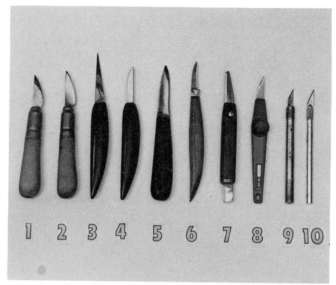

1-1

CARE OF TOOLS

To do their job, the carver's hand and power tools must be properly maintained. As a number of publications (some listed in the bibliography) deal extensively with the care and sharpening of tools, this matter will not be covered here. This should in no way minimize the importance of this very necessary part of wood carving. The beginner should study the publications on tool care and become thoroughly familiar, through actual practice, with the techniques described. In the case of power tools, the manufacturer supplies operating and maintenance instructions with each new tool sold. Should the carver buy used equipment, these manuals are usually available free from the manufacturer upon request.

1-2

USE OF THE KNIFE

There are many ways to remove the excess wood from a carving. The pocketknife or the replaceable-blade knife is the tool usually used by the beginner for carving.

To cut at right angles to the wood, the knife is normally held in a manner similar to that of holding a pencil and is pulled toward the body (Fig. 1-4). Unless the depth of cut desired is quite shallow, considerable downward and pulling forces are necessary. The knife is generally under control

1-1 *Knives. (1, 2) Nick Purdo knives; (3, 4) Knotts knives; (5) Wendell Gilley knife; (6) Dastra Tools; (7) Leichtung Inc.; (8) Stanley; (9, 10) Exacto. (See Appendix.)*

1-2 *Inexpensive knives, gouges, and chisels. X-acto and Japanese-made twelve-piece carving set.*

1-3 *Some type of workbench is almost a necessity.*

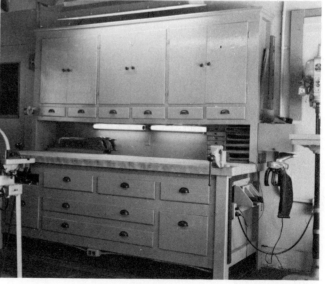

1-3

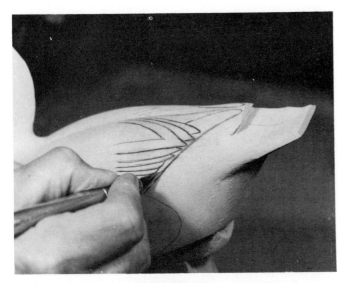

1-4

1-5

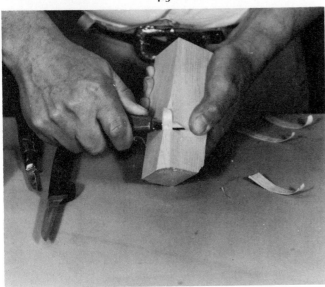

1-6

when used in this manner. One exception occurs when the cut is made to an edge and off the wood. As the downward and pulling forces applied to the knife are no longer resisted by the wood, the knife is out of control and dangerous. It is usually advisable to make the cut as it comes off the carving into a scrap piece of wood held by the other hand with the fingers out of the way (Fig. 1-5). Using the knife to cut at right angles to the wood is useful for individual feather carving where a cut is made outlining each feather. It is also useful for cutting out the crossed primaries, in carving the bill, and in many other situations.

The knife can also be pulled or pushed with the blade held at a small angle to the surface, so that the wood is cut and removed in a manner similar to wood planing. This method is, of course, commonly known as whittling. A carver using this procedure should give special consideration to control, ease of wood removal, and safety.

Whittling can be done in several ways, three of which are described here. It is suggested that the beginner take some scrap pieces of wood and experiment with these techniques, which are described below for a right-handed person. Reverse the instructions if you are left-handed.

First, try holding the block in the left hand and whittling wood off by moving the knife, held by the closed fist of the right hand, away from the body (Fig. 1-6). It will soon be apparent that it is difficult to control the length and depth of the cut. It will also be obvious that the knife, when no longer removing wood, is difficult to stop, and at this point is out of control and can be very dangerous. This technique is useful when fairly large amounts of wood are to be removed, as when roughing down the body of the carving. If the knife is used in this manner, it is advisable to rest the carving against a scrap piece of wood to arrest the movement of the knife as it comes off the carving.

Next, try holding the block again in the left hand, but this time grasp the knife (with its cutting edge pointed toward the body) by the first and second joints of the fingers of the right hand. Stretch the thumb of the right hand so that it rests against or near the end of the block nearest the body. Now, cut with the knife toward the thumb, using the finger muscles to supply the force in a motion similar to that of closing the hand (Fig. 1-7). Actually, this method is very natural and is exactly like paring a potato. Although the knife is moving toward the thumb, all the power is supplied by the fingers, and there is very little danger of cutting the thumb. This method provides excellent control, not only of the depth, but also of the length of the cut.

The third method of whittling involves holding the block by the left hand and the knife by the four fingers and thumb of the right hand. This time the cutting edge is pointed away from the body. The power is supplied by the thumb muscles of the left hand in the pushing motion (Fig. 1-8). Here, again, the knife and the cut are under good control. This method

1-4 *Cutting at right angles to the wood.*

1-5 *Cutting off the edge into a scrap piece of wood.*

1-6 *Whittling. Force is supplied by the arm muscles.*

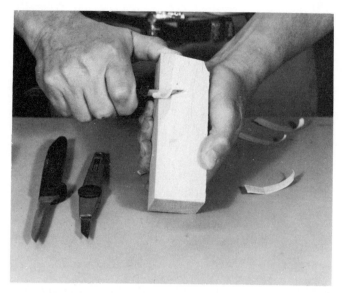

1-7 *Whittling. Force is supplied by the fingers.*

of whittling works especially well when the carving is held rigidly by a jig or vise, leaving both hands free to remove the wood.

Regardless of the method used, it is essential for good control that the knife edge cut down at a small angle to the grain of the wood. When the knife or any other sharp cutting tool is used in this manner, the wood is cut cleanly and there is no tendency for the wood to split or tear. This is commonly called, somewhat inaccurately, "cutting with the grain" (Fig. 1-9). If the cut is made angling up toward the grain, or even parallel to the grain, the wood will be split rather than cut. This is called "cutting against the grain," again not an accurate description. Sometimes, when a large amount of wood must be removed, it is desirable to cut up against or parallel to the grain and split off fairly large pieces. When this is done, considerable care must be exercised to prevent removing too much wood.

As the beginner progresses, the use of other carving tools will be discussed.

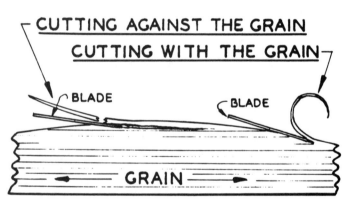

1-9 *Cutting with and against the grain.*

CARVING A HALF-BODY MALLARD DRAKE DECOY
(See Figure I-1, page 233.)

A half-body mallard drake decoy has been chosen for the first carving project. This is one of the simplest carvings, for problems connected with obtaining symmetry, both in carving and painting, are eliminated. Also, a mallard drake is a good subject for the first attempt at painting.

Three pieces of wood, a block 1¾ × 2¼ × 8 inches for the body, a piece ½ × 2¼ × 3 inches for the head, and a piece ¼ × ⅜ × 6¼ inches for the keel, are required. If cutting the material to size presents a problem, take the wood to a lumberyard or a cabinet shop and have the pieces ripped to size on a table saw. Although an inexpensive set of chisels

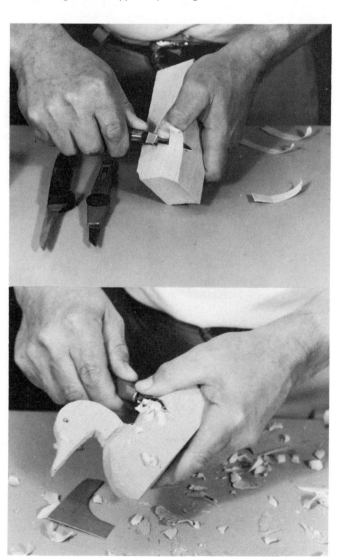

1-8 *Whittling. Force is supplied mainly by the thumb muscles of the left hand.*

1-10 *Mallard drake decoy.* ▶

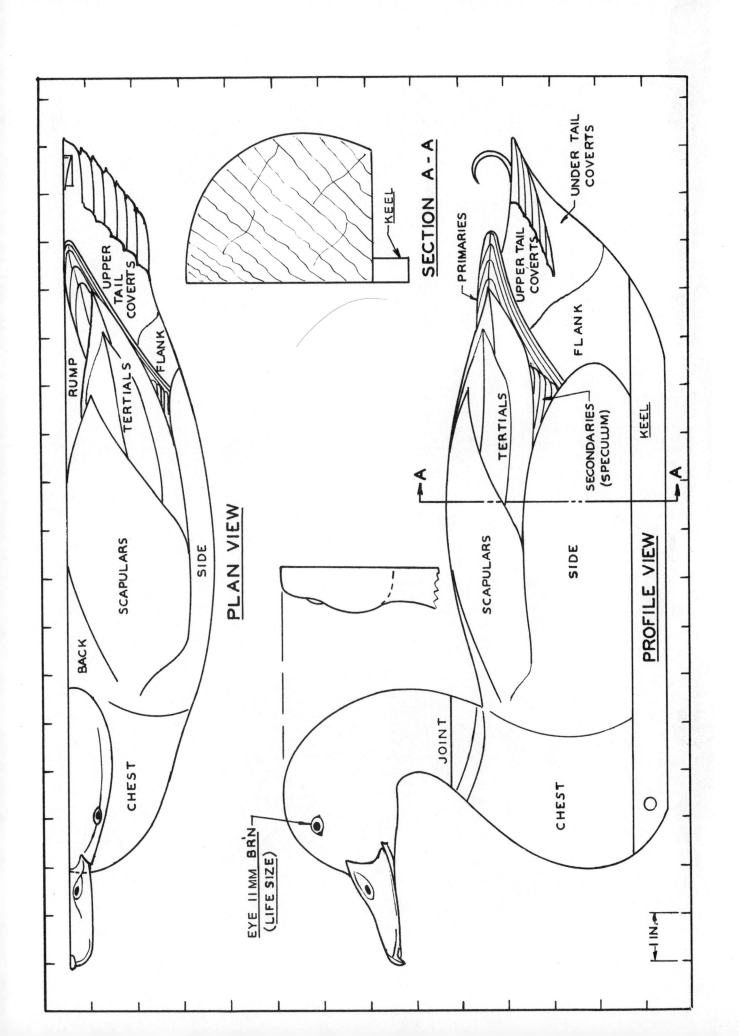

PLAN VIEW

RUMP

UPPER
TAIL
COVERTS

TERTIALS

FLANK

SCAPULARS

SIDE

BACK

CHEST

SECTION A-A

KEEL

PRIMARIES

UNDER TAIL
COVERTS

UPPER TAIL
COVERTS

FLANK

TERTIALS

SECONDARIES
(SPECULUM)

KEEL

A

A

SCAPULARS

SIDE

CHEST

JOINT

CHEST

PROFILE VIEW

EYE 11MM BR'N
(LIFE SIZE)

1 IN.

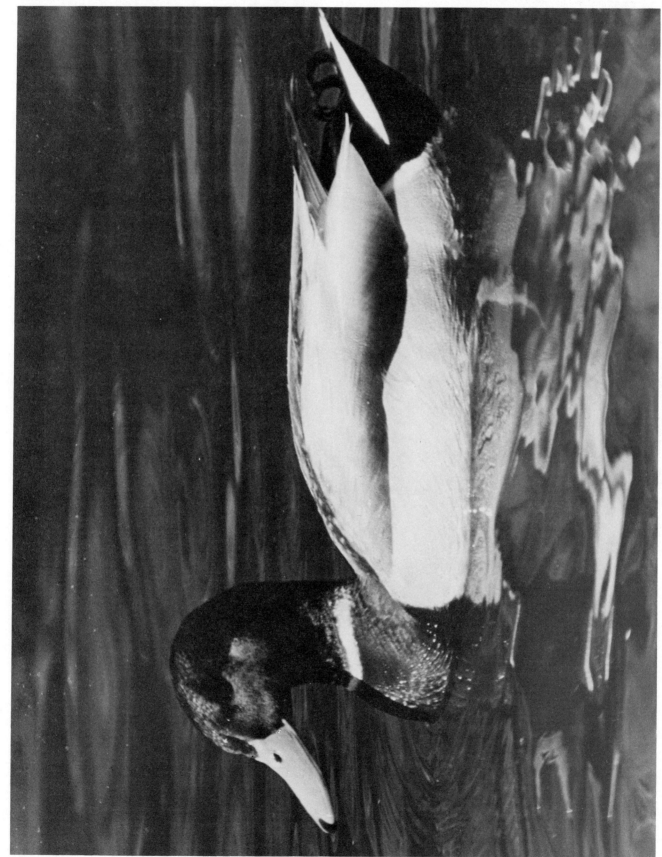

1-11 Common mallard drake.

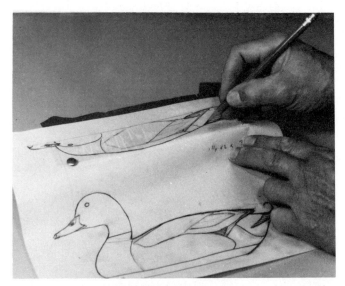

1-12 *Trace plan view to top of body block.*

1-15 *Sawed-out body showing removed parts.*

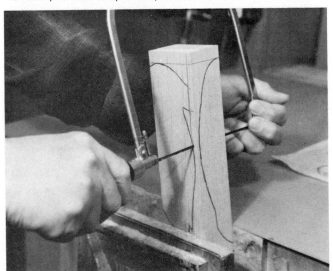

1-13 *Saw out the profile view with a coping saw.*

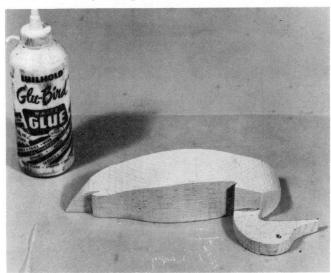

1-16 *Lay parts on waxed paper and glue head to body.*

1-14 *Reattach sawed off piece bearing plan view of body.*

would be helpful, about the only tools required are a coping saw and a knife. Other materials required include a 6-mm brown eye, some sandpaper (2/0 and 4/0), white glue, Plastic Wood, and a small piece of thin aluminum or other metal for the curled tail feather.

Figure 1-10 as printed is one-half life size, a good scale for the beginner's debut. First, make a tracing of the profile and plan view, also the cross-sectional view, directly from the drawing. After the tracing is completed, locate the profile view on the side of the body block and transfer the drawing to the block by means of carbon paper. Locate the plan view on the top of the body block, properly aligned with the profile view, and transfer it to the block in a similar manner (Fig. 1-12). Transfer the head drawing to the ½-inch-thick piece of wood, locating the head so that the bill is parallel to the grain.

Using the coping saw, carefully cut out the block to the the profile-view layout (Fig. 1-13). Reattach the sawed-off piece (which bears the plan view) to the body with small

1-17 *Start wood removal from midsection.*

1-19 *Sand carving occasionally to check overall progress.*

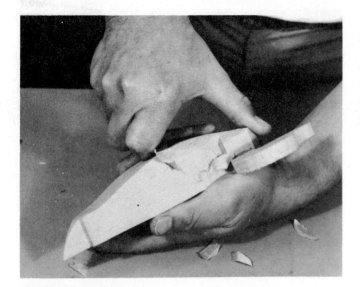

1-18 *Use the template to check body cross-sectional shape.*

1-20 *Carve the chest by rounding off this area.*

nails placed so that they will not interfere with the plan-view cut (Fig. 1-14), which is accomplished next. After the body is sawed to shape, saw out the head.

Place the sawed-out body on a piece of waxed paper laid upon a flat surface and glue the head in place (Fig. 1-16). While the glue is setting, transfer the cross-sectional view to a piece of cardboard or plastic and cut out as shown (Fig. 1-18). A cross-sectional template is not actually necessary when doing a carving that is not symmetrical, but its use provides good experience in working accurately to a predetermined shape.

Before starting carving operations, the beginner should make every attempt to study all available photographs of the bird being carved and, if at all possible, to study a live bird. Note particularly the cross-sectional shape of the head and body; the position and shape of the scapulars, tertials, and primaries; and the shape and position of the tail feathers and their coverts.

1-21 *Rough-carve the overall shape of the tertials and primaries.*

1-22 *Shape the undertail coverts and tail.*

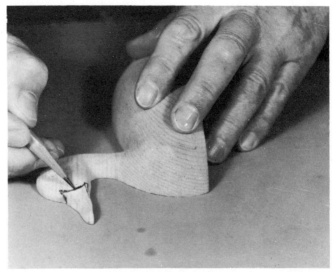

1-25 *Lay out intersection of the bill and the head.*

1-23 *Lay out and cut bill to the correct width.*

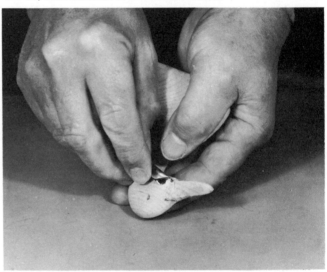

1-26 *Carefully carve the cheek to shape.*

1-24 *Reduce width of the head above the eye.*

Start by removing wood from the body near the midsection (Fig. 1-17), checking the body shape occasionally with the template to avoid removing too much wood. Make small, unhurried cuts with the grain, which will require turning the carving end-for-end from time to time. Sand the body at intervals as the carving progresses to obtain a better idea of the overall shape (Fig. 1-19). When the body shape matches the template, start removing wood from the chest (Fig. 1-20) and back areas (Fig. 1-21) until the desired shape is approached. Continue the body carving by shaping the flanks, under tail coverts, and bottom of the tail (Fig. 1-22).

Next, lay out the width and extent of the bill and remove the wood down to this line (Fig. 1-23). Shape the head and neck roughly, noting that the top part of the head, above the eye, is much narrower than the cheek area (Fig. 1-24). Lay out the approximate intersection of the cheek and bill (Fig. 1-25), carve the forward part of the cheek down to this line (Fig. 1-26), and round off the throat area (Fig. 1-27). Refer

1-27 *Wrap sandpaper around dowel for sanding throat area.*

1-28 *Carve as much bill detail as possible.*

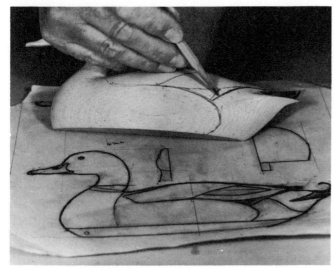

1-29 *Lay out the feather detail on the body.*

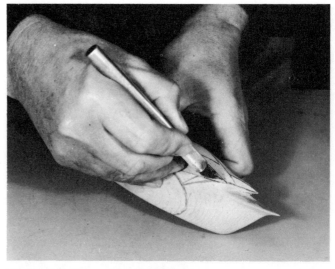

1-30 *Cut along the rear edge of the primaries.*

1-31 *Remove the wood from behind the primaries.*

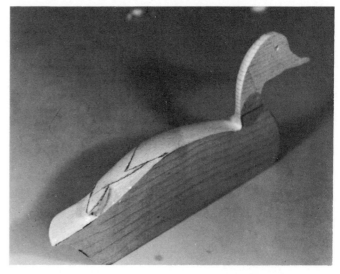

1-32 *Carve the forward side of the primaries and the rump area.*

12 ● *CARVING FOR BEGINNERS*

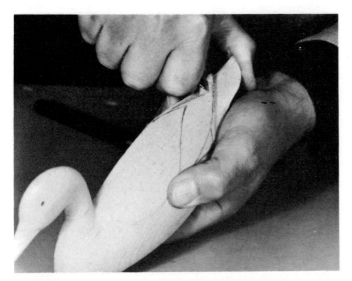

1-33 *Delineate the primaries by carving down the upper surface.*

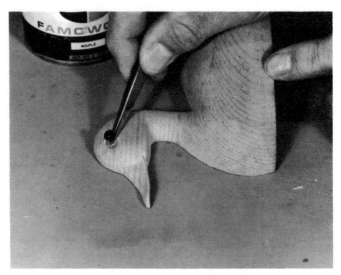

1-36 *Drill hole and install eye with Plastic Wood.*

1-34 *Carve the scapulars until they are prominent.*

1-35 *Locate and glue the curled tail feather in place.*

to the photographs of the mallard drake bill in Chapter 13 and carve the bill, incorporating as much detail as possible (Fig. 1-28).

Lay out the folded primaries as they rest over the flank and upper tail coverts. Also lay out the scapulars, tertials, and the outline of the extent of the side feathers (Fig. 1-29). Make a cut along the edges of the primaries and remove the wood in this area until the primaries stand out (Figs. 1-30, 31, 32). Carefully remove the wood from the rump and underneath the tips of the primaries. Make cuts around the outlines of the scapulars, tertials, and the speculum and remove the necessary wood to make them prominent (Fig. 1-34). Smooth off the rump, upper tail coverts, and the top of the tail. The individual primary feathers and the individual tail feathers may be carved or painted in, depending on the carver's ability and desires.

Cut the curled tail feather from a small piece of thin aluminum or other metal and bend to shape. Remove a small amount of wood the width and thickness of the metal and glue the simulated feather in place (Fig. 1-35).

Cut the keel to shape and glue it to the body using waxed paper in a manner similar to when gluing the head in place.

Sand the entire carving with 4/0 sandpaper until all toolmarks are removed.

Drill a hole of the proper diameter for the glass eye. (If a drill is not available, the hole can be made with a knife or small gouge.) Partially fill the hole with Plastic Wood and insert the eye to the proper depth (Fig. 1-36). After the Plastic Wood has dried, carefully scrape away the excess material until the eye has a natural shape. Sand the Plastic Wood around the eye until it is smooth, taking care that the sandpaper does not scratch the glass eye.

The beginner should now look at his creation with a critical eye. A mental note for future use should be made of any area where the carving could be bettered. If several areas need improvement, it would be wise to do another mallard drake carving and attempt to correct these imperfections.

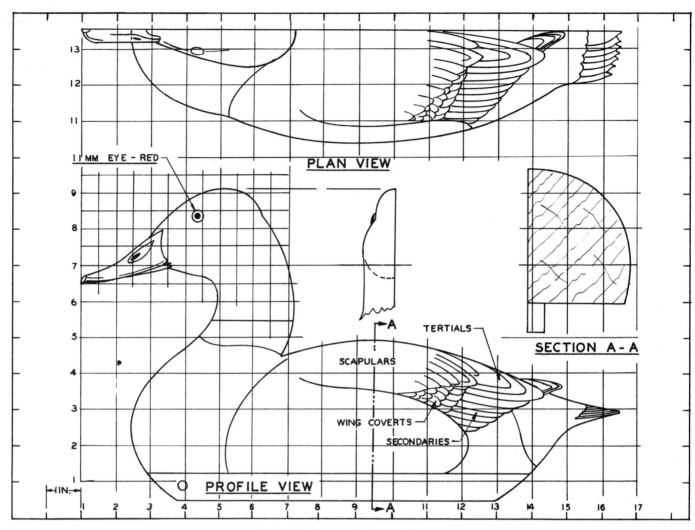

1-37 *Half-body canvasback drake decoy.*

ENLARGING OR REDUCING DRAWINGS

All of the drawings for carving projects in this book have marginal marks at intervals that represent one inch on the life-size bird. In most cases, depending upon the scale the carver wishes to use, it will be necessary either to enlarge or to reduce the printed drawing accordingly. One of the simplest ways to make this adjustment is by means of squares. First, connect the corresponding marks on the printed drawings in both the horizontal and vertical directions. Starting from the lower left-hand corner, assign numbers to both the horizontal and vertical lines as shown in Figure 1-37.

To make a life-size carving, make a layout composed of horizontal and vertical lines forming one-inch squares. Number the lines exactly the same as the lines on the smaller drawing. The life-size drawing is now easily made freehand by intersecting the numbered lines in the same manner as those on the drawing being enlarged. In areas such as the head and bill, where more accuracy is required, it is often advantageous to use smaller squares (Fig. 1-38).

If a drawing three-fourths life size is required, the layout is then made up of lines forming ¾-inch squares.

Suppose that the carver wishes to make a miniature carving of a canvasback drake with a body length of four inches. The life-size body length of the canvasback drake is approximately 14 inches. The size of the squares for the drawing of the miniature carving would then be 4/14 × 1.0 (size of squares on the life-size drawing) = .28, or ⁹⁄₃₂ inches.

HOLDING FIXTURES

Before starting the next project, a very useful homemade tool, the holding fixture, will be introduced. A holding fixture does the work of a third hand. It is simply a rigid support that can be easily attached by means of woodscrews to the carving. The fixture is in turn attached to the workbench or table by a vise or clamp.

Simple holding fixtures can reduce carving time and effort considerably and can actually improve the quality of

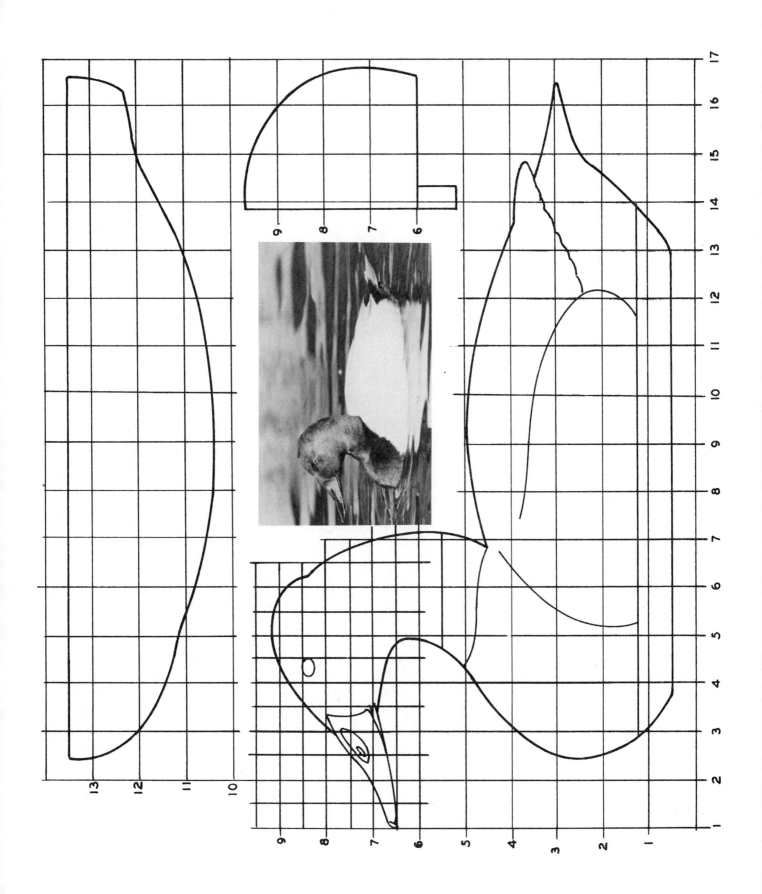

1-38 Canvasback drake drawing enlarged to one-half life size.

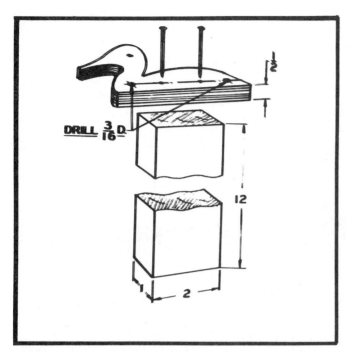

1-39 Holding fixture for half-body decoys.

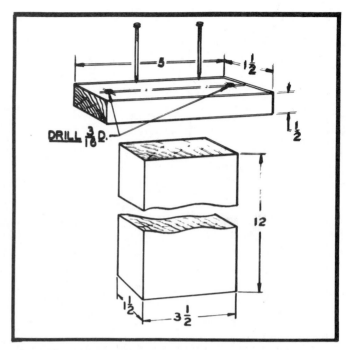

1-42 Holding fixture for full-body decoy.

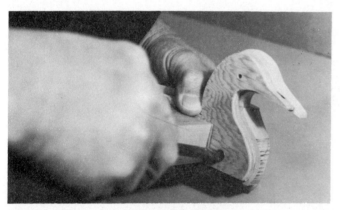

1-40 The carving is attached with woodscrews.

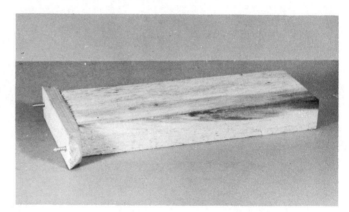

1-43 Completed holding fixture for full-body decoy.

1-41 Half-body decoys installed on holding fixture.

the carving by freeing both hands for guiding the wood-removing tool. In addition, a much greater selection of carving tools can be utilized when both hands are unhampered and when the block is rigidly held by the fixture. Furthermore, the larger the carving, the more important the holding fixture, for more wood removal is entailed. It is strongly recommended that the beginner take the time to make suitable holding fixtures for his carvings — they will pay for themselves many times over.

The construction of a simple fixture for holding a half-body decoy is shown in Figures 1-39, 40, and 41. A similar fixture for holding a full-body decoy is shown in Figures 1-42 and 43. The dimensions given in these drawings are only approximate and can be altered to fit different-size carvings or to permit the use of available scrap pieces of wood. Epoxy adhesive should be used to join the two pieces, for most ordinary glues and cements are not very effective in adhering to the end grain of wood. Other holding fixtures will be described and shown in Chapter 6.

USE OF OTHER CARVING TOOLS

The drawknife, Stanley Surform rasps, and the spokeshave are excellent tools for removing the wood down to the approximate final shape and are much more efficient and less tiring to use than a knife. Both hands are required to use these tools effectively; therefore, a holding fixture must be employed.

Drawknives are available with blades approximately six, eight, ten, and twelve inches long. (Refer to the Appendix for tool suppliers.) For roughing down the smaller-scale carvings, the six-inch blade is preferred. For larger, life-size carvings, the eight- or ten-inch blade can be used to advantage. Drawknives are normally pulled toward the body, with the blade held at a small angle to the surface (Fig. 1-45). Rather than turning the carving end-for-end so that the cut can be made with the grain, it is sometimes easier to reverse the tool and make the cut by pushing the drawknife away from the body (Fig. 1-46). Controlling the depth of cut with the drawknife is a little tricky, so its use should be limited to roughing operations only.

Once the carving has been cut down to its approximate rough shape, use a tool whose depth of cut can be more accurately controlled. The Stanley Surform rasp is excellent for removing wood safely down to the final shape. These fine rasps were introduced a number of years ago by Stanley Tools. They are made from very thin, hardened and tempered Sheffield steel and provide constant depth of cut, predetermined by design, which makes it possible to remove wood easily and quite safely from a surface that is curved in both directions, a difficult operation by almost any other means except sandpapering. In construction and manner of cutting, they are very similar to a kitchen grater. The many formed and sharpened teeth act as tiny wood planes, and each has an opening for the shavings to pass through, thereby eliminating clogging and assuring a clean cut with every stroke.

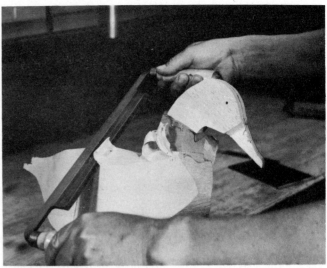
1-45 *Use drawknife to rough out the body.*

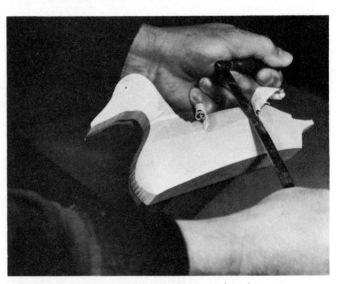
1-46 *The drawknife can also be pushed with good results.*

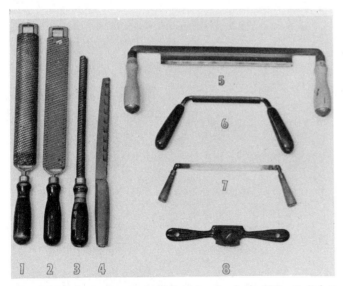
1-44 *(1-4, Stanley Surform rasps; (5) Greenlee drawknife; (6) Knotts Knives drawknife; (7) homemade drawknife; (8) spokeshave. (See Appendix.)*

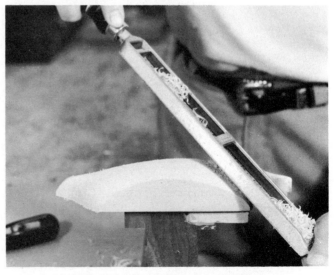
1-47 *Using the half-round Surform rasp to shape the chest.*

1-48 *The round Surform rasp is useful for shaping many hard-to-get-at spots.*

1-49 *Both the flat and half-round Surform rasps can be pulled effectively.*

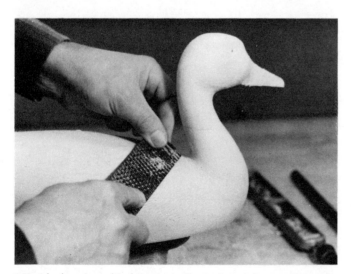

1-50 *A broken piece of Surform rasp is effective in removing wood from tight places.*

These rasps, like the conventional solid rasps, are normally pushed (Figs. 1-47, 48). However, if the direction of the grain permits, the author prefers to pull the rasp toward the body, with a motion similar to that used with the drawknife (Fig. 1-49). When the Surform rasp is used in this manner, the force required to remove the wood is more evenly divided between the arms and can be applied with less fatigue than when pushing. The Surform rasps are available in three basic shapes: flat, half-round, and round. The flat-rasp probably is the least used for bird carving; however, an unmounted flat Surform rasp (or a broken piece) is useful for removing wood in tight places (Fig. 1-50).

The spokeshave is very similar to the wood plane, except that its shorter base permits the tool to cut on a curved surface. The spokeshave is normally pushed by two handles located on either side of the blade. The depth of cut is determined by the exposed amount of blade, which is adjustable in a manner similar to that of a wood plane. The author prefers using Surform rasps rather than the spokeshave, mainly because the Surform rasps are more easily controlled and will cut end grain somewhat better than a spokeshave. This is strictly a personal preference, however, and not shared by all carvers.

OTHER HALF-BODY DECOY PROJECTS

Plans and photographs for two other half-body decoy projects — cinnamon teal and hooded mergansers — are included in this section. (Also see Figs. 1-37 and 2-49 for half-body canvasback drake decoy.) Actually, any of the full-body decoy drawings shown in this chapter and also in Chapter 8 can easily be adapted and used as half-body decoys. Half-body decoy drawings can also be used for full-body decoy carvings.

The half-body decoys featured here may be carved in the manner described earlier for the half-body mallard drake decoy. If a holding fixture, such as the one shown on page 16, is available, the easier and faster methods for removing excess wood discussed previously can now be used.

1-52 *Cinnamon teal. (See Figures N-1 and N-2, page 238.)* ▶

1-51 *Male cinnamon teal.*

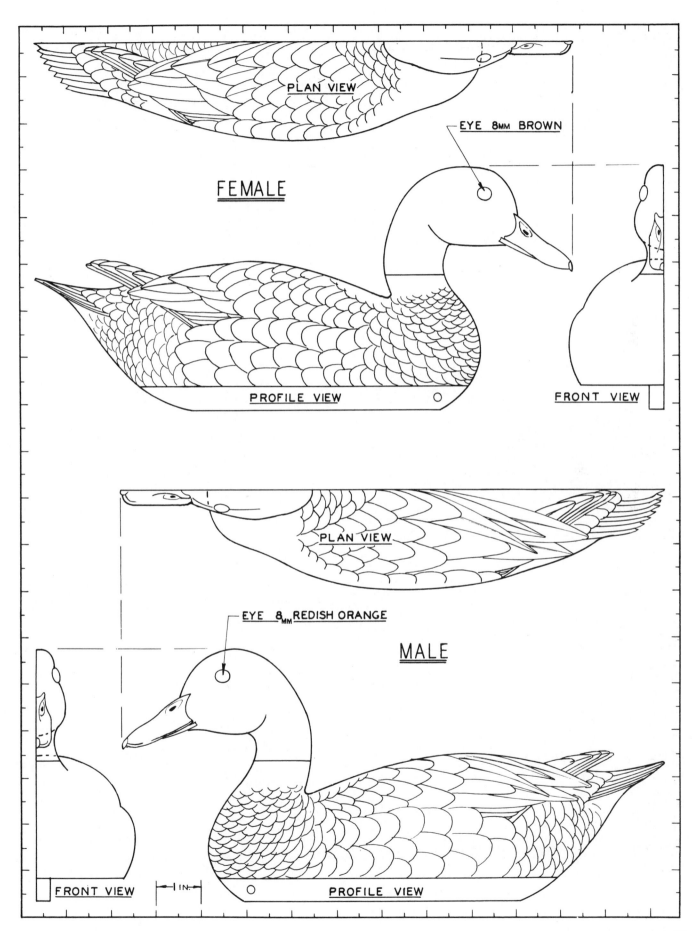

PLAN VIEW

EYE 8MM BROWN

FEMALE

PROFILE VIEW

FRONT VIEW

PLAN VIEW

EYE 8MM REDISH ORANGE

MALE

FRONT VIEW

1 IN.

PROFILE VIEW

1-53 *Female cinnamon teal ready for painting.*

1-54 *Male cinnamon teal ready for painting.*

1-55 *Finished female cinnamon teal.*

1-56 *Finished male cinnamon teal.*

1-57 *Hooded merganser plaque.*

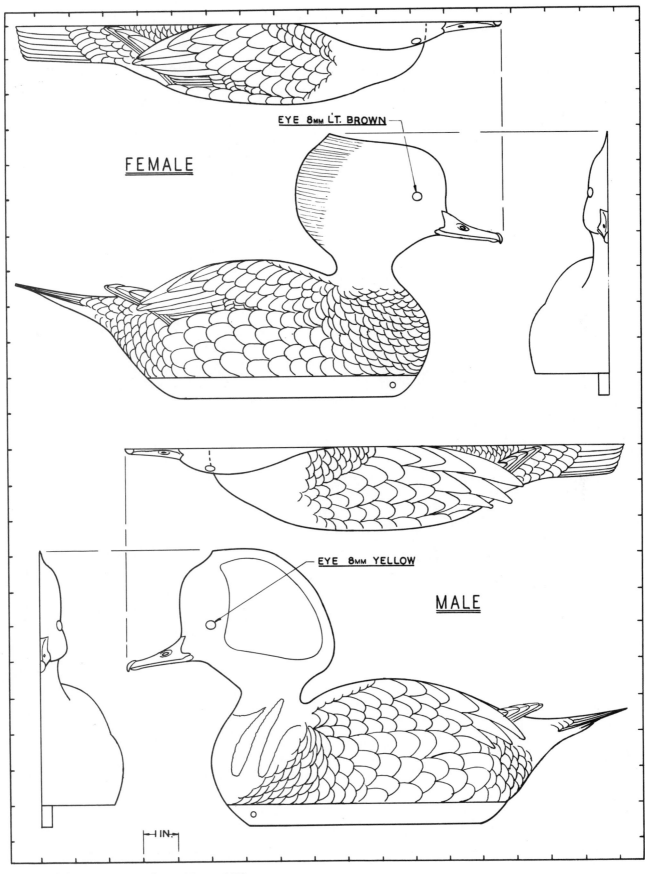

EYE 8MM LT. BROWN

FEMALE

EYE 8MM YELLOW

MALE

I IN.

1-58 *Hooded mergansers. (See Figure M-2, page 237.)*

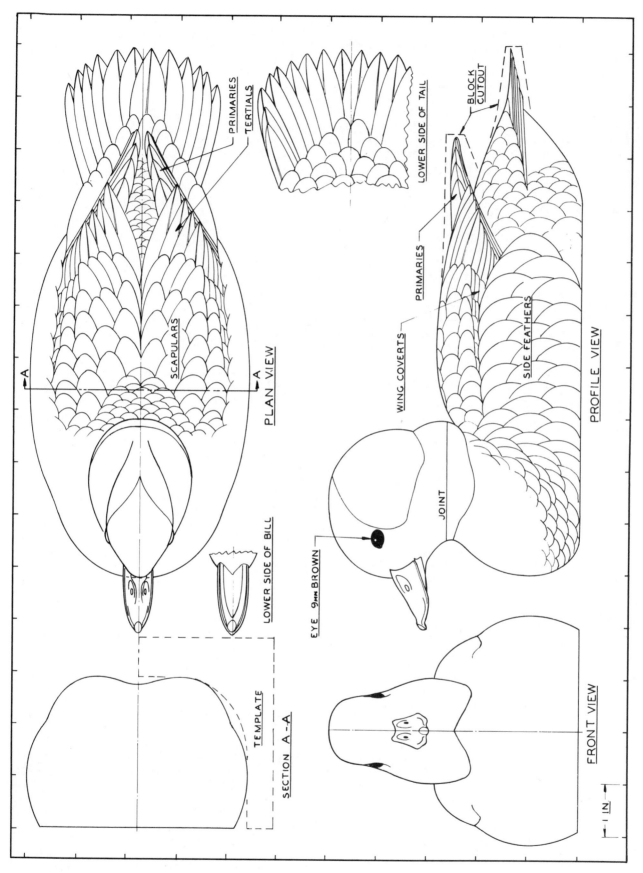

1-59 *Bufflehead drake. (See Figure K-1, page 235.)*

1-60 *Bufflehead drake.*

CARVING A FULL-BODY DECOY

If the detail is kept simple, carving a full-body decoy is not much more difficult than carving a half-body decoy and is an important step forward for the beginner. This type of carving gives him experience in obtaining symmetry, in carving the complete head and bill, and in carving the primaries of both wings when they are folded and fitted closely together. A life-size bufflehead drake has been chosen as a subject for the first full-body decoy, because of his small size and because he is somewhat easier to paint than many ducks.

The following materials are required for the carving: 3¼ × 4½ × 10½-inch block for the body, 2 × 3½ × 4½-inch block for the head, two 9-mm brown eyes, 2/0 and 4/0 garnet paper, and epoxy adhesive.

First, enlarge Figure 1-59 to life size. Then, establish a centerline on the upper side of the body block. Next, transfer the profile and plan views to the body block, maintaining proper alignment between the two views. Transfer the head drawing to the 2-inch-thick block of wood. Be sure that the bill is located parallel to the grain. Drill a small hole through the block at the eye location. This small hole will later facilitate the location of the full-size eyeholes after the head is carved. (A hole large enough to receive the eyes may be drilled at this time.) Although the body block and head can be sawed out with a coping saw (Figs. 1-13, 14, 15), considerable time and effort will be saved if a band saw is used.

1-61 *Bufflehead drake.*

1-62 *Bufflehead drake. Note shape of head as viewed from the front.*

1-63 *Locate and attach head with epoxy.*

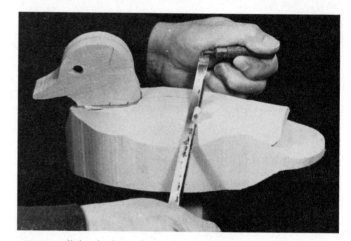

1-64 *A small drawknife can be used to rough-shape the body.*

Although many carvers hold the head block in one hand and completely carve the head before attaching it to the body, the author prefers to carve the head as an integral part of the carved bird. Since bird carving can be done easier, faster, and better if the piece is rigidly held, leaving both hands free for the actual carving work, attaching the head to the body block before carving the head generally works best. Also, more realistic neck lines can be developed when the neck and the body are carved as one. If extreme head positions make it difficult or impossible to carve the lower side of the bill, the author attaches the head with epoxy to a separate holding fixture (Fig. 6-35) and carves the entire bill and forward part of the head before attaching it to the body.

After the centerline of the head and of the body have been established and drawn in with a pencil, locate the head and neck fore and aft and sidewise (also, if desired, turned to one side or the other) and mark this location with pencil lines. Then attach the head to the body with epoxy adhesive (Fig. 1-63).

While the epoxy is curing, transfer the cross-sectional view to a piece of cardboard or plastic and make a template similar to the one shown in Figure 1-66. When the epoxy has properly cured, attach the assembled block to the holding fixture (similar to the one shown in Figs. 1-42, 43) with two woodscrews. Start removing wood from the midsection of the body (Figs. 1-64, 65) until both sides match the body template (Fig. 1-66). Continue roughing out the body by removing wood from the chest, flanks, and under tail coverts (Figs. 1-67, 68). Sand the body occasionally to check the overall progress.

To insure symmetry, it is important to retain the penciled centerline on the body and head until all detail has been completed. Whenever lines are partially removed by the wood-removing operations, draw the centerline back in before it is completely lost.

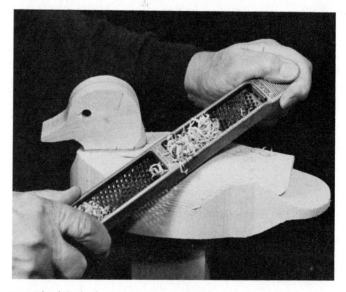

1-65 *Blend the body contours with the half-round Surform rasp.*

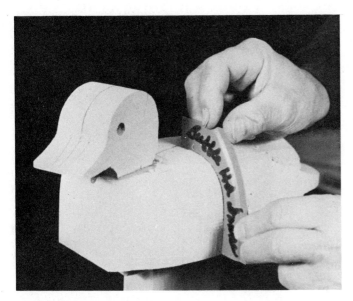

1-66 *Periodically check the cross-sectional shape of the body.*

1-69 *Rough form the upper part of the head.*

1-67 *Shape the breast by using the Surform rasp in the pulled position.*

1-70 *The overall shape of the carving has now been established. The head-body intersection and the extent of the side feathers are drawn in.*

1-68 *Shape the flanks and undertail coverts with the round Surform rasp.*

When the overall body shape has been established, make the plan-view layout of the bill and cut to shape with a coping saw and rough out the head (Fig. 1-69). Sand the entire carving smooth (Fig. 1-70).

Next, using a gouge, shape the concave intersection of the scapulars along the centerline of the back, the intersection of the scapulars and the side feathers (Figs. 1-71 and 1-59, Section A-A), and the intersection of the head and body (Fig. 1-72). Finish shaping the head (Fig. 1-73).

Now, lay out the individual tertial, secondary, and primary feathers on one side of the carving (Fig. 1-74). Trace this layout on a piece of transparent paper and transfer the layout, using carbon paper, to the other side of the carving (Fig. 1-75).

With the tip of a sharp knife, cut around the outline of the primaries and start removing wood with a chisel (Figs. 1-76, 77). Cut underneath the primaries, down to the rump, with a coping saw (Fig. 1-78) and remove this wedge-shaped

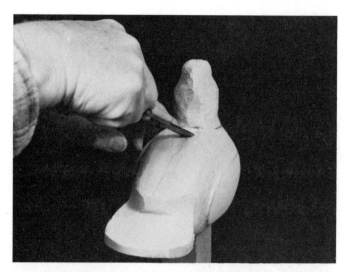

1-71 *Gouge out the rounded v-shaped depression at the centerline of the body.*

1-72 *Using a gouge, carve the intersection of the head and body.*

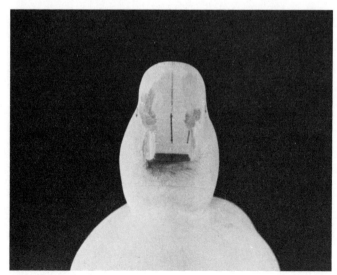

1-73 *Carve the head to its final shape.*

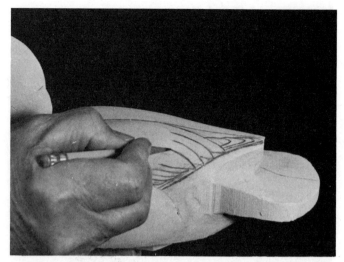

1-74 *Lay out the individual tertial, secondary, and primary feathers.*

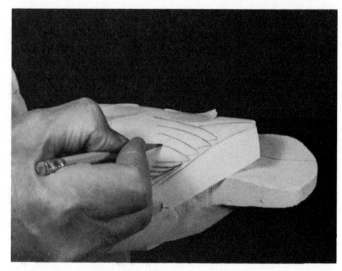

1-75 *Trace off the feather-pattern layouts and transfer them to the other side.*

piece of wood. Using a knife and chisels, carefully remove the wood from under the primaries until they are about 3/32 to 1/8 inch thick. Continue working in this area until the rump is smoothly shaped (Fig. 1-79). The primaries should now stand out realistically from the body. Carvers who wish to incorporate more detail may draw in the individual scapulars, exposed wing coverts, and other feathers. Cut around the outline of the individual tertial feathers and carve down the upper side of the primaries until they stand out from the tertials (Fig. 1-80). Continue by carving each feather of the tertial and secondary groups (Fig. 1-81), scapulars, and other feather groups (Fig. 1-87) if desired.

Individual feather carving is not as difficult as it looks. It is suggested that the beginner practice carving the individual feathers on a scrap piece of wood. First, sketch two or three feathers with a pencil on the surface. Then, using the point of a sharp knife, cut in the outline of each feather (Fig. 1-82). Next, remove wood from the bottom and right side of the

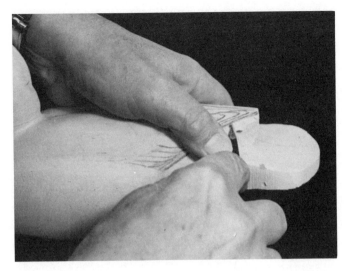

1-76 *Remove wood from the rear side of the primaries.*

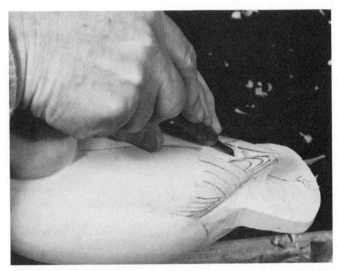

1-77 *Shape the rump with a small chisel.*

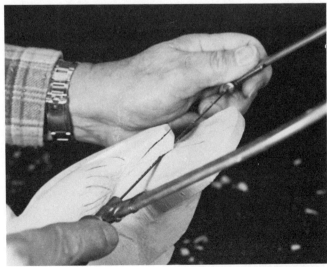

1-78 *Carefully saw out the wedge-shaped pieces from under the primaries.*

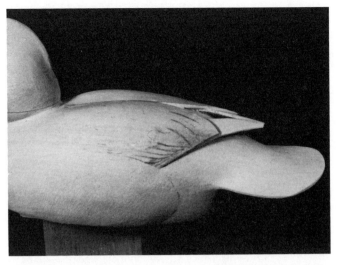

1-79 *Carve the primaries until they stand out realistically from the body.*

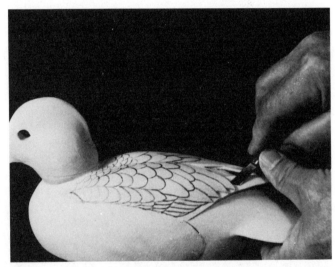

1-80 *Carefully carve the upper side of the primaries.*

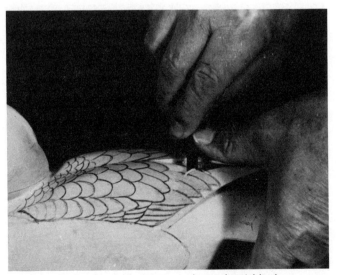

1-81 *Individually carve each of the secondary and tertial feathers.*

feather group so that the group stands out (Fig. 1-83). Start carving the first feather by removing wood at approximately a 45-degree angle next to the adjacent, overlapping feather (Fig. 1-84). Complete the feather by removing more wood on a flatter angle until the beveled cut extends across the entire feather (Fig. 1-85). Carefully sand each feather smooth (Fig. 1-86).

Lay out the tail feathers as shown in Figure 1-87. Support the tips of the tail feathers with a scrap piece of wood and cut them to shape (Fig. 1-88). Cut around the outline of each tail feather and carve them individually (Fig. 1-89).

Referring to Figure 1-59 and also the bufflehead bill pictured on page 267, lay out the ridge of the beak (culmen) and carve the cheeks and the bill roughly to shape (Fig. 1-90). Now lay out the intersection of the bill and cheek on both sides of the carving (Fig. 1-91) and carve the bill and cheeks down to this line (Figs. 1-92, 93). Cut along the lower edges of the upper mandible. Locate and mark the nostrils on both

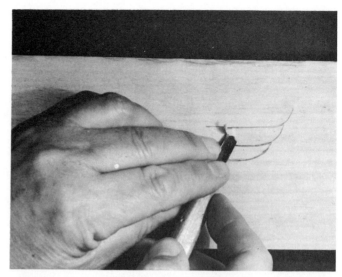

1-84 *Remove wood next to the adjacent feather at a 45-degree angle.*

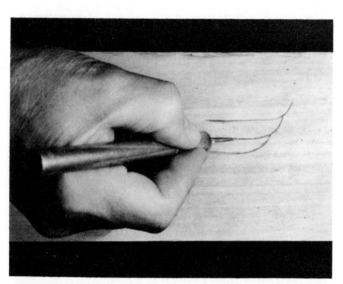

1-82 *Practice carving individual feathers.*

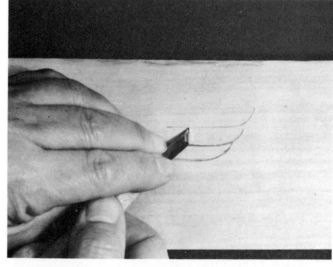

1-85 *Extend the bevel cut across the width of the feather.*

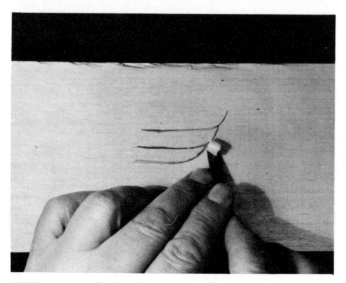

1-83 *Remove wood so that the feather groups stand out.*

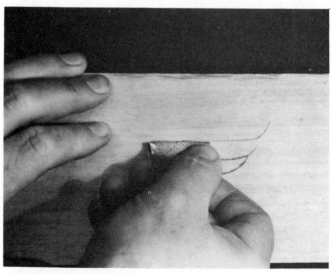

1-86 *Carefully sand each feather smooth.*

1-87 If desired, additional feathers may be carved.

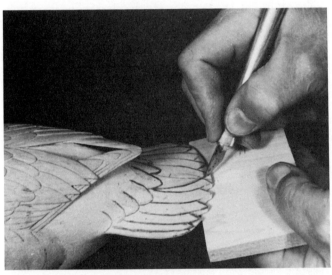

1-88 Support the tail with a scrap piece of wood while cutting the v-shaped notches.

1-89 Individually carve all of the tail feathers.

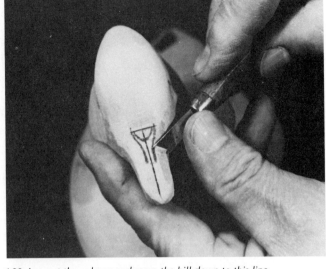

1-90 Lay out the culmen and carve the bill down to this line.

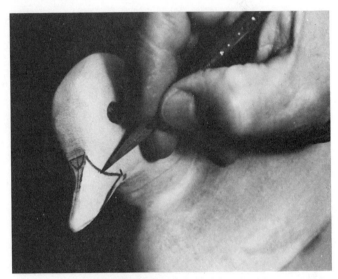

1-91 Lay out the intersection of the bill and cheek.

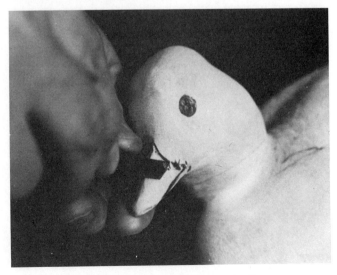

1-92 Carve the bill down to the bill-cheek intersection line.

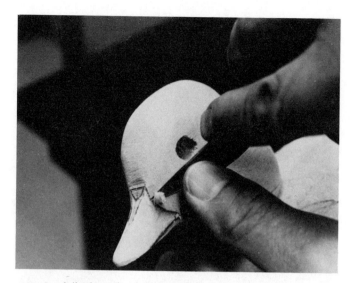

1-93 *Carefully shape the cheek in the bill area.*

1-96 *The carving is now ready to be painted.*

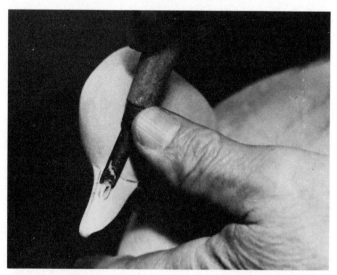

1-94 *Gouge out the small depression around the nostril.*

1-95 *Carefully shape the eyes.*

sides of the bill. Duplicate the nostrils by drilling small holes at their fore-and-aft extremities and by removing the wood between the holes to a depth of about $\frac{3}{32}$ inch. The nostrils on most waterfowl lie at the bottom of a small, oval-shaped depression which the carver can realistically reproduce by using a small gouge (Fig. 1-94). Make a shallow cut around the outline of the nail and make it just barely prominent by removing a small amount of wood around the cut. If desired, carve the underside of the bill in detail by referring again to the pictures on page 259. Complete the head and bill by carefully sanding smooth with 4/0 sandpaper. Drill full-size holes for the eyes and install them in the manner described on page 13.

Check the entire carving for toolmarks and sand smooth where necessary. The carving is now ready to be sealed and painted.

CARVING WORKING DECOYS

Although few hunters in this age of plastics still use wood decoys, the revival of competitive decoy contests in 1960, along with the appearance of many publications, plus the great popularity of antique decoy collecting have promoted the strong comeback of this American art form. Hundreds of working decoys are now entered by novices, amateurs, and professionals in a number of annual competitions. Many other decoys are carved and sold to collectors, and a fewer number are carved and sold as actual decoys, to be put into the water and shot over.

Probably every decoymaker, hunter, and collector has his own personal idea of what a good working decoy should look like. When some method of communicating directly with the ducks is developed, their reactions to different decoys can be polled, and if the ducks themselves agree, it will then be possible to design the'"perfect decoy." However, until that time, the designs of duck decoys, like those of fishing lures, will be influenced almost as much by their aesthetic appeal as by their ability to attract game.

1-97 *Lesser scaup.* ▶

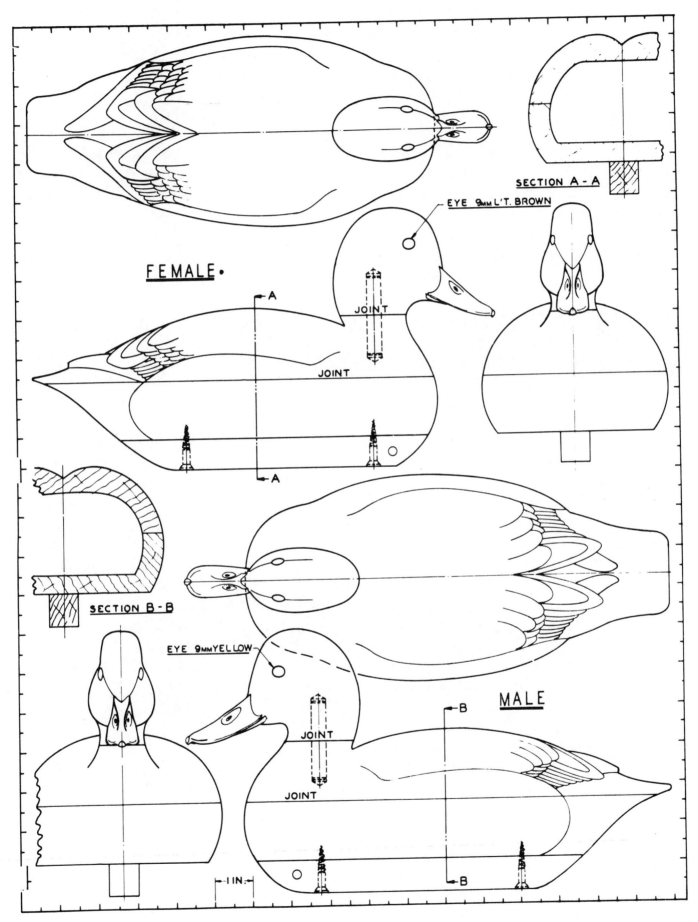

SECTION A - A

EYE 9MM L'T. BROWN

FEMALE.

JOINT

JOINT

A

A

SECTION B - B

EYE 9MM YELLOW

JOINT

JOINT

MALE

B

B

1 IN.

1-98 *Male lesser scaup.*

1-99 *Female lesser scaup.*

If there is disagreement on the design of working decoys, there is even more dispute on just what constitutes a good competition decoy. Owing to very keen competition, the working decoys entered in contests have become, for better or for worse, almost indistinguishable from decorative decoys. Most competitive working decoys are kept or sold as decorative decoys and end up on the mantel; they are so beautifully carved and painted and represent so much work that to expose these works of art to the elements would be unthinkable.

Competitive working decoys are usually judged on four characteristics: shape and form (likeness to species); seaworthiness (behavior in water); construction and workmanship; and painting and finishing. Present-day workmanship has reached such a degree of perfection that the contest judges in many cases are forced to make their final selections mainly on how the decoys look and perform in the tank. To the experienced eye, many species of waterfowl are recognizable at a distance just by the way they sit on the water. The position of the tail relative to the water and the amount and actual shape of the body profile exposed are some of the characteristics by which a particular species is identified. Most judges are experienced in these details and quick to note inconsistencies. Most of them also consider each entry on the basis of static characteristics (the ability of the decoy to right itself) and dynamic characteristics (usually referred to as roll and yaw stability).

The following overall standards for working decoy design are a guide for the beginner. I believe they meet generally accepted criteria. No attempt has been made to cover some of the controversial aspects of working decoy design, such as the extent of carving and painting detail, the most desirable attitudes of the bird to duplicate, and others.

The working decoy should closely resemble the species being depicted, both in shape and color, and should be constructed and finished to withstand hard usage. It follows that certain parts, such as the tail, must be stronger and usually thicker than the tail of a decorative decoy. Raised primaries and other detailed feather carving must be done in such a way that these parts cannot easily be broken. While this may not always apply to competitive decoys, the head and bill, the most vulnerable parts on actual working decoys, should be carved from a stronger wood. The head-body joint must be strong and withstand the adverse effects of water or weather. The decoy should be carved so as to prevent water collecting or pooling on the upper side of the body.

The decoy should float realistically: it must not list; the body must be at the correct fore-and-aft angle to the water; and the proper amount of the body must be exposed. Both the flotation angle and the exposed profile vary with different species. As mentioned above, the accurate duplication of the proper flotation angle and the correct amount of exposed profile for the species depicted is very important.

The decoy should have static stability, i.e., it should be capable of righting itself from any position. Static stability is usually obtained by locating a ballast weight under the body, normally in the keel. The decoy should also have reasonable stability around its fore-and-aft axis, which means that any rolling motion should be quickly self-damping. The most important factors contributing to good antiroll characteristics are the cross-sectional shape and the weighted keel. Some decoymakers also obtain additional roll stability by exaggerating the width of the body.

The decoy should neither yaw nor drift sideways excessively. Adequate directional stability and drift restraint are usually supplied by the keel if it is of sufficient depth and of a length almost, or equal to, that of the decoy body. Generally speaking, decoys used in deep, open water should have deeper keels than those used on ponds.

Provision must be made for the attachment of the anchor line to the decoy. Potential winners have been disqualified for the lack of a simple, drilled hole in the forward part of the keel.

The wood of both exterior and interior surfaces should be adequately sealed to prevent the absorption of water.

The painted finish of the decoy should be as nonreflective as possible.

The beginner who aspires to enter a winner in one of the decoy contests should start out by studying every winning decoy (actual decoys or photographs) that he possible can. He should try to attend some of the shows and gain first hand experience on how the decoys are judged and the winners chosen. He will find that his fellow competitors are a most friendly group and will, in almost all cases, go out of their way to help on any problems he may be experiencing. He will have the opportunity to examine closely many decoys and will be able to acquaint himself with the quality of workmanship required for the different classes. From this exposure he will be able to set realistic goals and proceed with a singleness of purpose to become a winner himself.

A drawing (Fig. 1-97) of a pair of lesser scaup (bluebills) has been included in this section to show the construction of a typical working decoy. This general configuration is also fairly representative of many competition decoys.

Because it is less detailed, the carving of a working decoy is usually simpler than that of a decorative decoy. However, the body of the working decoy is normally hollowed out, requiring a few changes in the carving procedure.

Over the years, wood has been removed from the interior of decoy bodies in a number of different ways. Probably the easiest and most effective is to make the body from two joined pieces of wood (Fig. 1-100). The two blocks are temporarily held together by two woodscrews. Unless the woodscrews are quite long, it may be necessary to counterbore the lower piece for the screwheads to get penetration of the screws into the upper block. After the screws are installed, transfer the profile and plan views of the drawing to the block and saw it out in the manner described earlier. Cut out the head next, and drill holes in it and the body to accommodate a dowel, usually ⅜ to ½ inch in diameter and two or more inches in length. Now, attach the head by means of epoxy adhesive, or carve and attach later, as you prefer (Fig. 1-101).

After the body has been roughed to shape, remove the woodscrews and hollow out the two body sections. The hollowing operation can be greatly facilitated by means of an approximately one-inch diameter wood bit driven by an electric hand drill or a drill press (Fig. 1-102). Obviously, care must be exercised in regulating the depth of the many drilled holes. After removing as much wood by this method as is

1-100 Make the decoy body from two pieces.

1-101 Drill for dowels and attach heads with epoxy.

1-102 Hollowing can be facilitated by use of a drill press.

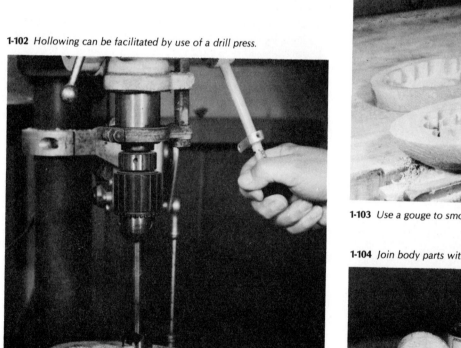

1-103 Use a gouge to smooth the interior of the body.

1-104 Join body parts with epoxy. Use small nails to hold parts in place.

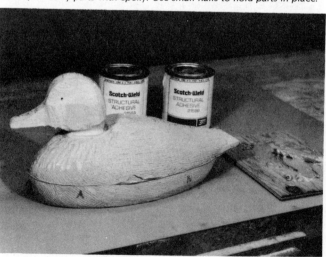

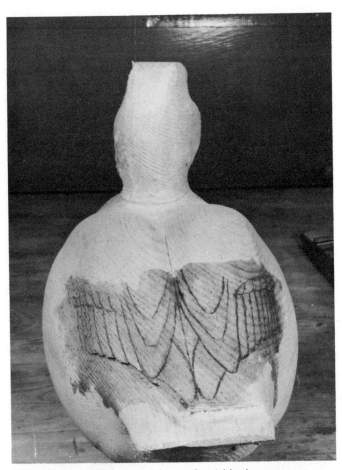

1-105 *Lay out the primary, secondary, and tertial feather groups.*

1-106 *Feather carving is usually less detailed on working decoys.*

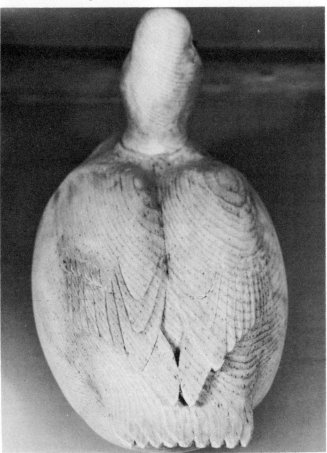

practical, gouge out the remaining material by hand (Fig. 1-103). In hollowing the body, it is important to leave sufficient wood for the final shaping.

When the hollowing operation has been completed, the inside of the two halves should be thoroughly sealed with lacquer sanding sealer or some other good quality sealer, as explained in Chapter 2. Then, join the two sections with an epoxy adhesive. Toenail four or five small nails to hold the parts in proper alignment (Fig. 1-104). After the epoxy has cured, begin the final shaping of the body.

Now draw in the primaries, secondaries, and tertials with pencil (Fig. 1-105). Carve the feather groups as previously described, except the depth of the feather carving is not as deep and the primaries do not extend out unsupported from the body (Fig. 1-106). Leave the tail quite thick for strength, and carve the individual feathers as desired. Complete the carving by shaping the head and bill.

Now, fill the screw holes in the bottom with epoxy. If the bottom section was counterbored for the screwheads, plug these holes with dowel stock, cemented in place with epoxy. Sand the entire decoy smooth and seal. When the sealer is dry, smooth with 4/0 sandpaper or 3/0 steel wool.

Next, make the keel. To get more weight below the body, some decoymakers use a denser wood, such as oak or one of the other hardwoods. The amount of weight required to obtain static stability depends on the location of the weight below the decoy body. Therefore, it is somewhat more efficient to use a lighter keel and to meet the static stability requirement by locating the necessary weight in the form of lead or some other dense material at or near the bottom of the keel. However, if the ballast weight is installed by pouring molten lead directly into a hole in the keel, it is very desirable to use the harder, tougher wood to withstand the heat. See Figure 1-107 for different methods of installing the ballast weight.

Now, float the decoy to determine how it rides in the water. If the carving is not symmetrical, or if the head is turned to one side or the other, the decoy will list. Correct the listing by relocating the keel slightly off the centerline toward the high side. Before this is done, check to see if the decoy rides with the proper fore-and-aft angle to the water for the species, and also note if the exposed profile is correct. If the fore-and-aft angle is correct, temporarily attach a lead weight (the amount has to be determined experimentally) near the center of the keel. If the decoy rides with its tail too high, locate the weight farther aft; if the tail is too low, locate the weight farther forward. Refloat the decoy and check its attitude, and at this time see if the decoy will right itself from any position. If it will not, add more weight or locate the weight farther below the body on a new, deeper keel. Several attempts, using a different size and location of the ballast, and probably of the keel, may be required to achieve the desired results.

These adjustments can usually be accomplished fairly easily. Making appreciable changes to the amount of exposed profile of the decoy is somewhat more difficult. If the decoy rides too low, either the weight of the decoy has to be decreased or the displacement of the decoy has to be increased. The obvious correction would be to reduce the amount of lead weight; however, this usually cannot be

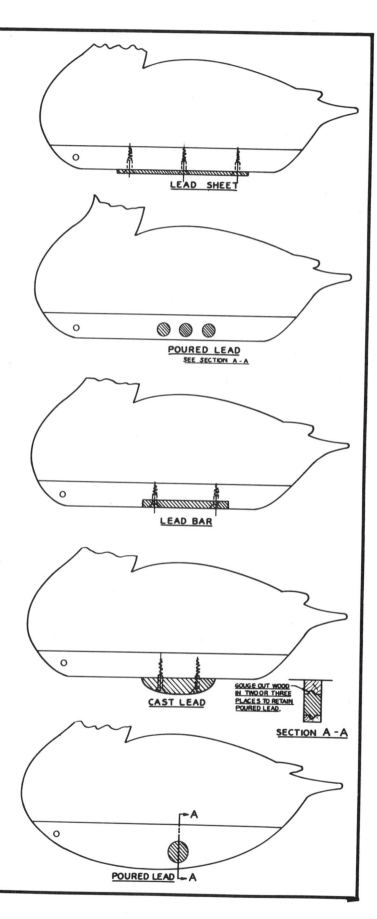

LEAD SHEET

POURED LEAD
SEE SECTION A-A

LEAD BAR

CAST LEAD

GOUGE OUT WOOD IN TWO OR THREE PLACES TO RETAIN POURED LEAD.

SECTION A-A

POURED LEAD

1-108 *Lesser scaup decoy (male).* ▶

done, inasmuch as this weight was determined as the necessary amount for static stability. The only other way to reduce the decoy's weight without affecting its exterior shape is to cut the body of the decoy in two again and remove more wood from the interior. Increased displacement can be achieved either by making the cross section of the keel larger or by attaching additional wood to the bottom of the decoy. When additional displacement has been obtained by either of these means, the amount of lead weight, being farther below the body, can usually be reduced.

If the decoy rides too high, either the decoy's weight has to be increased or the amount of displacement decreased. If only a small correction is needed, it may be possible to increase the amount of lead weight and/or reduce the cross-sectional width of the keel. Larger corrections would require reducing the body height of the decoy by cutting off a section of the body, parallel to the waterline, and attaching a new bottom.

When the proper attitude of the decoy in the water has been obtained, permanently attach the keel with epoxy. On competition decoys, it is sometimes preferable to attach the keel by two woodscrews only, so that the keel can easily be removed for conversion of the decoy into a decorative type. The decoy is now ready to be painted.

During the past few years, most decoy contests have featured decorative decoys rather than working decoys. These competition decoys are made to look as much like the real bird as possible, and very little consideration is given to their durability (strength of parts) and seaworthiness. They are floated, however, and must ride correctly but need not be self-righting or be required to have keels. Many recent decorative decoys are full-bodied, duplicating the cross-sectional shape of the bird, and some even have feet and tarsi. In some contests, action poses are preferred. Most of these carvings are hollow in order to obtain the proper profile on the water, but otherwise they are decorative carvings in every sense of the word — to call them decoys is a misnomer.

A carver interested in these competitions should first find out the rules for the particular contest that he wishes to enter. If possible, he should also talk to fellow competitors who are familiar with the contest and the criteria for judging.

1-109 *Lesser scaup decoy (female).* ▶

2

Painting for Beginners

Painting the carving can be every bit as interesting and absorbing as doing the actual carving. A bird's plumage is beautifully complex, not only in color, but also in texture and pattern; even to approximate its subtleties is difficult and time-consuming. This should not discourage the beginner, but only make him aware of the unlimited creative possibilities and the great challenges connected with this phase of realistic bird carving.

The painting of a bird carving can be very simple or extremely complicated, depending on the desires, ability, and patience of the individual carver-artist. If the beginning bird carver has never done any painting, it is wise on his first attempts to keep the painting detail as simple as possible; otherwise he will become frustrated and discouraged. As soon as he has developed some confidence, he should try to add a little more detail with each new attempt. Painting birds can only be learned by doing and by studying the actual bird and trying each time to come a little closer to the real thing. The novice (and also the advanced amateur and professional) should never be completely satisfied with his work; there will always be room for improvement.

This chapter covers only some of the easier techniques involved in the painting of realistic game birds. Those with some experience in painting should immediately turn to Chapter 7, "Advanced Finishing Techniques." Since a great number of authoritative books dealing with the mixing of colors are available, only information covering the mixing of a specific color on a particular bird will be included here. It would be wise, therefore, for the beginner to study some of the rudiments of color mixing.

The techniques involved in painting a realistic bird carving are not unlike those used by the illustrator-artist in painting very detailed, lifelike bird portraits with oils on canvas. The illustrator-artist must resort to shading and the use of highlights and shadows in order to create a three-dimensional effect. Although the carver-artist is already working on a three-dimensional object, he, too, has to use highlights and shading on occasions to make the painted bird appear natural. A *good* realistically painted carving generally requires more detailed work, extending over the bird's entire body, than a bird painted on canvas. The canvas painting can be viewed only from one side and normally at a distance; the painted carving is frequently subjected to very close inspection from all angles over its entire surface.

A lot about painting bird carvings can be learned by practicing on canvas or paper surfaces. Start out in this manner and then switch to the actual carving as soon as you have built up confidence in your painting ability. Painting, like almost everything else, requires practice, study, more practice, and a great deal of patience. Don't expect to become an expert overnight — no one else has.

MATERIALS AND EQUIPMENT

There are probably as many ways to go about painting a bird carving as there are suitable materials available to do so. Few carver-artists agree completely on the best techniques and materials. The materials and equipment listed below and the techniques described here and in Chapter 7 are certainly not the only ones. Although practically all realistic bird carvings are painted with either artist's oils or acrylic paints, the author has listed only oil paints. For the beginner, who has never painted, the slower-drying oils are easier to use than acrylics. After gaining some experience, the beginner can try acrylics, if he so desires.

Probably most carver-artists now use acrylics, and some obtain excellent results. On the other hand, some of the very finest bird carvings done today are painted with oils. About the only advantage acrylics have over oils is their faster drying time, although to some of us this is a disadvantage. Acrylics dry in just a few minutes, giving the artist very little time to blend colors and make corrections. They also have a disconcerting property of drying somewhat darker than the mixed color, and compared to oils, they have poorer covering qualities. Oils are slow drying and give ample time for the mixing and blending of colors and for the duplication of feather detail with brushmarks. They dry the same color as mixed and the colors on the palette remain usable for hours — a distinct advantage over acrylics.

However, many carver-artists become frustrated and impatient waiting for oil paints to dry. The drying time of oil paints can be reduced somewhat by modifying certain slow-drying colors with fast-drying colors. For example, black and white are two of the slower-drying colors. Mixing a small amount of raw umber into white and burnt umber into black not only reduces the drying time of these colors considerably but also subdues the starkness of white and black. Drying time can be further decreased by the use of fast-drying painting mediums (thinners) and dryers, which will be discussed later. The drying time of oil paints, of course, is increased by low temperature and high humidity. If these two factors are partially controlled, a substantial reduction in drying time can be achieved.

In 1976, Windsor and Newton, a British firm, introduced a new medium called Artist's Alkyd Colours. All colors of this paint dry overnight and combine the advantages of both oil and acrylic paints. Alkyd Colours are of high quality, and the use of alkyd resin in them, instead of the linseed oil used in artist's oils, has virtually eliminated the yellowing that occurs with age in white oil paints. They also have the advantage of being completely compatible with oil paints and oil-painting mediums, although some of these mediums do tend to increase drying time. Alkyd Colours can be mixed with oils to reduce the drying time of oil paint. Unfortunately, at the present time Alkyds generally are available only in larger art supply stores and are a little more expensive than artist's oils.

The author recommends using Alkyd Colours, at least to a limited degree. With the exception of white (which is used

---

Sealer
  1 pint
Undercoat – Grumbacher's Hyplar or equivalent
  8 oz. white   2 oz. burnt sienna
  2 oz. black   2 oz. raw sienna
  2 oz. burnt umber
Oil paint
  1½ × 6 tube
    titanium white
    Grumbacher's M G white or Windsor and Newton
      Alkyd white
  1 × 4 tube
    Ivory black   burnt sienna
    burnt umber   raw sienna
    raw umber   yellow ochre
  Small tube
    Thalo blue   cadmium orange
    cadmium yellow,   cadmium red, deep
      medium   alizarin crimson
Brushes
  sable brights, sizes 1, 2, 8
  round sables, sizes 0, 00, 000
  nylon flat ¾ inch wide (for applying Hyplar undercoat)
  bristle flat ¾ inch wide (for applying sealer)
  red sable or badger-hair fan blender, small and medium
  white bristle fan blender, small and medium
Other equipment
  palette knife
  palette (multiple sheet, throw-away type)
  turpentine
  medium
  brush cleaner – Silicoil jar and Cleaning Fluid (manu-
    factured by the Lion Co., 428 Ormsby, Louisville,
    Kentucky)

---

to modify most colors), the earth colors – the umbers and the siennas – are used for bird painting more than any other colors. Since these colors are all fast drying, there is no advantage in substituting alkyds for oils in these colors. At the start, if the artist-carver used only black and white alkyds, he would reduce drying times considerably. Later he can add more Alkyd Colours to replace most of the other slow-drying oil colors, such as cadmium yellow, Thalo blue, cadmium red, and alizarin crimson.

Except for those situations in which acrylics can be easily used (for example, when applying undercoats or when little or no blending of colors is required), the painting instructions in this book assume the use of oil paints. Some of the basic materials and equipment required for painting realistic game bird carvings are listed below. More can be added as the novice progresses.

SEALERS AND UNDERCOATS

Before applying any paint to the sanded carving, the wood should be sealed. While sealer does not actually hermetically close off all the wood pores, it does reduce considerably the rate at which the wood gains or loses moisture, which is important in the prevention of checks. Sealing also helps prevent the wood from exuding pitch. In addition, when sanded or steel-wooled, the sealer helps fill the open grain of the wood.

A number of wood sealers are available at paint stores. The author prefers lacquer sanding sealer, which can be either sprayed or brushed on. Under normal temperatures, lacquer sanding sealer dries and is ready for sanding in less than one half hour. "Deft," a brushed-on lacquer, is quite similar to lacquer sanding sealer.

After the wood is sealed and sanded (or steel-wooled), apply either an oil paint or an acrylic paint undercoat to the carving. The color of the undercoat should approximate that of the final coat. The author prefers to use an acrylic-base paint, not only because it dries in less than one half hour, but also because it has excellent bonding characteristics. Grumbacher's Hyplar is one acrylic paint readily available in a variety of colors. The undercoat paint, regardless of the type used, should be thinned to reduce brushmarks to a minimum.

MEDIUMS AND DRYING AGENTS

Oil paint from the tube is normally mixed with a painting medium. The painting medium can modify the oil paint in one or all of the following ways: reduce the consistency of the paint for easier application; make the paint more translucent; affect the flatness or the gloss of the dried paint; and decrease drying time. There is probably more disagreement among carver-artists on the selection of painting mediums and the amount to use than on any other points.

Turpentine and linseed oil, or a mixture thereof, are the

most popular painting mediums. Turpentine tends to make the dried paint flatter (less shiny) and reduces drying time. Linseed oil adds sheen to the dried paint and increases drying time. The author prefers to use Copal Painting Medium, made by Grumbacher, mixed 50–50 with turpentine. This mixture produces a very slight sheen and reduces drying time considerably. If alkyds are used, Windsor and Newton have a medium called Liquin that complements the fast drying qualities of Alkyd Colours.

A number of painting mediums and drying agents are available at artist's supply stores. Experiment with these products until you obtain the finish you prefer.

PAINTING THE MALLARD DRAKE
(See Figures I-1 and I-3, page 233)

Preparatory to any actual painting, assemble all photographs of mallard drakes, especially those in color, that you possibly can. In addition, make every attempt to study the actual bird. Then, familiarize yourself with the basic colors of the plumage, giving special attention to areas such as the tertials, where the colors blend.

Some means must be provided to support the carving while it is being painted and to facilitate handling while the paint is wet. A holding fixture (Fig. 2-1) is simple to make; almost any scrap of plywood larger than the carving will suffice. Add another piece of plywood, smaller than the carving, for spacing the carving away from the holding fixture. Attach the carving by means of two woodscrews.

Seal the wood before applying the undercoat. Lacquer sanding sealer, thinned about 50 percent with lacquer thinner, works well, dries in a very short time, and can be applied with either a brush or a cloth. When the sealer is dry, sand lightly with 6/0 sandpaper or 3/0 steel wool (Fig. 2-2). Be careful not to scratch the eyes of the decoy.

It is usually desirable to make the undercoat approximate

2-2 *After sealing, sand or steel wool lightly.*

2-3 *Apply an undercoat of white Hyplar.*

2-1 *Simple holding fixtures for painting half-body decoy.*

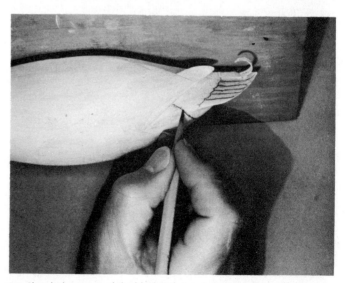
2-4 *Sketch the extent of the black tail coverts lightly with a pencil.*

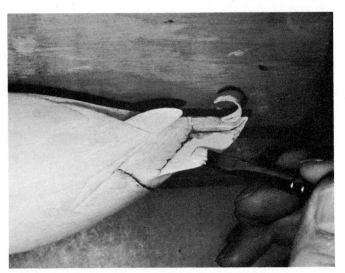

2-5 *Apply white paint to the tail feathers.*

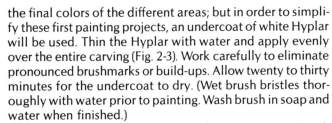

the final colors of the different areas; but in order to simplify these first painting projects, an undercoat of white Hyplar will be used. Thin the Hyplar with water and apply evenly over the entire carving (Fig. 2-3). Work carefully to eliminate pronounced brushmarks or build-ups. Allow twenty to thirty minutes for the undercoat to dry. (Wet brush bristles thoroughly with water prior to painting. Wash brush in soap and water when finished.)

Because of the overlapping of the feathers, the finish painting must start at the tail and proceed forward. The upper edges of the side feathers overlap the scapulars, tertials, and secondaries; therefore, paint these areas before the side feathers.

First, sketch the rearmost extent of the black upper and lower tail coverts lightly on the carving with a pencil. Also, mark the forward extent of the black area on the tail coverts (Figs. 1-10 and 2-4).

Squeeze out some titanium white and raw umber onto the palette. Add a very small amount of raw umber to the white and mix thoroughly with a palette knife. The raw umber will make the white color more natural and will also decrease drying time appreciably. Add a drop or two of painting medium (equal parts of linseed oil and turpentine will do nicely for this first attempt) and work evenly into the paint.

Now, using a flat sable brush, apply the paint to the tail-feather area, both upper and lower surfaces (Fig. 2-5). Smooth the paint with diagonal, outward brushstrokes (Fig. 2-6). Delineate each tail feather with a fine line of raw umber, mixed with white and medium, applied with a 00 or 000 round sable brush (Fig. 2-7). When making these fine lines over the wet paint, wipe the brush clean after every stroke. If desired, the lines delineating the tail feathers can be added after the tail area is dry; however, as the amateur progresses, he will be using the *alla prima* (wet-on-wet) technique more and more. Adding these delineating lines while the paint is still wet will give him his first experience with this technique.

BRUSH MARKS

2-6 *Smooth tail paint with diagonal, outward brushmarks.*

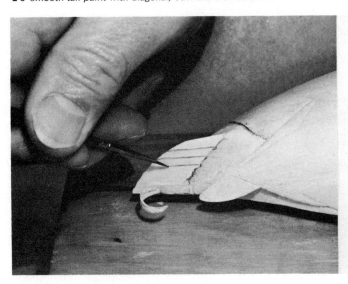

2-7 *Delineate each tail feather with a fine line.*

2-8 *An excellent way to clean brushes.*

2-9 Paint the bill next.

2-12 Paint the primary feathers next.

2-10 Paint the black rump and upper and lower tail coverts.

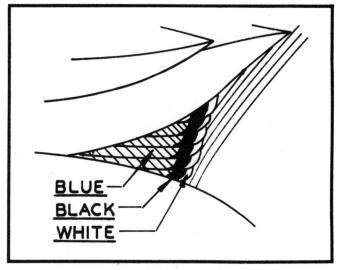

BLUE
BLACK
WHITE

2-13 Layout and colors for the secondaries (speculum).

2-11 Terminate the tail coverts in fine, irregular lines.

2-14 Paint the secondaries in accordance with Figure 2-13.

Use a brush for each color, if desired, or quickly clean the brush for the next color. In cleaning the brush, first wipe off the excess paint with a paper towel or cloth. Then, stroke the bristles across the coils of a Silicoil cleaning jar filled with Silicoil brush cleaning fluid until they are clean (Fig. 2-8). Wipe the bristles dry. Clean all brushes thoroughly after each painting session. The Silicoil jar is highly recommended for fast cleaning and conditioning of the brush. If not available, almost any jar filled with turpentine or paint thinner can be used. In this case, stroke the brush bristles against the side of the jar and wipe with paper towels or cloth until the brush is clean.

Continuing with the painting of the mallard, draw in the outline of the white neckband (the white neckband does not go completely around the neck but tapers to nothing on each side near the back of the neck). Paint this area with the paint mixed for the tail and smooth out any paint ridges. Paint the upper side of the bill next with cadmium yellow, medium (Fig. 2-9). Mix a small amount of black into the yellow and paint the underside. The white neckband and the bill are painted out of sequence so that they will be dry at the time the head and chest are painted.

Next, mix a small amount of the burnt umber into some black; add medium, and paint the rump and the upper and lower tail coverts, including the curled tail feather (Fig. 2-10). Carefully paint back to the white tail feathers. Using a 00 or 000 round sable brush, drag the black paint, with single brushstrokes, back into the white paint to duplicate realistic, feathery edges of the tail coverts (Fig. 2-11). Here, again, wipe the brush clean after every few strokes. Brush the forward edge of the black area smoothly so that no ridges of paint remain. Allow this area to dry before painting the flanks.

Proceed now to the primaries. Paint this feather group, including the edges and the underside, with burnt umber mixed with a small amount of raw umber and white. (Always add a small amount of painting medium to each color.) Delineate the individual feathers with black paint in the manner described for the tail feathers (Fig. 2-12). Sketch in the secondary feathers (Fig. 2-13). Paint the white area first, the black next, and the blue (Thalo blue mixed with a small amount of white) last. Delineate the individual feathers with black paint (Fig. 2-14).

Move along to the painting of the tertial feathers. The tertials on a mallard are large feathers, dark brown on the outer parts, blending into brownish gray on the inner parts. Painting the tertials provides good experience in the blending of colors. Using white and small amounts of black and burnt umber, mix a light brownish-gray color. Apply burnt umber along the outer parts of the feathers and paint the remaining areas with the brownish-gray mixture (Fig. 2-15). Using a flat sable brush, carefully stipple the two colors together (Fig. 2-16). Stippling is accomplished by tapping a dry brush perpendicular to the surface. Wipe the brush clean and dry after every few stipple strokes. After roughly blending the two colors by stippling in the general area where the two colors meet, further blend them by brushing over the area, from the burnt umber into the gray, *very* lightly with a sable or badger-hair fan blender (Fig. 2-17). If desired, a fine

2-15 *Apply paint to the tertials.*

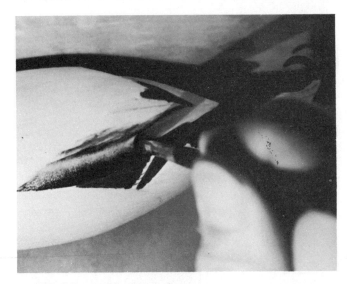
2-16 *Blend the two colors by stippling.*

2-17 *Further blend tertial colors with a dry badger-hair fan blender.*

line of burnt umber, representing the shaft of the feather, may be added to each tertial.

Sketch in the V-shaped back area (Fig. 1-10) and paint the scapulars in a manner similar to that described above for the tertials (Figs. 2-18, 19).

The back area, which is painted next, is composed of brown feathers with lighter-colored edges. First, paint this area with burnt umber mixed with a small amount of white. Then, add a stripe of raw sienna around the edges of the feathers (Fig. 2-20). Now, using a dry fan blender, drag the dark brown back into the lighter-colored edging. Carefully do one feather at a time, starting from the rear (Fig. 2-21). This technique of individual feather painting is used often in painting bird carvings.

Next, the flank and side. After the black upper and lower tail covert area has dried, add the narrow, tapering white band that outlines the forward side of the black area. Using a small, round sable brush, drag the white paint back onto the black to create a feathery edge. Mix a light brownish-gray color, similar to that used on the tertials, and paint the flank area ahead of the white stripe. Lightly drag some of the gray paint into the white using a fan blender (Fig. 2-22). Draw in the rearmost extent of the chest feathers and paint the side area back to the flank with the gray paint. Drag the gray paint up onto the scapulars in fine lines to create the effect of irregular feather edges (Fig. 2-23).

The chest of a mallard drake is a rich chestnut color. To achieve this, mix burnt sienna with a small amount of black and paint the chest area (Fig. 2-24). Be careful not to extend this paint onto the white neck. Using the fan blender or a small, round sable brush, carefully drag the chestnut-colored paint back into the gray paint on the sides. Wipe

2-19 *Blend the scapular paint with the fan blender.*

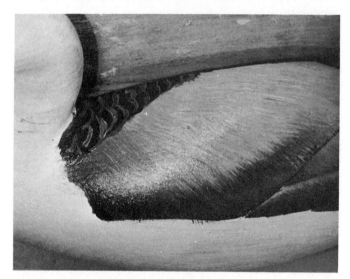

2-20 *Outline each back feather with raw sienna.*

2-18 *Apply paint to the scapular area.*

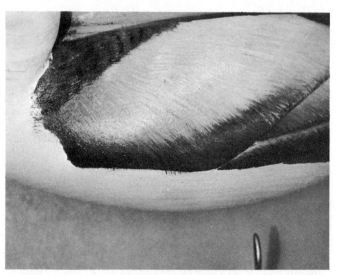

2-21 *Blend the two colors of the back feathers lightly.*

2-22 *Add brushmarks to the flank area with the fan blender.*

the brush clean after every stroke. Some of the chest feathers near the rear edge have gray-colored edgings. If carefully done, the gray edging can be applied over the wet chestnut-colored paint (Fig. 2-25). Drag fine lines of the chest paint up into the white neckband edge.

Painting the head on the mallard drake is another exercise in blending colors. Rather than use a prepared green, mix Thalo blue and cadmium yellow, medium. The resulting green color can then be easily varied from a bluish green to a yellowish green. Mix small amounts of these two colors by varying the amount of Thalo blue. Also, mix another small amount of Thalo blue and black. Apply the paint (Figs.

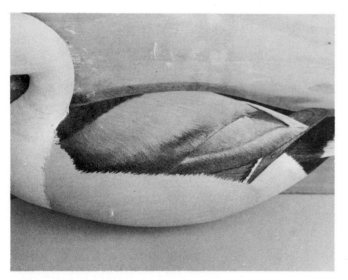

2-23 *Paint the side and drag paint lightly upward.*

2-25 *Edge some of the chest feathers with gray paint.*

2-24 *Drag the chest paint back onto the gray side paint with irregular lines.*

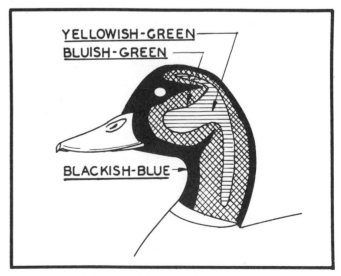

YELLOWISH-GREEN
BLUISH-GREEN
BLACKISH-BLUE

2-26 *Approximate location of the head colors.*

2-26, 27, 28, 29). The highlight in the green area can be made more pronounced by adding more yellow. Blend the colors very lightly with the fan blender. Drag the head paint into the upper edge of the white neckband in very fine lines (Fig. 2-30).

Paint the nail of the bill black, also the nostril. Carefully scrape away any paint that may have gotten onto the glass eye accidently. If desired, add additional paint to the white neck band and drag onto the chest paint with a fine brush after the chest paint has dried. Inspect the carving for missed spots and touch up if necessary. Allow the paint to dry before removing the carving from the holding fixture.

2-29 *Apply the yellowish-green paint last.*

2-27 *Apply the blackish-blue paint first.*

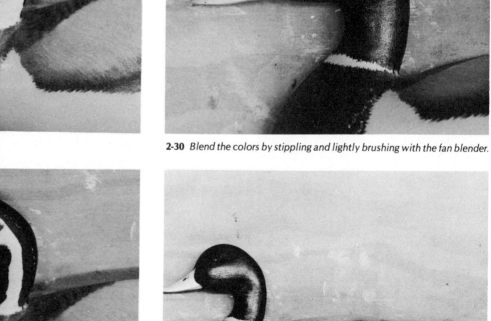

2-30 *Blend the colors by stippling and lightly brushing with the fan blender.*

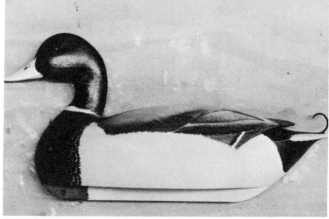

2-28 *Next, apply the bluish-green paint.*

2-31 *Finished mallard drake.*

PAINTING THE CANVASBACK DRAKE

(See Figure J-1, page 234.)

Painting the canvasback drake is very similar to painting the mallard drake. In this instance, however, the entire bird will be painted without permitting certain areas to dry before proceeding.

Attach the carving to the holding fixture and seal the wood with lacquer sanding sealer, thinned with lacquer thinner. Sand lightly or rub with 3/0 steel wool. Brush an undercoat of white Hyplar, thinned with water, over the entire surface of the carving.

After laying out the rearmost extent of the tail coverts, paint the upper and lower surfaces of the tail with a mixture of black and burnt umber to which a small amount of white has been added. Smooth the paint with diagonal, outward brushstrokes and delineate each feather with a fine line of burnt umber. Lay out the forward extent of the black tail coverts and rump areas and paint with black, mixed with a small amount of burnt umber. Drag the black paint into the wet tail paint to create the feathery edges of the tail coverts (Fig. 2-32).

Mix a medium gray color, using white and black, and paint the secondaries, but do not paint the edges of the two upper secondary feathers. Smooth the paint with diagonal brushstrokes and paint the edges of the two upper feathers with the black used for the tail coverts (Fig. 2-33). The upper and lower surfaces of the bill may also be painted with this same black at this time.

Now, mix a small amount of black into white to duplicate the basic body color of the male canvasback. Add more black to a small amount of this mixture and brush this paint onto the flank, just ahead of the black area. Paint the rest of the flank with the light gray body paint. Blend the two

2-32 *Paint the tail and tail coverts first.*

2-33 *The two upper (inner) secondary feathers have black edges.*

2-34 *Canvasback drake.*

2-35 Blend the light gray flank paint into the darker gray.

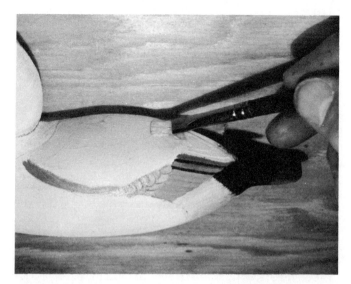

colors with the fan blender and drag the medium gray paint back into the black tail covert paint (Fig. 2-35).

Paint the exposed wing covert feathers next with the medium gray paint used for the secondaries. Lightly delineate the edges of these feathers with a darker mixture (Fig. 2-36). Paint the primaries with burnt umber mixed with raw umber and lightened slightly with white. Delineate the individual feathers with black.

Using the light gray body mixture, paint the entire area of the tertials, scapulars, and the back (Fig. 2-37). Apply a small amount of medium gray paint just above the side feathers and blend this paint into the scapulars to delineate the two feather groups. Then add brushmarks with the fan blender, starting from the rear and working forward (Fig. 2-38).

Paint a triangular area at the lower forward part of the side feathers with white, always adding a small amount of raw umber (Fig. 2-39). Paint the rest of the side feathers with

2-38 Blend the paint and add brushmarks with a fan blender.

2-36 Paint the exposed wing coverts next.

2-39 Paint the lower front side feathers white.

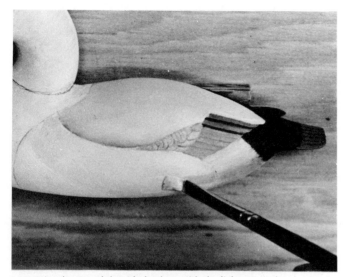

2-40 *Paint the rest of the side feathers with the light gray paint.*

2-41 *Blend the side feather paint and add brushmarks with a fan blender.*

2-42 *Extend the black chest paint into the gray side paint with fine lines.*

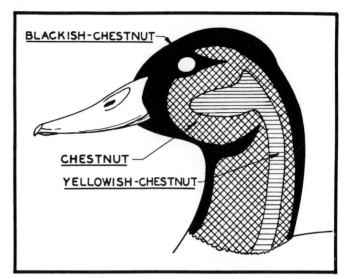

2-43 *Approximate location of head and neck colors.*

the basic light gray paint (Fig. 2-40). Using a fan blender, smooth out the side feather paint and add brushmarks. Drag the side feather paint along the upper edge into the scapulars, wing coverts, and secondaries with fine brushstrokes (Fig. 2-41).

Lay out the line separating the chestnut-colored neck from the black chest and back. Carefully paint the black area just back to where it touches the gray body paint. Use a fan blender to smooth the paint, again using short, rearward strokes (downward on the front of the chest) and proceeding in the forward and upward directions. Carefully drag the black paint into the body paint to create a soft, feathery edge (Fig. 2-42).

Squeeze two small piles of burnt sienna and yellow ochre onto the palette and mix the two paints to make a rich, chestnut color. Add a considerable amount of black to a portion of this mixture and more yellow ochre to another portion. Paint the head with three colors (Figs. 2-43, 44, 45).

2-44 *Apply the dark head paint first.*

2-45 *Apply the lighter head colors last.*

2-47 *Finished canvasback drake except for vermiculations.*

Blend the colors by stippling and further blend and add brushmarks with the fan blender. If stronger highlights are desired, add more yellow ochre to these areas and blend in with stippling (Fig. 2-46).

The bird can be considered finished at this point. However, for those who would like to progress and to strive for more realism, now would be a good time to try adding vermiculations. Canvasbacks (and also a number of other duck species) have fine, wavy lines called vermiculations over much of their bodies. First, read the explanation of vermiculations on page 161, and practice making these rather difficult feather-markings on a flat surface. In this example, the author used gray oil paint, thinned with turpentine to about the consistency of ink, and applied the thinned paint with a drawing fountain pen. Allow the painted carving to dry thoroughly before attempting to add the vermiculations (Figs. 2-48, 49).

2-48 *Vermiculations can be added with a drawing fountain pen.*

2-46 *Blend the head colors by stippling and add brushmarks with the fan blender.*

2-49 *Finished canvasback drake.*

2-50 *Lay out the areas of the dark colors lightly with a pencil.*

2-51 *Make the undercoat approximate the final colors.*

PAINTING THE BUFFLEHEAD DRAKE
(See Figure K-1, page 235.)

The handsome little bufflehead male is an interesting painting subject. Painting both sides of this full-body decorative decoy will also give the beginner experience in applying the paint symmetrically.

After sealing the carving, apply thinned white Hyplar over the entire surface. When the white Hyplar has dried, lay out the areas of dark color lightly with a pencil (Fig. 2-50) and paint them with black Hyplar (Fig. 2-51). Add some white Hyplar in the upper tail covert area and blend this gradually into the black of the rump area. Again, the undercoats should be thin, and brushmarks and build-ups in the paint should be carefully eliminated.

Mix raw umber and a small amount of black into white. Apply this gray paint to the tail feathers, on both the upper and lower surfaces. Smooth the paint with diagonal, outward brushstrokes so that the resulting brushmarks duplicate the barbs of the feathers (Fig. 2-53). Repeat this operation for the underside of the tail. Using a small sable brush, add white to the tips of the tail feathers (Fig. 2-54). Mix a small

2-52 *Male bufflehead in alert position.*

2-53 *Add brushmarks to duplicate the barbs of the feathers.*

2-55 *Paint in the shafts of the tail feathers.*

amount of burnt umber and black and paint in the exposed shafts (Fig. 2-55).

Add a little white to a portion of the dark gray tail mixture and apply this paint to the upper tail covert area. Mix some burnt umber into black and paint the forward part of the v-shaped rump area. Blend the gray upper covert paint into the blackish rump paint, making a gradual change in color. Add white to the tips of the upper coverts (Fig. 2-56). Using a fan brush, blend the gray covert paint into the white tip areas (Fig. 2-57). Add a small amount of raw umber into white and paint the under tail coverts and flank area on both sides. Blend the white with the gray upper covert and rump areas.

Mix a small amount of black and white into burnt umber and paint the primaries, both upper and lower surfaces.

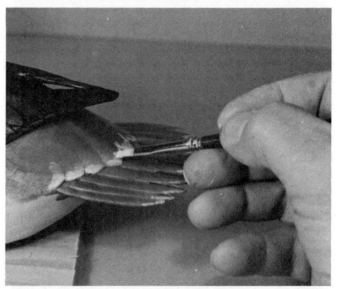

2-56 *Add white to the tips of the upper covert feathers.*

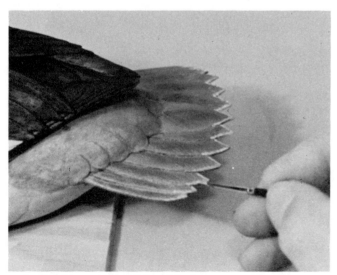

2-54 *Add white to the tips of the tail feathers.*

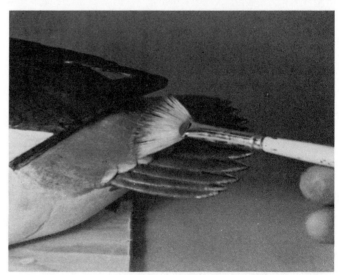

2-57 *Blend these areas and add brushmarks with a fan blender.*

2-58 *Paint the sides and chest and add brushmarks with the fan blender.*

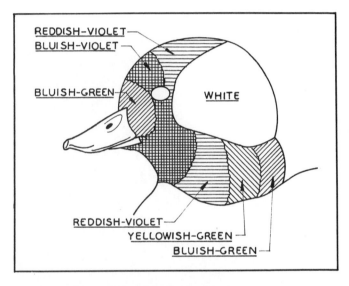

REDDISH-VIOLET
BLUISH-VIOLET

BLUISH-GREEN

WHITE

REDDISH-VIOLET
YELLOWISH-GREEN
BLUISH-GREEN

2-59 *Approximate location of the head colors.*

2-60 *Add brushmarks to the white paint on the head.*

2-61 *Blend the edges of the head colors by light stippling.*

Add more white to this mixture and delineate the individual primary feathers. Duplicate the shafts of these feathers with black paint.

Paint the back and inner scapular areas next with black mixed with a small amount of burnt umber and Thalo blue. (The blue will make the black a richer, more natural color.) Also, paint the dark areas of the head at this time. Allow this paint to dry before proceeding.

After the black paint has dried, paint the exposed secondary (speculum), wing coverts, and outer scapular feathers with white paint to which a small amount of raw umber has been added. If the wing covert feathers have not been carved in, delineate them with the gray tail paint.

Mix a small amount of raw umber and painting medium into Grumbacher's M G white for the sides and chest of the carving. Grumbacher's M G white has a much thicker consistency than regular white paint. It is used to emphasize brushmarks and thereby create more texture in the solid white areas. Since this white paint dries quickly, mix small amounts. Apply the paint to one side of the carving, smooth out immediately, and add brushmarks with a badger-hair fan blender. Starting from the rear, use rather short, rearward and slightly upward brushstrokes. Drag the paint back onto the flanks, secondaries, wing coverts, and scapular areas (Fig. 2-58). Repeat this procedure on the other side of the carving; then paint the breast and neck areas, adding brushmarks to duplicate the feather texture. Using the same paint, paint the white area of the head and feather out the edges (Fig. 2-60).

The head of the bufflehead male is highly iridescent with bluish-green, yellowish-green, bluish-violet, reddish-violet, and blue shades. While it is impossible to duplicate these iridescent colors exactly with paints, they can be approximated fairly well (see Chapter 7). The violet color can be roughly duplicated with a mixture of alizarin crimson and Thalo blue. By adding more red and blue, respectively, the reddish-violet and bluish-violet shades can be obtained. The bluish- and yellowish-green shades are created by

varying the amounts of Thalo blue and cadmium yellow, medium. Apply these colors in the general areas shown in Figure 2-59. Blend the colors at their intersection points only by stippling (Fig. 2-61). Lightly brush areas of the same color with a badger-hair fan blender, but be careful not to mix the colors. Using a small sable brush, drag the head paint down into the white neck paint to duplicate the feathery edge. After the head has dried, touch up the white head paint, as required.

The upper side feathers of the bufflehead male are delicately edged with black. Duplicate this black edging with individual strokes of a small sable brush (Fig. 2-62).

Mix a small amount of black and a very small amount of Thalo blue into white for the bluish-gray bill. Lighten the forward part of the bill by adding more white. Paint the nail a dusty color using burnt umber, black, and white. Complete the carving by painting the nostrils black.

2-62 *Paint the black edging of the upper side feathers with individual strokes.*

2-63 *Finished bufflehead drake.*

PART II

Planning the Carving

Once he has developed some skill and confidence in his work, the resolute carver should never knowingly copy another's carvings or use another carver's drawings. All man-made creations, including artist's drawings and paintings, should serve only as aids. Make every effort to work from actual birds and photographs. This is the only way to develop your own style and produce carvings that truly represent your creativity. With the exception of the first few projects for the beginner, all of the drawings and photos of carvings in this book are presented only to help the carver plan his own work. Obviously they will not serve this purpose if they are directly copied.

The success of a realistic bird carving primarily depends on four factors: how well the carving is planned during the drawing stage; how expertly and accurately the actual carving procedure is executed; how realistically the carving is painted; and how artistically the carving is displayed.

The planning and drawing stages that precede any actual work on the wood block are every bit as important as the actual carving and painting. Unfortunately, this all-important part of carving is often relegated to a minor role. Lack of originality, awkward poses, inaccurate dimensions, anatomical errors, and other undesirable characteristics can usually be traced back to improper planning.

A realistic bird carving must obviously be dimensionally and anatomically accurate. A good realistic bird carving must also capture a graceful, natural pose. An infinite number of bird positions may be completely natural; however, some are not graceful and, if duplicated, will not make pleasing carvings. The carver's success largely depends on his ability to select and accurately duplicate the poses that accentuate the naturally graceful and beautiful lines of the bird he is attempting to depict.

The serious carver must acquire a comprehensive knowledge of the various positions of game birds: relaxed, alert, sleeping, preening, stretching, displaying, landing, taking off, and others. Whenever possible, study the live bird from every aspect and record all observations, preferably on the spot. Sketches may be made, but photography is the only method by which important structural details and position can be accurately discerned and recorded. Much more on the subject of photography will be included in Chapter 4.

Information and suggestions presented here and in subsequent parts of this book will aid the game bird carver in working out some of the planning problems mentioned above and, in addition, will help him to consolidate these ideas into a drawing. Again, remember that the planning of a carving, like everything else, reflects the amount of study, research, and effort that went into it.

(3A) *Five pintail drakes and one hen — courtship flight.*

3

Bird Anatomy for Carvers

Some knowledge of bird anatomy is necessary for planning a successful realistic bird carving and for the proper execution of the carving work itself. Even a smattering of bird anatomy will help the carver to improve his carvings and also to appreciate more fully the absolutely fantastic physical adaptations and the superbly efficient and beautiful construction of these marvelous creatures.

As there are few anatomical differences between game birds and other birds, a great deal can be learned about game bird anatomy while dressing domestic fowl or even when carving the Thanksgiving turkey. Much more can be learned, however, by carefully skinning a game bird specimen, studying the feather groups on the removed skin, and then, by dissection, becoming acquainted with the important bones, joints, and muscles.

From one viewpoint, the exterior anatomy of birds is somewhat more complex than the corresponding anatomy of mammals. In most mammals, except for some very long-haired or wooled species, the skin and hair do not contribute greatly to the overall shape. On most birds, waterfowl especially, the contour feathers, including the down feathers, are quite thick over much of their bodies and modify the skeletal-muscular-skin configuration considerably. The extent of this modification varies, for the bird, by using an estimated twelve thousand feather control muscles, can at will alter its overall exterior body shape by fluffing out or pulling in part or all of its body-contour feathers. The strutting turkey gobbler is a familiar example of this exquisite feather control. The exterior appearance of a bird is further complicated by the fact that the overall body shape is modified by the wings when they are in the folded position.

From another viewpoint, the overall body shape of the bird is simplified to a degree in comparison to the mammal's in that the feathers refine the rather irregular basic body form, in most cases, into more smoothly flowing lines.

Although the game bird carver's knowledge of bird anatomy need not be extensive, it should at the very least cover individual feather construction, major feather groups, and the more important bones, joints, and muscles.

FEATHERS

The intricacy of bird plumage almost defies description. Since a great deal of the time spent on a realistic bird carving is devoted to the simulation of feathers, the construction of the individual feather will be described briefly (Fig. 3-1).

The exterior part of the feather is called the vane. The main structural member is called the shaft. It runs lengthwise from the quill, which is embedded in the skin, to the tip of the vane. Branching out from the shaft at an angle on both sides are the many barbs, each a minute feather in itself. On one side of the barb, too small to be seen with the unaided eye, are the straight barbules. On the other side of the barb, projecting out in a similar manner, are the barbules with tiny, hooklike projections called barbicels. The barbicels hook themselves to the straight barbules of the adjacent barb and hold the vane together in an amazingly strong, continuous, and flexible manner. If the barbs become separated, they will rejoin not just once, but time and time again. It is well worth the time and effort to examine a bird's feather under a high-power magnifying glass or microscope.

On the flight feathers, tail feathers, and certain other feathers, the barbs are held together along their entire length by the tiny barbicels. On most of the body-contour feathers, the barbules apparently do not have the barbicels (or at least they are ineffective) out near the edges of the vane. As a result, the barbs separate and are seen as fine lines, giving the feather's edge a very soft and delicate effect. Both wing and body feathers, which are more or less solidly vaned, are generally referred to as contour feathers.

The coloring of the feathers is just as complex as their structure. Blacks, browns, most reds, and yellows are produced by pigments. Blues, some yellows and reds, violets, glossy blacks with a bluish or greenish tint, and whites are structural colors. Structural colors are produced by the microscopic surface structure of the feather reflecting portions of the color spectrum. The iridescent colors, which are structural, are produced by the interference of light waves by the

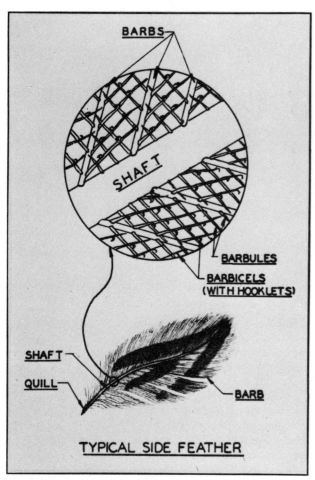

3-1 *Feather details.*

mer. Many duck specimens taken during the normal hunting seasons have not yet gotten their full breeding plumage. The carver should be aware of this and the molting process when using male duck specimens for feather pattern and coloration. F. H. Kortright's fine book, *The Ducks, Geese, and Swans of North America*, thoroughly covers this subject.

FEATHER GROUPS

At first glance, the contour feathers of the game birds appear to be quite evenly distributed over their entire bodies. A closer inspection reveals that the contour feathers originate from groups, or tracts, on the skin and that there are certain other areas with no contour feathers, although they may be covered with downy feathers. This distribution of the contour feathers, called pterylosis, is complex and varies somewhat between the different groups of birds.

The serious carver need not be familiar with all of the feather tracts (pterylae) and the areas where there are no contour feathers (apteria) inasmuch as the contour feathers overlap and appear to be continuous. He should, however, be familiar with some of the more prominent feather groups, both wing and body, for several reasons. First, the external shape of the bird's body is modified greatly by its feathers. Second, in some cases, the overall shape of the feather group must be carved prior to the carving of the individual feathers. Third, it is sometimes difficult without this infor-

different surfaces of the barbules while pigment granules located below the surface of the barbules absorb the light waves not reflected. More will be said on this subject in Chapter 7.

FEATHER MOLTS

Birds from time to time replace their worn feathers by molting. This is of little consequence to the carver except in the case of ducks. In the Northern Hemisphere, a special, or eclipse, molt occurs after the females start incubating their eggs. At that time the bright breeding plumage of most male ducks is replaced with a plumage very similar to the females. Shortly after this molt is completed, a second molt starts, and the female-type plumage is very gradually replaced over a period of several months by the breeding plumage.

Male ducks are almost always carved and painted in breeding plumage. However, the ruddy duck is one exception as his most attractive plumage occurs during early sum-

3-2 *Scapulars on a green-winged teal.*

mation to distinguish feathers of one group from those of another. A good example of a situation of this kind would be the overlapping of the scapulars with the tertials and, in turn, with the primaries and secondaries of the folded wings of a green-winged teal (Figs. 3-2, 3).

If available, an actual fresh or unfrozen specimen can be a great help in acquainting the beginner with the different feather groups. The feather groups on a specimen should first be studied with the wings outstretched. Particular attention should be paid to the position of the scapulars and tertials in this position. Next, the wings should be correctly folded and the new position of the feather groups noted.

The position of the folded wing and the amount of wing exposed vary not only with the different game birds but also on a particular bird, depending on its activity. In the case of waterfowl, the wings are normally neatly folded under the side feathers and scapulars. The long primaries extend on back under the secondaries and tertials and normally lie crossed above the tail or upper tail coverts. (On some of the smaller geese, the crossed primaries actually extend beyond the tail.)

Compared to waterfowl, upland game birds have much shorter and broader wings. Although their folded wings normally lie under the side feathers and scapulars, the primaries of upland game birds are not crossed but rest along the bird's flank, sometimes extending to the upper tail coverts, and are covered to a large extent by the secondaries, tertials, and scapulars. The folded wings of pigeons and doves remain almost completely outside the body-contour feathers.

On these birds, the primaries, which are largely covered by the secondaries, tertials, and scapulars, normally meet at a point above the tail coverts.

Folding the wings of a specimen also graphically shows the carver how the wings should appear in this position and, very roughly, the movements required of the bird to accomplish this remarkable feat. Of equal importance, this exercise clearly shows how the shape of the bird's body is modified by the folded wings. As mentioned, waterfowl, especially geese, have much larger wings relative to their body size than, for example, upland game birds. The shape of the goose's body will be altered to a greater extent by the folded wings than that of a quail's.

After noting these exterior features, carefully skin the specimen and identify and study the feather groups on the removed skin.

Primary Flight Feathers

These large, strong-shafted feathers, always ten to each wing, are the most important flight feathers. In the flight configuration, they are also the most prominent feather group on most game birds. The primaries are attached to the "hand" part of the wing structure and are controlled individually and as a group by a complex system of muscles and tendons. During the upstroke, the individual feathers are rotated and are opened to permit the air to pass through them; on the downstroke, they close and overlap to prevent the flow of air. Movement of the individual primaries is accompanied by the movement of the wing as a whole and the primaries as a group through wrist movement. These movements of the wing and of the individual primary feathers are so complex that even experts do not fully understand how they contribute to the bird's flight. The above oversimplified statements were not intended to describe the flight of a bird, but only to point out some of the detail the carver must consider when attempting to duplicate the bird's wing in the flight configuration. Consideration must also be given to the bending or deflection of the primary feathers caused by the high air loads developed during the downstroke. Many fine pictures that stop the fast-moving wing in its various flight positions are now available in a number of publications. The carver should familiarize himself with the basic wing and feather movements of the bird in flight.

Even when the wings are folded, the primaries significantly affect the overall shape and detail of the bird's body. Because the primaries of waterfowl, pigeons, and doves lie under the secondaries and tertials, and extend to or beyond the bird's plan-view centerline, they affect the overall contour of the back more than in the upland game birds.

Secondary Flight Feathers and Tertials

The secondary flight feathers are attached to the forearm of the wing and are in effect a continuation of the primaries. Unlike the primaries, they are not individually controlled, and they act more like the wing on an airplane to maintain lift and to stabilize flight. The two or three innermost secondaries, usually longer and/or different in shape and color,

3-3 *Tertials on a green-winged teal.*

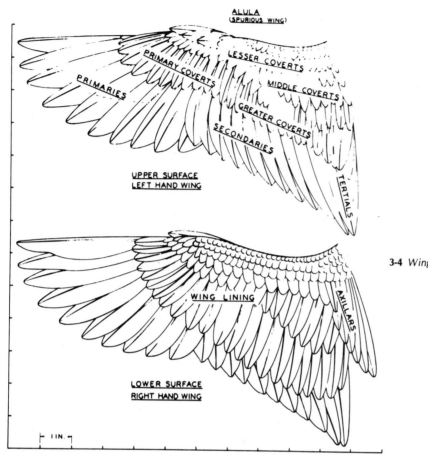

ALULA
(SPURIOUS WING)

LESSER COVERTS

PRIMARY COVERTS

MIDDLE COVERTS

PRIMARIES

GREATER COVERTS

SECONDARIES

UPPER SURFACE
LEFT HAND WING

TERTIALS

WING LINING

AXILLARS

LOWER SURFACE
RIGHT HAND WING

1 IN.

3-4 *Wing of a cinnamon teal.*

3-5 *Typography of a goose.*

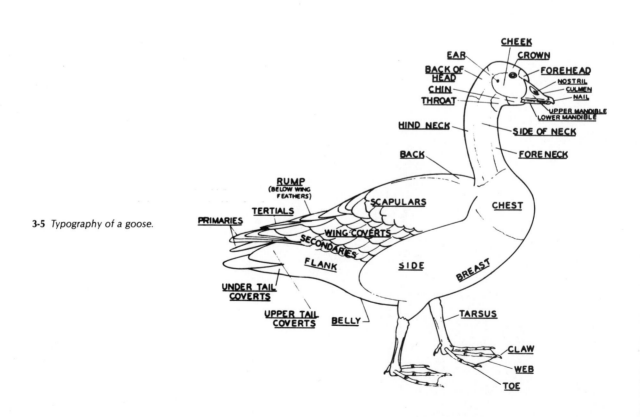

CHEEK

EAR

CROWN

BACK OF HEAD

FOREHEAD

NOSTRIL

CULMEN

NAIL

CHIN

THROAT

UPPER MANDIBLE

LOWER MANDIBLE

HIND NECK

SIDE OF NECK

BACK

FORE NECK

RUMP
(BELOW WING FEATHERS)

SCAPULARS

CHEST

TERTIALS

PRIMARIES

WING COVERTS

SECONDARIES

FLANK

SIDE

BREAST

UNDER TAIL COVERTS

UPPER TAIL COVERTS

BELLY

TARSUS

CLAW

WEB

TOE

are the tertials. On many ducks several of the secondary feathers are brightly colored, more often than not iridescent, and are referred to as the speculum. The secondaries and the tertials form a prominent feather group when the wings are outstretched.

When the wings are folded, varying amounts of the secondaries are exposed, depending on the species. Ducks display all of the tertials and often some of the speculum, although in many cases, the side feathers completely cover all of these secondary feathers. Most of the secondaries and all of the tertials of the different goose species are exposed when the wings are folded. Some of the secondaries on the upland game birds, pigeons, and doves are usually exposed; on quails and partridges, however, the secondaries are almost all covered by the scapulars. The tertials are much more conspicuous on waterfowl than they are on the other game birds.

Wing Coverts

The wing coverts, on both the upper and lower wing surfaces, are arranged in rows and are overlapped like the shingles on a roof (Fig. 3-6). The primary coverts overlap the primary feathers, and the greater coverts extend over the secondary feathers. The primary and greater coverts are in turn overlapped by the middle coverts, which are partially covered by the lesser coverts. The wing coverts, especially the primary and the greater, are usually quite distinct when the wing is outstretched and, on geese, are always noticeable when the wings are folded.

Alula (Spurious Wing)

The alula is composed of three feathers attached to the articulated "thumb" of the wing. These feathers act in a manner similar to that of a slat on the leading edge of an airplane wing, which reduces the stalling speed by locally speeding the airflow over the upper surface of the wing. These feathers are important to flight and are discernible during certain conditions of flight, at which time they are extended forward of the wing's leading edge.

Axillars

The axillars are a fan-shaped group of feathers located on the underside of the wing in the "armpit" area. These feathers, usually elongated, help close the gap between the inboard wing feathers and the body during flight. This feather group is, of course, seen only when the wings are outstretched.

Scapulars

The scapular feathers, often elongated and sometimes differently colored and/or marked, are located on either side of the back in the "shoulder" area, just inboard of each wing.

3-6 *Wing of a common Canada goose.*

The scapulars overlap the tertials in the flight configuration and help streamline the wing-body intersection; in addition, they help cover the folded wings. The overall body shape is modified somewhat by the scapulars, depending on the position of the wings and also by muscular control of the scapulars themselves. Regardless of the bird's position, the scapulars as feather groups can never be ignored by the carver.

Side Feathers

This conspicuous group of large feathers, often strikingly marked, not only cover the bird's side and legs, but they also help cover the folded wings.

Tail Coverts

The tail coverts overlap the tail feathers and complete the streamlining of the bird's body. These feathers, especially the upper tail coverts, often have distinctive color and markings. The upper tail coverts of the wood duck and pheasant are outstanding not only for their coloration but also for their length.

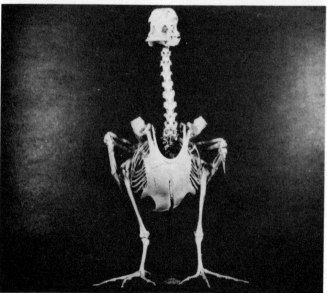

Tail Feathers

The tail feathers are extended or fanned out during certain flight maneuvers (see Chapter 5). At other times and when the bird is at ease on either ground or water, the tail feathers are normally compressed together and are much less conspicuous. (The tail feathers on brant and on some of the quails and partridges are often almost, or completely, covered by the tail coverts.) This feather group is of special importance to the carver, because its position almost always reflects the activity of the bird: jumping, landing, flying, turning, stretching, preening, or displaying.

BONES, JOINTS, AND MUSCLES

The bird's skeleton is a remarkably strong and extremely lightweight structure (Figs. 3-7, 8, 9). Nature has fused most of the back vertebrae to provide strength and rigidity for flight, and compared to man's, the bird's skeletal structure (except for neck and tail) is quite rigid. The main part of the bird's skeleton is somewhat analogous to the fuselage of an airplane: it provides a rigid structure between the wings and tail, articulated points of attachment for the wings, legs (landing gear), and tail, and a rigid structure for the attachment of the heavy pectoral flight muscles (engine mount and engine).

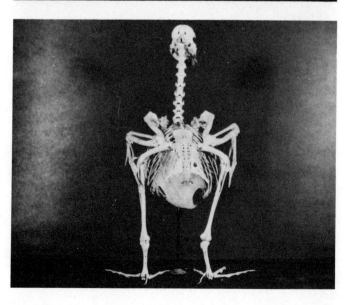

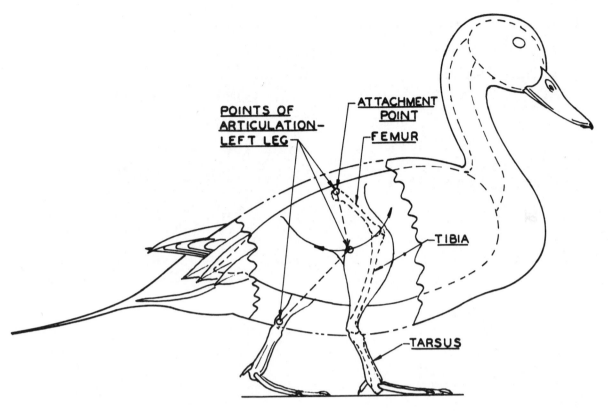

3-10 *Leg movement and leg musculature of a pintail.*

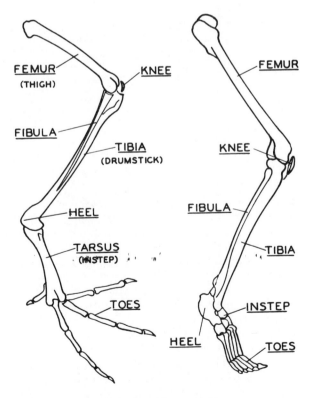

3-11 *Comparison of a duck's leg with a man's leg.*

A bird stands on its two legs, as does man, but there is little similarity between the two as far as posture is concerned (Fig. 3-11). For a human to simulate a bird's posture, he would have to stand on his tiptoes, draw his knees close to his chest, and bend his body forward until it was almost parallel to the ground. Obviously, this posture, if assumed by man for more than a few moments, would become quite uncomfortable. The bird assumes this position easily by virtue of its almost rigid back structure, long pelvis, short and heavily muscled forward-pointing thighs, and long, highly developed toes. Some birds (the partridge and quail families are good examples) can also stand, walk, and run, seemingly without effort, in an almost erect manner. However, with most birds, this upright position is usually assumed in an attempt to gain more visibility when they are alerted.

Unlike man's, the bird's thighbone (femur) is quite short and is articulated in a limited forward and backward direction only (Fig. 3-10). The thighbone is in turn articulated with the shinbone (tibia) at the knee in a similar manner to that of man's; however, due to the very short, forward-pointing thighbone and its high attachment point, the bird's knee is located against its body and, being completely covered by the side feathers, is never seen. The bird's thighbone superficially appears to be more a part of the body than of the leg. In the case of game birds, the muscled shinbone, or

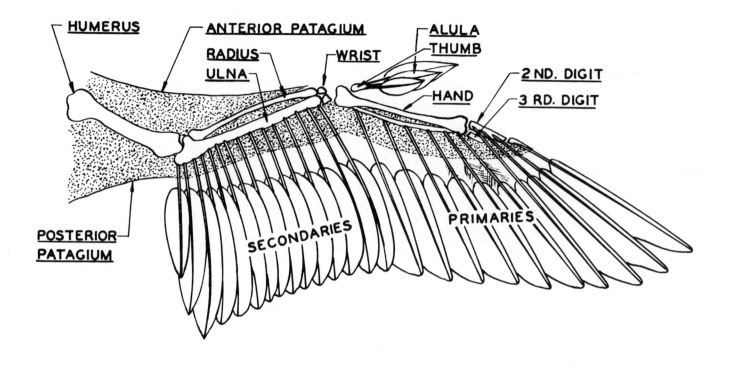

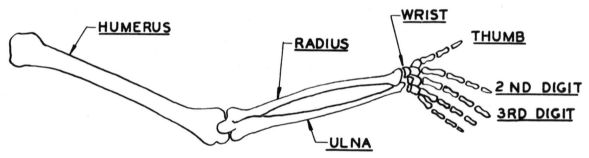

3-12 *Comparison of a duck's wing with a man's arm. The attachment of the flight feathers is also shown.*

drumstick, is also almost completely covered by the side feathers when the bird is standing. When the bird is walking or running, a larger part of the shinbone is exposed. Under most conditions, the unexposed part of the muscled shinbones modifies the overall body shape and, for that reason, must be noted by the carver.

The bird walks on its toes; the actual heel joint (commonly but erroneously referred to as the knee) is located close to the body, in some cases actually touching or hidden by the body-contour feathers. The metatarsal bones (the arch of man's foot) are fused on the bird into a single bone called the tarsus, which is almost always incorrectly called the leg. All game birds have three forward-pointing toes. Including the attachment joint, the outer toe has four joints, the middle toe three, and the inner toe two. On game birds, doves

and pigeons excepted, the fourth toe, called the hind toe, is relatively undeveloped and serves very little useful purpose.

Because of the large number and shape of the cervical vertebrae, the bird's neck is remarkably flexible in all directions; a common Canada goose has approximately twenty vertebrae compared to a giraffe's seven. A bird can move its head almost 180 degrees in either direction and can reach practically any part of the body with its beak. Since the bird's eyes are immovable, this flexibility of the neck is of great importance in detecting danger. It also aids the bird in obtaining food, feather-preening, and many other tasks. The long neck of a duck or goose is the ultimate in gracefulness; unfortunately, this attribute is seldom accurately duplicated in carvings. The carver should study these smoothly flowing, almost serpentine convolutions, at every opportunity.

The tail is supported and articulated in all directions by six caudal vertebrae terminating in a flattened bone (pygostyle) to which the tail feathers attach. The bird, by adept muscular control, can not only move its tail in any direction, it can fan out or compress its individual tail feathers, make them concave or convex, and can raise one side and lower the other (see Chapter 5). Understanding the significance of these various tail configurations is important in duplicating the bird's activity and imparting the feeling of motion.

The bird's wing, with its incomparable structure and matchless muscular control, represents one of nature's most marvelous adaptations. It is almost inconceivable that something so very light in weight, so superbly functional and durable, and so beautiful could have evolved over eons of time from the foreleg of the bird's reptilian ancestors.

The wing's skeletal structure is incredibly small in comparison to its total area and is located well forward, almost at its leading edge. The upper arm (humerus), the forearm (composed of two bones, the radius and the ulna), and the elbow are quite similar to man's (Fig. 3-12). The joints of a bird's wing also articulate in a manner very similar to man's. The bones of the bird's hand have been reduced to the second and third fingers, fused together, and a small thumb.

The ten primary feathers are attached to the hand and second and third fingers. The secondary feathers originate from the rearmost bone of the forearm (ulna). The thumb is articulated and bears the three feathers of the spurious wing, or alula. The primary, greater, middle, and most of the lesser coverts are attached to a long, flat membrane lying behind the bones of the hand and forearm. Stretching between the shoulder and wrist is another membrane (anterior patagium), which forms the leading edge of the wing in this area and is covered by small covert feathers. To the rear of the upper arm, a third membrane (posterior patagium) stretches from the elbow to the body.

The muscular control of the wing as a whole and of the individual flight feathers is extremely complex. How a bird instinctively masters the intricacies of flight is almost incomprehensible. There are muscles that extend, retract, and fold the wing; others control the wing fore and aft; and still others can rotate the wing as required. Small muscles and tendons located in the membrane along the rear of the fused fingers control the individual primary feathers. The major pectoral muscle — the large breast muscle that supplies the tremendous power for the downstroke — attaches to a ridge on the front face of the upper arm near where it is articulated with the body. The minor pectoral muscle, which supplies the much smaller, but vital, power for the upstroke, is located between the major pectoral muscle and the keel. How can a muscle located well below the wing possibly raise it? Nature has ingeniously supplied this muscle with a long tendon that passes up through a hole formed by the three shoulder bones and attaches to the top side of the upper arm. This hole acts as an efficient pulley for the tendon to work over. The pectoral muscles, both in weight and dimension, comprise a very large percent of the bird's body. They are important to the carver, for they can, and do, modify the body shape, especially in the bird's flight configuration.

4

Collecting Data

A certain amount of basic information on the particular bird to be carved is an absolute necessity before planning any serious carving. Ideally, this information should include overall dimensions of the bird and certain detail dimensions; the characteristic shape of the head, bill, neck, body, wings, tail, and feet; the color and markings of the plumage; the color of the bill and feet; and actual photographs of the bird showing its natural configuration in the pose to be duplicated. Unfortunately, most carvers are almost always forced to work with considerably less information. In too many instances, carvings are planned, carved, and painted from information limited to only one or two photos or illustrations. Obviously, the more information available for the planning, carving, and painting stages, the better the finished product will be.

COLLECTING PICTURES

First, acquire and save every actual game bird photograph that you can. *Audubon, National Wildlife, National Geographic*, many official state magazines, and the various sports magazines are all potential sources of good bird photographs. Many excellent bird books are available now (some of which are listed in the bibliography) which feature actual photographs, rather than artist's illustrations. This is not to suggest that you should not collect books illustrated by drawings and paintings, for many of these books can be

very helpful. Most artists and illustrators make every effort to portray the bird accurately, but small errors and a little artistic license are inevitable. It must be remembered, too, that the artists until recently had relatively few good action photographs to work from and had to rely completely on their ability to retain what they saw. Use actual photographs whenever possible. Man-made illustrations and photos of others' carvings should be used only as an aid for working out details difficult to obtain from actual bird pictures.

Conscientiously search for good game bird pictures and save all you find, and you will be amazed at the fast growth of your collection. Obviously, some systematic means of filing these pictures must be provided if they are to serve their purpose.

Don't attempt to save complete magazines with good bird photos, not only because of the storage problem involved, but also because of the difficulty of finding a particular picture in a large pile of publications. Instead, cut out important pictures and attach them by means of rubber cement or other adhesives to a fairly heavy 8½ x 11-inch sheet of paper and insert these sheets into looseleaf notebooks. The pictures of the male and female of only one species are put on a page. When the cut-out pictures are pasted up in this manner, the pages showing one species can easily be filed in one section of the notebook or in a separate notebook covering that species or a group of similar species. At present, the author has separate notebooks for geese, ducks, upland game birds, marsh birds, and shorebirds. These will be further broken down as the present books become full.

As you increase the number of bird books and other bound publications in your collection, it becomes very difficult to remember the location of the various good pictures of a certain game bird. One way to overcome this problem is to have a blank page, or part of a page, assigned to each species and to insert it in the notebook next to the corresponding page on which the pictures of that species are pasted. The location by publication and page number of each good picture of this species is then written on this page. The same could be accomplished with a small card file. Another method is to photographically copy the better pictures and paste the prints in the notebooks along with the cut-out pictures.

Another very important aspect of data collection is a systematic filing of all pertinent information used to make a particular carving. The author uses a file consisting of 9 × 12-inch envelopes, one for each game bird species, containing all drawings and sketches, detail feather-pattern drawings, and cross-sectional templates required to make the carving. If several carvings of a particular species have been made, the individual sketches and drawings are identified and dated accordingly.

BIRD SPECIMENS

There is no better source for data than an actual specimen (Figs. 4-1, 2, 3). Game bird carvers have one advantage over other bird carvers: specimens can be collected legally during the open hunting seasons. Specimens can also be pur-

4-1 *Black duck mounted by author.*

4-2 *Dried mountain quail wing.*

4-3 *Study skin, skinned head, and dried feet prepared by author.*

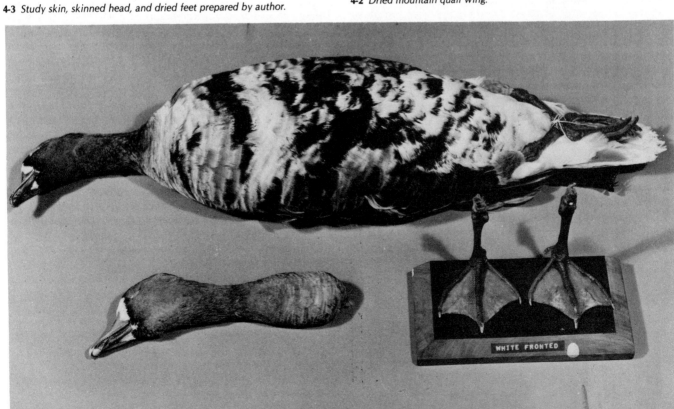

chased from game bird farms. Even the carver who does not hunt usually has hunter friends who normally are glad to help out. Heads, wings, and feet – some of the most difficult parts of the bird to carve – are discarded when the bird is cleaned.

Specimens and parts can be preserved for a short time by freezing; however, providing the necessary freezer space and using the frozen specimens for reference eventually present problems. The serious carver who wishes to retain specimens for use over the years should make a special effort to learn how to permanently preserve the whole bird and bird parts he acquires. Several publications on this subject are listed in the bibliography.

AMATEUR PHOTOGRAPHY

Amateur photography can aid in collecting carving data in at least two ways. First, the serious carver will soon want either to give some of his carvings to friends or to sell them. Once the carving is gone, it is amazing how soon the pertinent details of the carving are forgotten. With photographs of his carvings for reference, the carver can see where he has been, so to speak, and these pictures can help immeasurably in improving future work. Also, it is almost a necessity to have photos of his work available if he intends to exhibit or sell.

Second, by amateur photography the carver can build a file of live bird pictures to which he can refer for planning and carving data. As previously mentioned, it is practically impossible to recreate by sketching or to retain in memory the myriad details of a bird's structure, position, feathering, and coloration. Only the camera can capture and accurately record these all-important features.

The photographing of wild birds in their natural habitat can be very difficult, time-consuming, and expensive; however, taking pictures of these same bird species in parks, zoos, private aviaries, game refuges, and game farms is much easier, and good results can usually be obtained with considerably less effort and expense.

There is available today a bewildering array of cameras, lenses, and accessories, most of which meet the requirements of the carver-photographer. The larger formats (2¼ × 2¼ inches and bigger) are best for taking good portraits of bird carvings, but they have several drawbacks when photographing live birds.

One of the biggest difficulties in bird photography is getting the camera close enough to the subject so that the bird's image, recorded on the film, will be sufficiently large to produce a usable print without excessive enlarging. In almost all cases, longer focal length (telephoto) lenses, which magnify the subject, must be used. If the camera-to-subject distance remains constant, lenses of the same focal length produce images of the same size, regardless of the format size of the camera. Therefore, in order to utilize the negative of the larger format camera to advantage, the camera either has to be moved closer to the subject or a lens of a much longer focal length must be used. If all other factors, such as

resolving power of the lens, sharpness of focus, proper exposure, film quality, and quality of processing remain constant, in the final analysis the actual size of the image on the film is much more important that the size of the negative itself. Long focal length lenses with adequate covering power for the larger format cameras are very expensive; the range of focal lengths and their availability are extremely limited; and they are bulky and heavy. Except when used on the larger single-lens reflex cameras, the long focal length lenses present formidable viewing and focusing problems.

Considering original cost and availability of camera, lenses, and accessories, cost of film and processing, and portability, the 35-mm camera, featuring interchangeable lenses, is probably the best single piece of equipment for photographing both carvings and live birds.

There are two basic types of 35-mm cameras from which to choose, both capable of meeting the carver-photographer's requirements: the rangefinder (RF) type and the single-lens reflex (SLR) type. The fundamental differences and some of the advantages of these two types of 35-mm cameras will be discussed below.

35-mm Rangefinder Camera

Viewing and focusing are accomplished in the rangefinder camera by an optical-mechanical system that is completely separate from the camera lens. There are disadvantages connected with this arrangement. As the viewer must be located at a distance above the lens centerline, the photographer sees the object or scene being photographed slightly differently than the camera lens sees it. This difference is referred to as parallax. The designers of late-model RF cameras overcame this problem with a mechanical linkage, operated by the focusing mechanism, which automatically corrects the scene observed in the viewer to coincide with the picture recorded on the film.

The field of the viewer is correct for only one focal length of lens. If lenses are interchanged, either accessory viewers must be used to show the correct field for each lens, or the built-in viewer must be designed to permit the selection of several different fields. On most late-model rangefinder cameras, the change of field with a built-in viewer is either automatic with the change of lens or must be made manually. The Leica M4, for example, automatically shows the correct fields of view for the 35-mm, 50-mm, 90-mm, and 135-mm focal length lenses. Most popular RF cameras do not provide a built-in viewer for use with a lens with a focal length exceeding 135-mm.

Although there are many long focal length lenses available for 35-mm cameras, there are very few (probably none over 180-mm focal length) that can be easily adapted for direct use on the rangefinder camera. Some manufacturers of photographic equipment have designed an accessory, called a reflex housing, which attaches between the camera body and the lens and permits viewing and focusing through the lens. In effect, this device converts the rangefinder camera into a single-lens reflex camera and permits the use of a few special lenses, some of them in the 200-mm to 640-mm focal length range. The reflex housing is not cheap, and it is

4-4 *A modern single-lens reflex camera featuring automatic exposure with manual override control.*

bulky and heavy. In the author's opinion, it would be more economical and practical to buy a good SLR body (camera less lens) for use with the long lenses.

The rangefinder camera, when equipped with the proper lens and viewing-focusing means, will take excellent pictures. Fine, used cameras of this type often can be purchased for a fraction of their original cost; however, it is strongly recommended that the amateur acquaint himself with all of the problems mentioned here, especially those involving the use of long focal length lenses, before he invests his money in a camera of this type.

35-mm Single-Lens Reflex Camera

Practically all of the problems of the rangefinder camera have been eliminated in the design of the modern SLR camera (Fig. 4-4). Also, one additional feature, vital to bird photography, has been incorporated.

Viewing and focusing are accomplished in the SLR camera through the lens itself. The parallax problem inherent in the RF camera is eliminated, as is the necessity of providing a viewer for each different focal length lens used. Viewing through the lens is done by means of a hinged mirror, located just behind the lens, which reflects the image 90 degrees upward to a ground-glass focusing screen. The mirror swings out of the way automatically when the picture is taken. This image on the ground glass is normally viewed through another optical system, called the pentaprism, which corrects the reversed image on the ground glass and permits the photographer to view the scene as he would normally see it. The photographer thus views the exact picture that the camera records on the film. Another important advantage of the SLR camera is that the lenses (and there are many from which to choose) can be readily interchanged and the photographer can view and focus without any alterations to the camera or the need of special accessories.

A significant advantage of the newer SLR camera over the RF camera is behind-the-lens exposure meters. The actual intensity of the light reaching the film is accurately measured regardless of the focal length of the lens or its focusing distance. This feature is particularly valuable when long lenses are used with extension tubes for close focusing distances or when tele-extenders are used for increased focal lengths. These arrangements require a not-easily-determined increase in exposure, since the light has to travel farther.

Many of the newer model SLR cameras incorporate automatic exposure control. On the better cameras, this automatic feature can be overridden, and the shutter speed and aperture adjusted manually to obtain the correct exposure. On a few cameras, the automatic feature can be compensated manually to correct for extreme conditions, such as strong back lighting. Most cameras with automatic exposure incorporate either shutter-preferred exposure or aperture-preferred exposure (on at least one model, either method can be selected). With the shutter-preferred system, the desired shutter speed is selected manually and the aperture (diaphragm) is controlled automatically. On the aperture-preferred system, the aperture is selected manually and the shutter speed is controlled automatically.

When taking pictures of birds that seldom remain still for long, the amateur photographer needs every convenience that he can get for fast, accurate focusing and exposure control.

Selecting Camera and Lenses

So much 35-mm camera equipment is available today and at such a range in price that the selection of a camera and lenses becomes very confusing. Take your time and become thoroughly familiar with some of the different popular makes of cameras. Visit a number of camera stores, if possible, state your specific needs, and obtain recommendations from a number of camera salesmen. Using the actual recommended equipment, try focusing on objects of the size and at the distance that will exist under actual conditions; familiarize yourself with the exposure control; try changing lenses; and perform any other operation that may be necessary for the particular camera. In addition, it is strongly advised that the amateur rent the camera and lens of his choice (many camera stores rent equipment) for a short time and use the equipment in the field before buying.

In selecting a camera and a standard lens (usually 50- to 58-mm focal length), an important point to consider is how close to the subject the lens will focus. This minimum focusing distance varies considerably with different makes of cameras. It is almost always desirable to fill the negative, and it is also desirable or necessary at times to take detailed, close-up pictures – for example, the head and bill or feet of the carving. The amateur should try to anticipate the smallest object he may wish to photograph and try to pick a camera-lens combination that will handle the situation. To photograph quite small objects, it may be necessary to buy accessories such as close-up lenses or even extension bellows.

Before deciding on a particular camera and lens, the amateur should test the camera's viewing and focusing capabilities with a telephoto lens of at least 400-mm focal length. Focusing screens that work well with the normal lenses

(50- to 58-mm) are usually inadequate for use with longer lenses. Most bird photographers prefer to use plain ground-glass focusing screens. The split-image microprism focusing feature, which is standard on most SLR cameras, tends to black out when used with lenses whose focal length is 200- to 250-mm or more. A few SLR cameras have interchangeable focusing screens, and there are usually a number of screens from which to choose. When selecting a camera, the amateur should definitely pick one whose focusing screens can easily be interchanged.

For photographing live birds, a telephoto lens of at least 200-mm focal length for the 35-mm camera is normally required. The amateur should not overestimate the magnifying power of the long lenses. For example, when using a 35-mm camera equipped with a 200-mm focal length lens, it is necessary to be within ten feet of a bird the size of a mallard in order to fill the negative. This distance would increase to twenty feet when a 400-mm focal length lens is used and to approximately thirty-five feet with a 640-mm lens. Minimum focusing distance is also a very important consideration when selecting the telephoto lens. There is nothing to be gained by going to a 400-mm lens, if, because of minimum focusing distance it becomes necessary to back away from the object being photographed until only one half of the negative is used. The same results could be obtained much less expensively with a 200-mm lens, provided that this lens has a minimum focusing distance one half that of the 400-mm lens.

The minimum focusing distance on most telephoto lenses can be reduced somewhat by the use of an extension tube inserted between the camera body and lens. This reduction in minimum focusing distance is gained at the expense of not being able to focus on objects at distances that approach the infinity end of the focusing range. For example, the 400-mm Novoflex Nesting Tele Lens has a minimum focusing distance of approximately fourteen feet. When an extension tube 21-mm in length is inserted between the lens and camera body, the minimum focusing distance is reduced to approximately eleven feet. The maximum focusing distance is reduced from infinity to approximately sixty feet.

Tele-zoom lenses have been improved greatly during the past few years, and many good ones now are available in the 80- to 210-mm focal length range, and at least one each in the 85- to 250-mm and 100- to 300-mm ranges. These lenses usually have a minimum focusing distance of about six feet — about one half of that on most telephoto lenses — and are ideal for photographing birds that can be closely approached.

Also improved are tele-converters, or extenders, which are small, optical devices that can be inserted between the camera and the lens to increase the focal length of the lens. These extenders double (2X) or triple (3X) the focal length of the lens on which they are used. There are advantages and disadvantages connected with use of extenders. On the plus side: great increases of focal length with small increases in size, weight, and cost and without increasing the minimum focusing distance (very important for close-up photography). On the minus side: decreased speed of the lens (with a 2X extender, the lens speed is cut in half) and the magnification of the optical deficiencies of the lens plus

the addition of some new ones. On the whole, the better extenders do a fair to good job. Some of the higher priced tele-zoom lenses have matching extenders that are designed to give optimum performance. If the lighting conditions permit a lens with a 2X converter to be stopped down to f/8 or smaller (the effective diaphragm opening thus becoming f/16 or smaller), satisfactory results can be gotten. However, although a converter is inexpensive, light, and convenient, it will not produce results comparable to a telephoto lens whose focal length is the same as the telephoto-converter combination.

A number of SLR camera manufacturers now have power winders (autowinders) available at a reasonable cost. These battery-powered units are capable of advancing the film and releasing the shutter at speeds up to about three frames per second. They are very useful for bird photography and permit the amateur photographer to get many shots he would normally miss while manually advancing the film.

Owing to the magnifying ability of the long focal length lenses, any camera movement is also magnified; therefore, it usually becomes necessary, unless a very fast shutter speed is used, to provide a support for the camera when lenses longer than 150-mm focal length are required. Even when the camera is mounted on a sturdy tripod, some shake or vibration can still exist, and it is advisable to use a shutter speed of 1/125 second or faster when using lenses with focal lengths in excess of 300 mm.

Because of practical limitations of size, weight, and cost, long focal length lenses are much slower than standard focal length lenses. The terms "fast" or "slow" when used in reference to a lens indicate in general terms the light-gathering ability of the lens. The speed of the lens (not to be confused with the shutter speed) is dependent on the diameter of the lens, or more accurately, the maximum aperture of the lens. For example, if a 400-mm focal length lens were designed to have the same light-gathering capability, or "speed," of a standard 50-mm, f/8 lens, the 400-mm lens would be in excess of nine inches in diameter. This lens would obviously be a costly and heavy piece of equipment.

Under actual usage, it soon becomes very apparent that the slow, long focal length lenses, combined with the necessary faster shutter speeds, have very definite limitations in regard to available light. This limitation can be offset, to a degree, by using films with fast emulsion speeds (high ASA ratings). Generally speaking, however, the faster the emulsion speed, the grainier the film, and the smaller the amount the negative can be enlarged and still produce a usable print.

Practically all of the normal focal length lenses purchased as standard equipment on SLR cameras have automatic diaphragms. An automatic diaphragm permits the photographer to compose the picture and focus with the lens at its maximum opening. With the lens at maximum opening, the image is at its maximum brightness and the depth of field (the distance in front of and behind the subject within which all objects are in focus) is at its minimum. These are conditions for optimum focusing. When the shutter is released, the diaphragm stops down to a preselected opening.

Although a very desirable feature, many telephoto lenses

do not have automatic diaphragms; some have preset diaphragms; others have single, manual, click-stop control rings.

The most important considerations in selecting a telephoto lens, in addition to general overall quality, are ease and accuracy of focusing, diaphragm control, minimum focusing distance, and lens speed (maximum aperture). The amateur should be very deliberate in his selection, and, again, he should try to use the lens of his choice under actual field conditions before buying.

Photographing Bird Carvings

While it is important to photograph the carving from an angle that will produce the best picture for sales or publicity purposes, it is necessary to take pictures from several different angles so that a complete photographic record of the carving is made. The pictures should include a direct profile view, three-quarter front and rear views, front view, rear view (preferably taken from a fairly high angle so that the back of the carving will be shown), and any detail shots that seem important.

There are at least two simple, popular ways of photographing a bird carving. One is to photograph the carving against a perfectly plain background, attempting to eliminate distracting shadows. When taking black-and-white pictures, it is also desirable to eliminate or reduce any differentiation in shade between the horizontal surface upon which the carving rests and the vertical surface forming the background. This may not always apply when photographing in color. The other method is to photograph the bird carving in a natural background (Figure 4-6). In this case, shadows are usually desirable, provided they do not detract from the carving itself.

One of the simplest ways of lighting the subject is to photograph the carving in the shade, using only available outdoor light (Fig. 4-5). When this method is used, shadows are subdued or reduced to a minimum. For black-and-white pictures, a light-colored background (light gray works well) should be used. For color pictures, a background paper of a contrasting color, which adds interest to the photograph, may be desirable.

When it is not convenient to take pictures outside, or if the weather does not cooperate, the amateur has to resort to an artificial light source. Although either flashbulbs or an electronic flash can be used, there are two disadvantages. First, unless the flash is bounced off the ceiling or some other reflective surface, the resulting picture will be quite flat, and there will often be harsh, distracting shadows. Second, it is usually difficult to accurately determine the proper exposure except by trial and error.

Good, consistent results can be quite easily obtained with the use of two inexpensive photoflood lights and reflectors (preferably supported by stands) when the camera, lights, and subject are arranged as shown in Figure 4-7. The background paper is continued from the vertical onto the table as before. The photoflood light reflectors are pointed straight up and the light is bounced off the ceiling. If the ceiling is reasonably reflective, the carving will receive a soft light and shadows will be practically eliminated. If

shadows are desired, the photoflood lights (or light) can be placed and directed at the subject in many ways, giving a variety of effects. Also, a combination of indirect and direct lighting can be used to give pleasing and sometimes dramatic effects. However, direct lighting is generally harsher and produces a more contrasty picture that often does not show the carving to its best advantage.

When taking pictures in artificial light, the exposure time is increased, requiring slower shutter speeds. Therefore, a tripod or some other support for the camera is an absolute necessity.

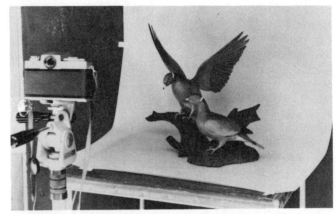

4-5 *Photographing a bird carving with natural light.*

4-6 *Photographing a bird carving using natural background.*

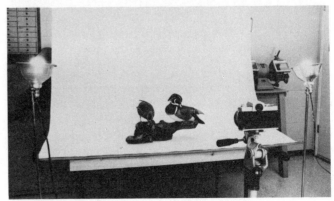

4-7 *Photographing a bird carving with artificial light.*

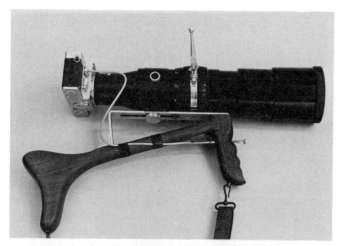

4-8 *Homemade gunstock type mount for 500-mm telephoto lens.*

4-9 *Homemade gunstock type mount for 85- to 250-mm zoom lens. Camera equipped with power winder. An ideal setup for photographing birds when they can be approached closely.*

Photographing Live Birds

Before attempting to photograph live birds, thoroughly familiarize yourself with your equipment. Practice focusing on objects the size of a bird located at a distance likely under actual conditions. Focusing the long lenses is extremely critical, and birds seldom stand still for long, if at all; learn to focus quickly and accurately. Also, practice using the exposure controls (diaphragm and shutter speed) until all of these operations become more or less automatic.

The long lenses and the camera must be supported by a tripod or by some other means. As the birds are generally moving, the camera cannot be locked into one position on the tripod. It is usually desirable to tighten the pan control (azimuth) and the elevation control until there is a slight restraint to movement. The camera can then be moved the necessary amount to follow the bird's movements. The shutter release should be carefully squeezed — like the trigger on a rifle — to reduce movement of the camera.

Unless the photographer is operating from a fixed position, such as a blind, a tripod is very cumbersome to transport, set up, and use. Furthermore, in many instances a tripod does not provide sufficient flexibility, for example, when photographing birds in flight — a difficult task even under the most ideal conditions. When the subject is moving rapidly, better pictures can be gotten by mounting the camera and lens on a structure similar to the stock of a gun, which is held by both hands and braced against the shoulder, thereby reducing unwanted camera movement (Figs. 4-8, 9). When this equipment is used, shutter speeds of 1/250 second, or faster, must be maintained. Shutter speeds of 1/500 second, or faster, are required to stop the rapid wing movement of birds in flight.

While the gunstock mount is a necessity for photographing birds in flight, it also works well for photographing sitting, standing, or swimming birds and gives the photographer much greater mobility. When photographing birds, ease of movement is of great importance; if the photographer is loaded down with equipment, he will spend more time moving this equipment than taking pictures. The author learned this the hard way and now limits his equipment to the gunstock mount, one lens (usually an automatic diaphragm 500-mm telephoto), two camera bodies (one loaded with black-and-white film and the other with color), and plenty of film.

If the carver has actual specimens available for color reference, there is not much to be gained by taking color pictures. Black-and-white film generally has more latitude (greater allowance for error) than color film and is, of course, much cheaper to use. Contact-size proofs can be inexpensively made of all the black-and-white film that has been exposed, and if a magnifying glass is used for making the selection, only sharp, well-exposed pictures need be enlarged. Two popular American black-and-white films produce good results: Kodak Plus X (ASA speed 125) and Kodak Tri X (ASA speed 400). For most lenses with focal lengths of over 400 mm, it is often mandatory to use the faster Tri X film so that shutter speeds of 1/125 second or faster can be used in conjunction with smaller apertures which produce greater depths of field and in turn make focusing somewhat less critical.

When taking pictures of a particular bird, try to get shots from different angles: profile, front and rear, three-quarters front and rear, and from overhead, if possible. Also try to get pictures of the bird in different poses: alert, swimming, preening, sleeping, stretching, and others.

MUSEUMS AS SOURCES

Another source of information commonly overlooked is the natural history museum. Museum curators and preparators are especially helpful in passing a wealth of information on to the carver.

Many museums not only have fine reference libraries, they usually have on display mounted specimens of all the game birds, and, in addition, large collection of study skins. In some cases, if the proper contacts are established, it may even be possible to borrow some of their study skins. Some museums are in need of certain specimens to complete or to provide more depth to their collections. It is possible that the carver can reciprocate the museum's generosity by supplying some of these specimens when they can be legally taken.

CHAPTER

5
Making the Drawing

The success of a realistic bird carving greatly depends on how well it was planned in the drawing stage. Unless the original cut-out of the rough block is made from a drawing based on accurate dimensions and proportions and a graceful, natural pose of the bird, no amount of good carving and painting will save the finished product from looking amateurish. It is possible to make some corrections during the carving procedure by removing more wood than originally planned; however, adding wood is often a real problem. Some carvers attempt to work out the important lines and details of the carving as they proceed with the actual wood removal. While this "by guess and by golly" method of carving may occasionally turn out fairly well, depending on the carver's experience, ability, and luck, more often than not the end product betrays the lack of early thought and planning. This does not mean that every detail of the carving has to be worked out on the drawing prior to doing any work on the carving itself. Such details as feather-pattern layouts can usually be more easily accomplished on the curved surface of the carving after its overall shape has been established. The drawing does not have to be a thing of beauty in itself. Its primary purpose is to produce a good carving; its secondary purpose is to provide a record for possible future use.

The aspiring bird carver does not use his full creative ability until he plans his own carvings and makes his own drawings. As long as he uses other carver's drawings and attempts to duplicate other carver's work, his carvings will not be truly original, and his own distinctive style will not develop.

ALTERING EXISTING DRAWINGS

If the beginner has little drawing experience and possesses limited dimensional and structural information on game birds, it may be to his advantage to start by altering other carvers' drawings before attempting a completely original drawing. However, this practice should be discontinued as soon as he has gained some confidence in his own ability to plan a carving. Carving planning, like the actual carving, can only be learned by doing.

When altering an existing drawing that is not your own, realize that you may be copying another's mistakes; therefore, attempt to check such important points as overall dimensions, shape, etc., as thoroughly as possible within the limits of the data you possess.

For all practical purposes, the position of the head on a decoy carving establishes the activity of the bird: relaxed, alert, sleeping, preening, feeding, drinking, displaying, attacking, or others. On standing carvings, the position of the body, legs, wings, and tail are also very important and complement the head position in duplicating the attitude of the bird.

A simple change in the head position of the bird is probably one of the most common alterations to an existing drawing and suitable for a first attempt. Extreme head positions are very difficult to work out accurately on paper, and usually some cutting, fitting, and other alterations are required during the actual carving procedure.

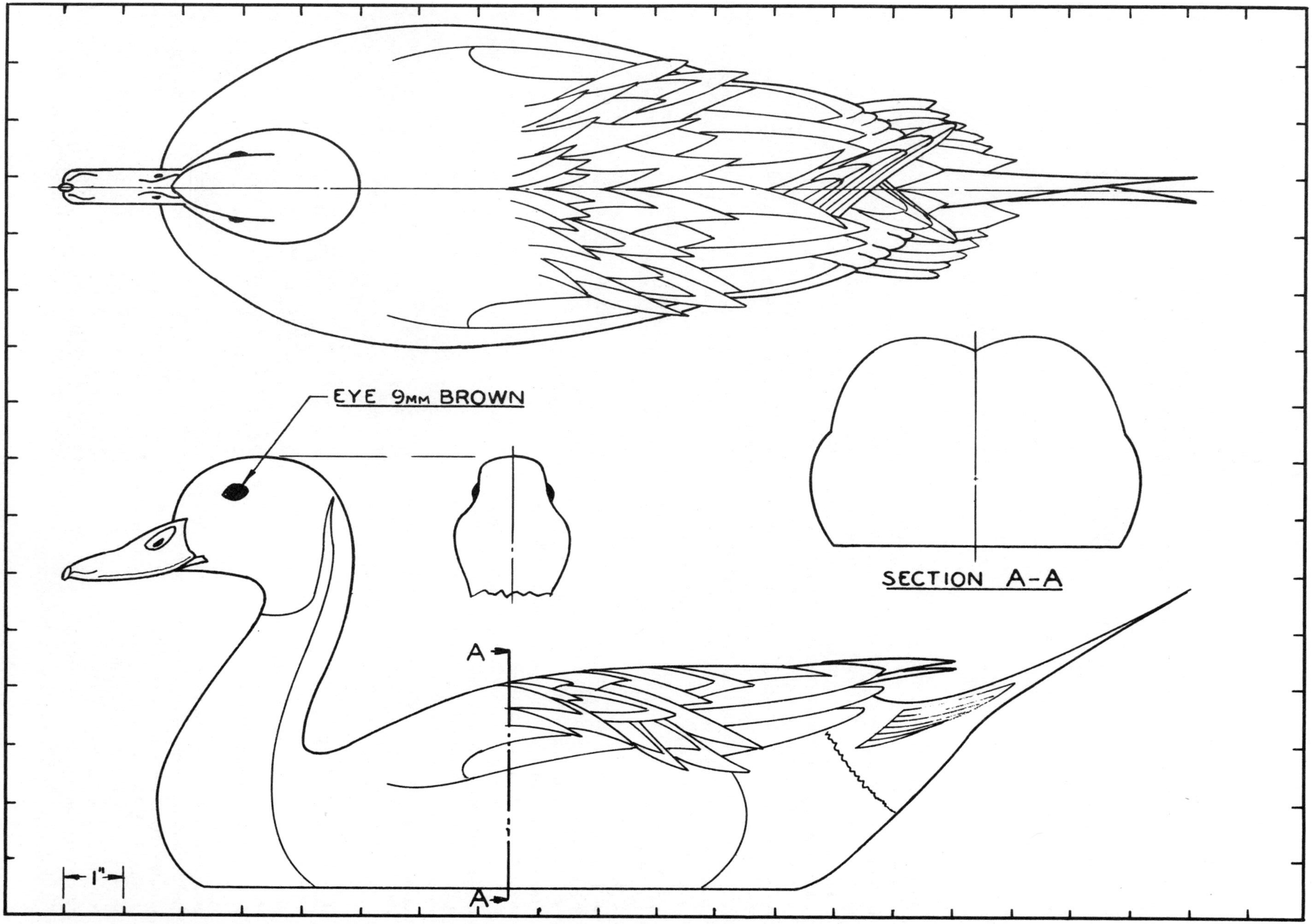

SECTION A-A

EYE 9MM BROWN

5-4 Pintail drake drinking or feeding.

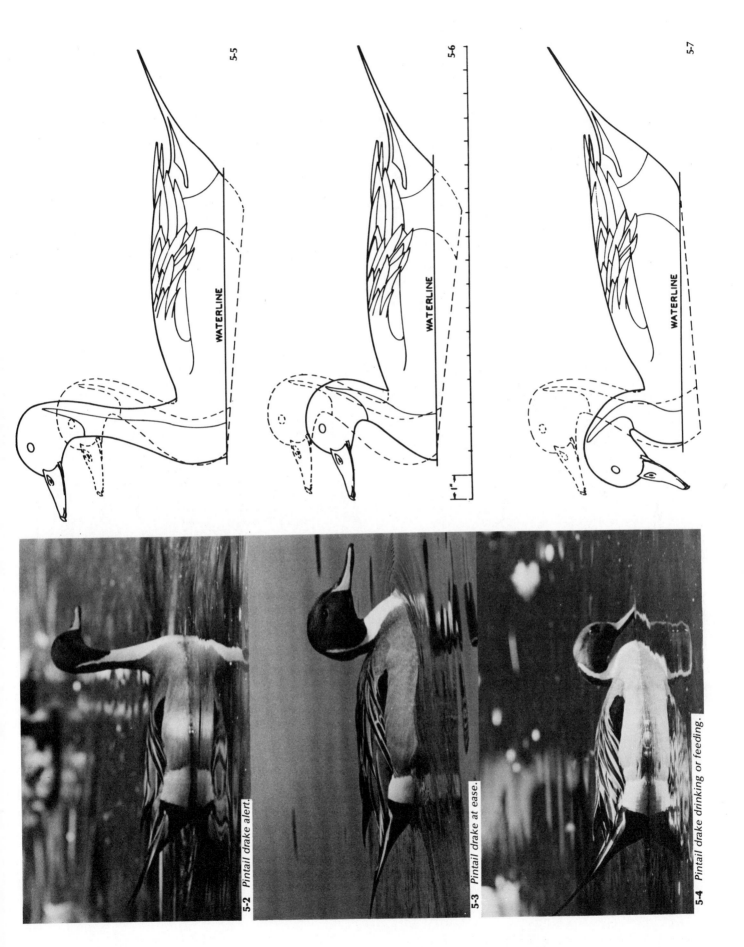

5-5

5-6

5-7

WATERLINE

WATERLINE

WATERLINE

1"

5-2 *Pintail drake alert.*

5-3 *Pintail drake at ease.*

5-4 *Pintail drake drinking or feeding.*

Start by making a layout (preferably on vellum or other thin, transparent paper) of the drawing to be altered. The drawing can be enlarged or reduced by means of squares, a method described in Chapter 1. After the drawing has been copied to the desired scale, trace off the head and part of the neck on a separate piece of paper and use this tracing as an overlay (or underlay) on the drawing to determine the new head position. Now, move the overlay drawing around until the head appears to be in the required position. Transfer the head in its new position to the drawing and blend the neck and chest lines into the original drawing. It is often necessary to try several head positions before obtaining one that looks right.

Except in the case of some extreme head positions, it is much easier to work out the new position with the head pointed directly forward. If the head is to be turned to one side or the other, the head-to-body joint should be made parallel to the water or to the ground, depending on whether the carving is a decoy or standing. The head can be rotated on this plane without introducing another, possibly undesirable, angle.

To provide an example, a drawing of a pintail drake (Fig. 5-1) has been altered to portray the three different head positions shown in Figures 5-2 through 5-4.

Other alterations to the profile view, such as changes in the body position, tail position, and, on standing and flying carvings, leg and wing positions, can usually be accomplished by the overlay method. Before attempting to alter any drawing, the beginner should make every attempt to find an actual photograph showing the bird in the approximate position that he is trying to duplicate.

MAKING ORIGINAL DRAWINGS

One of the better ways to work out a good drawing is to obtain dimensions from a fresh or frozen specimen and to determine the natural shape and position from actual photographs. For those who do not have access to acutal specimens, some of the more important dimensions of the various game birds have been included in Chapter 11. Mounted birds are excellent studies for establishing feather pattern and color and also for procuring bill, foot, and tarsi shape and dimensions, but they are seldom accurate enough for determining body form, position, and overall dimensions.

Since it is easier to make a drawing for a decoy carving, a drawing of a male Barrow's golden-eye decoy will be made step-by-step as an example.

Before starting a drawing, first assemble all of the study data (specimens, actual photographs, artist's drawings and paintings, etc.) available on the particular species to be portrayed. However, in this example the Barrow's golden-eye drawing will be made entirely from information contained in this publication.

The Barrow's golden-eye is of the subfamily called sea or diving ducks, more commonly called divers. In Chapter 10, the diving ducks are described generally as having a low body profile when in the water. Their bodies are usually

parallel to the water, and their tails are often close to the water or actually touching it, as shown in Figure 5-8.

The profile (side) view should be worked out first. As Figure 5-8 shows a direct side view, a fairly accurate profile drawing can be made by tracing or sketching directly from this photograph (Fig. 5-9). After the drawing has been made from this photograph, enlarge it to the desired size of the carving, which in this example will be life size. Lay out lines on the traced drawing or sketch forming squares of .2 inches. (The squares could be larger or smaller, but in this case this size of square gives about the number of lines required to make an accurate enlargement.) Number the horizontal and vertical lines as shown. The approximate body length for a male Barrow's golden-eye as given in Chapter 11 is 13.0 inches. The body length of the bird in Figure 5-8 is 2.6 inches. The size of squares required to produce a life-size drawing

5-8 *Male Barrow's golden-eye.*

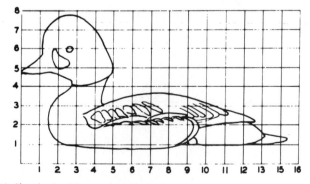

5-9 *Sketch of golden-eye from Figure 5-8.*

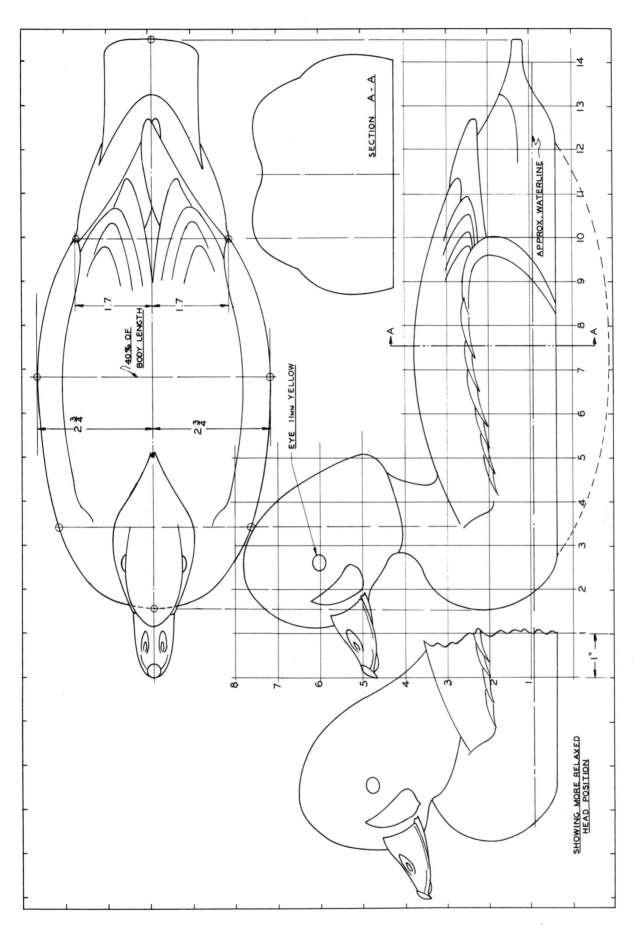

SECTION A-A

40% OF
BODY LENGTH

1.7   1.7

2 3/4   2 3/4

EYE 11MM YELLOW

A   A

APPROX. WATERLINE

14 13 12 11 10 9 8 7 6 5 4 3 2

1"

8 7 6 5 4 3 2 1

SHOWING MORE RELAXED
HEAD POSITION

5-10 *Barrow's golden-eye drake decoy.*

is determined by simple ratio and proportion:

.2 inches = the size of squares on the drawing to be enlarged.

Let x = the size of squares required for the life-size drawing.

$$\text{Then } \frac{2.6}{13.0} = \frac{.2}{x} \text{ or } x = \frac{13.0 \times .2}{2.6} = 1.0 \text{ inches}$$

A drawing composed of 1.0-inch squares can now be made, and the horizontal and vertical lines are numbered in the same manner as on the small, traced drawing. The life-size profile of the bird is drawn in freehand in the manner described in Chapter 1 (Fig. 5-10). A tracing should now be made of the life-size bill profile of a male Barrow's golden-eye shown in Chapter 13. Use this tracing to correct, if necessary, the bill on the enlarged, life-size profile drawing.

Next, make the plan view of the drawing. Photographs showing the top views of waterfowl are very scarce; therefore, a certain amount of improvising almost always has to be done in establishing this view. First, draw a centerline above the profile view and parallel to the waterline. Then, project the body length of the profile view up to this centerline. The overall width of the body (with the wings folded) of a male Barrow's golden-eye is given in Chapter 11 as 5.5 inches. Lines parallel to the centerline, located at 2.75 inches on either side, are now drawn. The maximum body width of most waterfowl occurs at approximately 40 to 50 per cent of the body length. Locate this general area on the plan view. Project up from the profile view a line from the rearmost side feather. (These feathers are edged in black and are difficult to see in the photograph.) Also, project a line from the approximate intersection of the foremost side feathers and the scapulars. The body width of waterfowl decreases quite rapidly in the flank and chest areas. Referring to Figure 5-11, the maximum body width is measured as 1.3 inches. The width of the body at the termination of the side feathers measures .80 inches. The life-size width of the body in the forward flank area can now be determined.

Let x = the life-size body width in the forward flank area,

$$\text{then } \frac{1.3}{5.5} = \frac{.80}{x} \text{ or } x = \frac{5.5 \times .80}{1.3} = 3.4 \text{ inches}$$

Locate this width on the plan-view drawing.

The width of the tail is rather hard to discern in Figure 5-11, but it is much narrower than the forward flank area. In any case, waterfowl, by means of muscular feather control, can alter the width of the relaxed tail, at will. As a very rough approximation, the width of the relaxed tail on diving ducks runs around 40 per cent of the body width. For puddle ducks and geese, this percentage is somewhat greater, probably around 50 per cent. The general planform shape of the tail of divers and most geese is nearly rectangular, while the tail shape of the puddle ducks is more nearly triangular.

Now, add the planform of the tail in the plan view. The width of the chest also varies because of muscular feather control but probably approximates 80 percent of the body width. Draw the chest in the plan view as one half of an oval or ellipse. Now, complete the planform shape on one

side of the centerline by drawing smooth curves connecting the points shown. (On any symmetrical view or section, it is always advisable to work out one side of the drawing first, then trace it off, and transfer it to the other side of the drawing.) The plan-view drawing at this point is sufficient for making the block cut-out. If the beginner desires, he can add other details, such as the plan view of the head and bill and feather detail. As mentioned before, it is usually easier to work out the various feather patterns on the carving itself after the overall body shape has been established.

Now, draw a cross-sectional view through the maximum body section. Fortunately, Figure 5-11 gives an almost direct view of the body shape. This photo can be traced or sketched and then enlarged in a manner similar to that described for the profile view. Actually, when a rectangle representing the width and height of the life-size body section is drawn, it is relatively easy to sketch the body shape without resorting to the square method.

5-11 Rear view of a Barrow's golden-eye drake.

Figure 5-11 can also be used for determining head widths. The maximum head width is measured as .44 inches. The width of the head above the eyes is measured as .33 inches. The measured width of the body is 1.35 inches, and the actual life-size width of the body is 5.5 inches. The head widths can now be found by ratio and proportion:

Let x = the maximum head width,

$$\text{then } \frac{1.35}{5.5} = \frac{.44}{x} \text{ or } x = \frac{5.5 \times .44}{1.35} = 1.8 \text{ inches}$$

Let y = the head width above the eyes,

$$\text{then } \frac{1.35}{5.5} = \frac{.33}{y} \text{ or } y = \frac{5.5 \times .33}{1.35} = 1.35 \text{ inches}$$

Figure 5-12 shows male Barrow's golden-eyes in a more relaxed position. By using the procedure covered earlier in this chapter it now is easy to alter Figure 5-10 so that it approximates this new position.

Figures 5-13 through 5-17 provide subjects for practice in making original drawings of decoys.

5-12 Four Barrow's golden-eye drakes try to gain the attention of a female.

5-13 Female shoveler.

5-14 Male shoveler.

5-15 Rear view of a male shoveler.

5-16 Ruddy duck drake.

5-17 Front view of a ruddy duck drake.

DRAWINGS FOR STANDING CARVINGS

Next, attempt a drawing for a standing carving. These drawings are not much more difficult to make than drawings for decoy carvings, except that some knowledge of the placement and size of the bird's tarsi and feet is required.

The direct, profile view of a male pintail shown in Figure 5-18 can be copied and enlarged by using the procedure described earlier. (See Figure 5-19.)

In this example, the tarsi location is easily obtained from Fig. 5-18. However, it is sometimes necessary to rework a decoy drawing into a drawing for a standing carving or to work from a picture of a floating bird. As an aid to the carver, the length of the tarsus and the overall length and width of the feet are included in Chapter 11. The approximate tarsi locations are shown in Chapter 12. The tarsus length given is the distance from the bottom of the foot up to the first joint. On most waterfowl and also marsh and shore birds, the entire joint and also some of the lower part of the tibia (drumstick) is covered with scales and is usually exposed. About 10 to 20 per cent of the tarsus length given in Chapter 11 should be added to obtain the approximate overall length of the exposed "leg" on these species. The tarsus length for the pintail drake is given as 1.87 inches, to which 20 per cent, or .37 inches, is added, giving an overall length of the exposed "leg" of 2.25 inches. This dimension is now used to establish the groundline in the profile view of the drawing.

The feet and tarsi of birds in the same game bird family are similar, except for size. By using dimensions given in Chapter 11, in conjunction with photos or sketches shown in Chapter 12, it is fairly easy to approximate the size and shape of the tarsi and feet. However, more realistic results can be obtained with much less effort if actual specimens are available for reference. Avoid making the feet of waterfowl in an exactly triangular shape, so often seen on standing carvings; under the bird's weight, the toes spread out to the extent the web will permit and, being jointed, form anything but straight lines. Most birds are quite pigeon-toed; take this into consideration when locating the feet on the carving. Also, the tarsi of most birds are cambered, i.e., closer together at the ground than at the body. The camber angle is approximately 3 to 5 degrees, measured from the vertical. This angle should be duplicated when the leg holes are drilled.

The proper positioning of the tarsi and feet relative to each other can be very important in imparting the illusion of movement, or inactivity, as in carvings of sleeping birds. The static or stiff appearance of some standing carvings is often caused by the improper positioning, and sometimes the improper location, of the tarsi and feet. Generally,

5-18 *Pintail drake.*

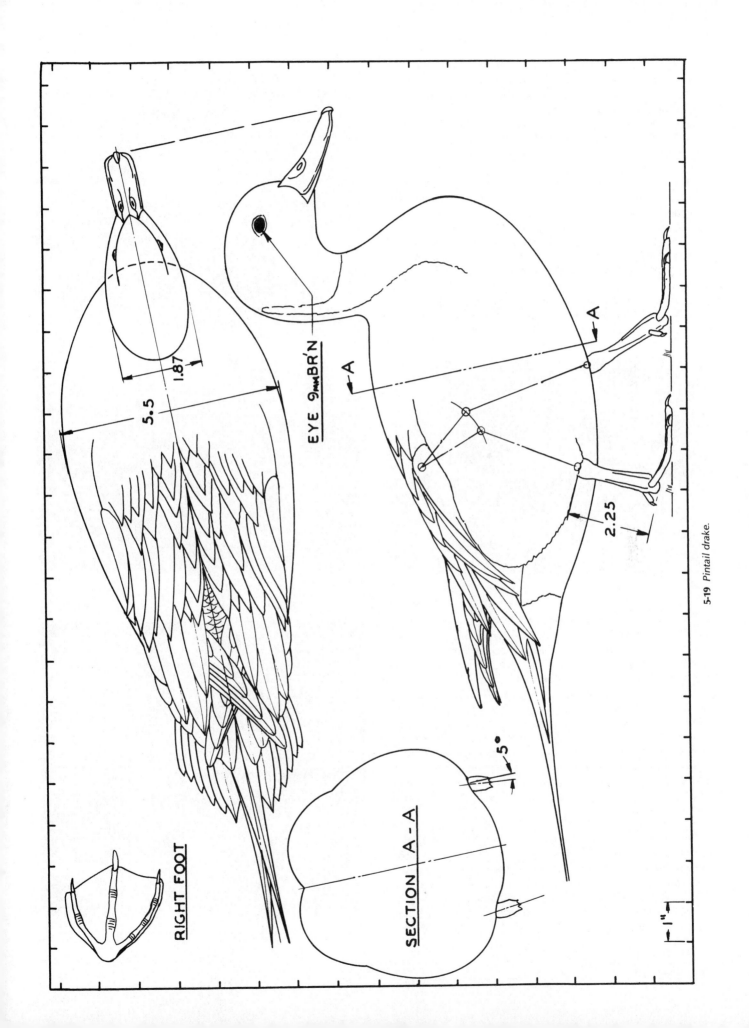

5.5

1.87

EYE 9mm BR'N

A

A

2.25

RIGHT FOOT

SECTION A-A

5°

1"

5-19 *Pintail drake.*

both tarsi should not be located at the same angle and position. When extreme leg positions are used, it is advisable to locate points of articulation and lines representing the position and location of the femur and tibia on the drawing, in addition to showing the tarsus and foot. (See Figure 3-10.) A careful study of photographs and live birds will help eliminate the problems caused by incorrect positioning of tarsi and feet.

When working out the tarsi angles and positions of the feet, consider also how the carving is to be mounted. This is usually of secondary importance if the carving is mounted on a flat surface, but is very important if the carving is mounted on an irregular surface such as a piece of driftwood or another similar mount. In almost all cases, it is advisable to select the actual base or mount while the carving is still in the drawing stage. If this is done, the location and angles of tarsi and feet can be accurately determined to fit the mount. Furthermore, the carving itself, both its pose and positioning, and the mount can be selected to complement each other. (See Chapter 9.)

5-21 *Front view of a pintail drake.*

5-20 *Rear view of a pintail drake.*

5-22 *Side view of female pintail.*

By referring to Figures 5-20 and 21 and the body-width dimension in Chapter 11, the plan view and the cross-sectional view can now be constructed, and the head and neck width can be determined in a manner similar to the procedure described in the preceding section.

Figure 5-24, an alteration of Figure 5-19, duplicates the pose shown in Figure 5-25. This pose does not compliment the bird; it is not pleasing to the eye; and it looks stiff. The long neck of a pintail is very graceful, and its beauty should be accentuated. Figures 5-26 and 27 show the same basic pose except that the neck has now been curved. Much of the stiffness has been eliminated, and the effect of motion has been created by a simple change in the position of the feet and tarsi.

By altering Figure 5-19 again, Figure 5-28, which duplicates the pose in Figure 5-30, is obtained. Here, the bird is about to enter the water, and by opening the bill, the feeling of aggressiveness was added to this already dynamic position. Figure 5-29 shows still another alteration, this one duplicating the relaxed, striding pose shown in Figure 5-31.

For practice, make a drawing depicting the female pintail's pose shown in Figure 5-22, aided by Figure 5-23.

5-23 *Front view of female pintail.*

5-25 Pintail drake in an alert pose.

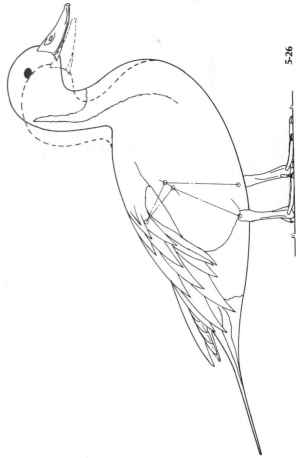

5-27 Pintail drake in a semi-alert, graceful pose.

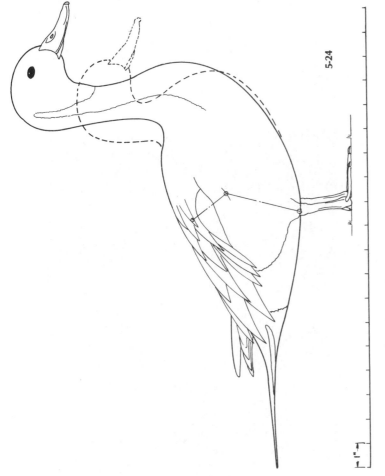

5-24

5-26

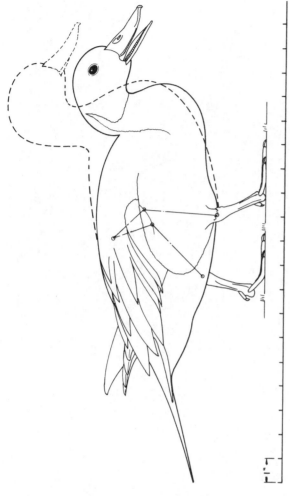

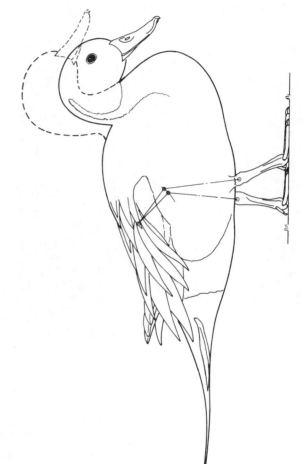

5-28

5-29

5-30 Striding pintail drake about to enter water.

5-31 Pintail drake in a relaxed, striding pose.

DRAWING WINGS AND FLYING BIRDS

Before starting the drawing for a carving with extended wings, first decide on the general overall configuration desired. How the carving is to be supported for display will influence this decision. Flying-bird carvings are extremely difficult to display in a realistic manner without sacrificing some authenticity of the bird's overall shape and position.

The wall mount is one of the more popular methods of supporting the flying carving. For a mount of this type, the bracket supporting the carving is attached so that it is hidden by either a wing or the body. Birds landing or taking off are often depicted with their feet touching the mount and actually supporting the carving. In other cases, flying carvings are supported by some extrinsic means, such as a rod, a piece of wood carved to represent marsh grass, or some other type of support. Many methods have been used to support the flying carving, but few of them display the ingenuity and artistry necessary to create the all-important illusion of free flight.

The complicated up-and-down, fore-and-aft, and rotational movements of the bird's wing in flight are accompanied by changes in the wing's planform shape. The complexity of the wing movements and shapes cannot be fully appreciated until the flight of a bird is seen in slow motion or in individual photographs taken with a high-speed camera. The late Edgar M. Queeny's superb book, *Prairie Wings*, contains many excellent pictures showing waterfowl in flight.

Most carvers attempt to duplicate only the simpler, classic wing positions: the standing bird stretching or preening (Fig. 5-32); gliding with fixed wings (Fig. 5-33); or in the landing or take-off position (Figs. 5-34, 35). There are an infinite number of graceful and artistic wing positions, and the

5-33 *Pintail with wings in a gliding position.*

5-34 *Pintail with wings and body in a landing position.*

5-32 *Shoveler hen stretching wing and leg.*

5-35 *Pintail with wings and body in a typical take-off position.*

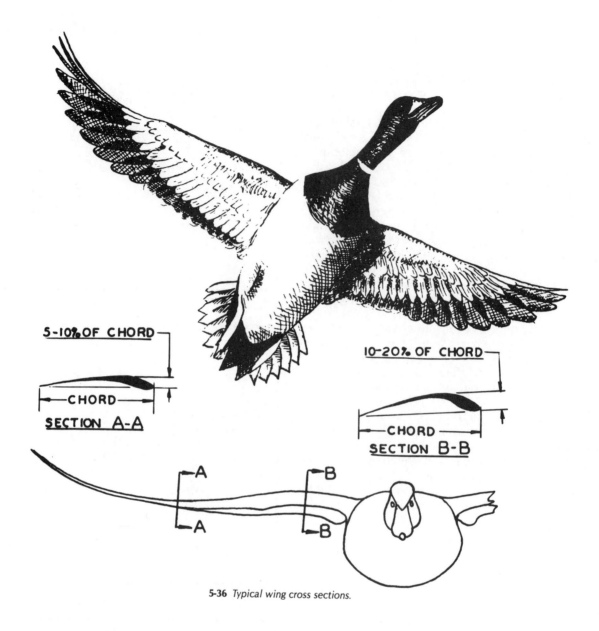

5-36 Typical wing cross sections.

carver can find unlimited possibilities in depicting some of these seldom, if ever, copied wing positions.

Before attempting to draw or to carve a bird's wing, first study thoroughly the wing's skeletal structure (including the points and limits of articulation) and the feather patterns. (See Chapter 3.) Next, make an accurate, full-size drawing of the plan view of the wing in the desired position. If a specimen is available, lay the actual wing on a piece of paper, stretch and pin in the proper position, and trace the overall planform shape and the location of the tips of the primaries, secondaries, and tertial feathers directly onto the paper. By taking measurements from the specimen, all of the feathers can be located and accurately drawn in. When the upper surface has been completed, make a tracing of the wing outline on another piece of paper and add the feather pattern of the lower surface. Also, draw at least one cross-sectional view, taken near the wing's root (Fig. 5-36).

Next, determine the shape of the wing in the front view,

5-37 Classical wing position for upland game when gliding.

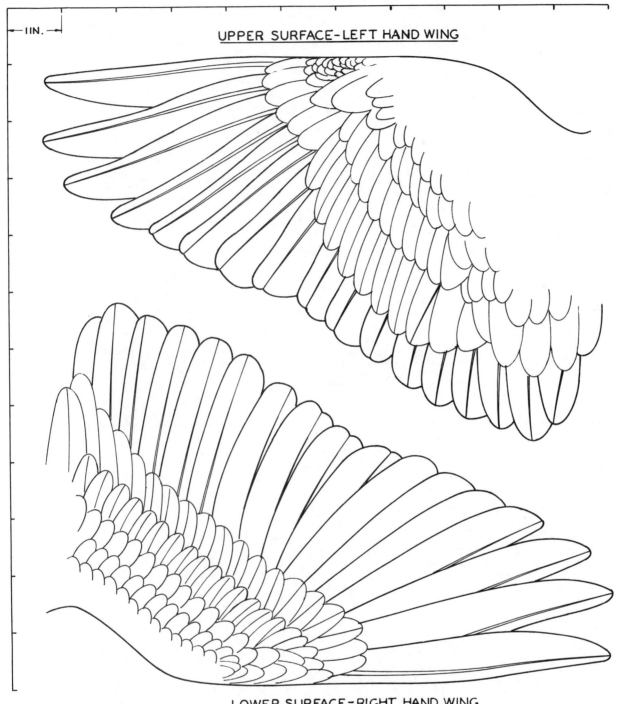

UPPER SURFACE–LEFT HAND WING

|–1 IN.–|

LOWER SURFACE–RIGHT HAND WING

5-38 *Wing of a band-tailed pigeon.*

including the spanwise curvature. The spanwise curvature of the wing, especially in the area of the primaries, largely depends on the amount of wing extension and the air load exerted upon the wing. It follows that the upward spanwise curvature will be much greater during the downstroke than at any other time. When there is no air load, for instance when the bird is stretching or preening, considerable curvature still exists in the primary feathers, but in the opposite direction. This is because the bird's primaries are curved downward, probably not only to fit its body when the wings are folded but also to reduce the amount of upward deflection during the downstroke. Flying upland game birds are

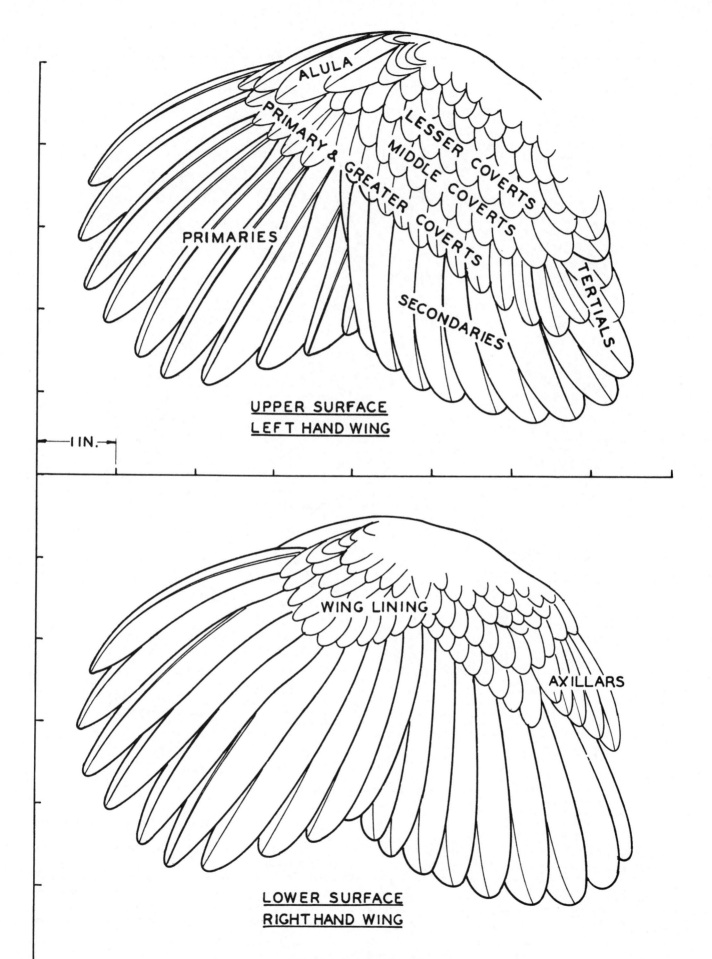

ALULA

LESSER COVERTS

MIDDLE COVERTS

PRIMARY & GREATER COVERTS

TERTIALS

PRIMARIES

SECONDARIES

UPPER SURFACE
LEFT HAND WING

I IN.

WING LINING

AXILLARS

LOWER SURFACE
RIGHT HAND WING

5-39 *Wing of a mountain quail.*

often portrayed with their wings in a fixed, gliding position. In this configuration, their primaries have a very definite downward curvature (Fig. 5-37).

The thickness of the wing in the front view is determined by the chordwise (fore-and-aft) curvature, often referred to as camber. Most of the camber of a bird's wing occurs in the area of the secondary and tertial feathers, as this part acts very much like the wing on an airplane to provide lift and stabilization. The thickness of the wing in the direct front view decreases rapidly outboard of the wrist joint and reduces to the thickness of one feather at the extreme tip.

The bird's body during straight and level flight has smoothly flowing lines and is fairly easy to draw, especially if a specimen is available. In this configuration, the body cross section becomes somewhat flatter and conforms quite closely to the shape of an ellipse. When drawing the plan view, the fore-and-aft location of the wings is one of the more important details to consider. The approximate wing location for the different game bird families is given in Chapter 11.

Drawing the bird in the landing or take-off position is considerably more difficult. Tremendous power, which is reflected in every part of the bird's body, is required for these maneuvers. The body position sometimes approaches the vertical, and extreme head and neck positions are required in order to maintain balance and to gain visibility. The wings move in a much larger arc, almost 180 degrees. The tail extension and position and the tarsi and feet positions are very distinctive. There are many good photographs available showing birds in the landing and take-off configurations; they should be carefully studied before attempting a drawing depicting these modes of flight (Fig. 5-40).

The bird's head always remains level, i.e., an imaginary line drawn through the center of both eyes is almost always parallel to the horizon, and is usually pointed in the general direction of flight. This is of special importance when carvings of flying birds are to be displayed on the wall.

5-41 *Mallard drake banking. Note position of its head.*

5-42 *Mallard dropping in for a landing.*

5-40 *Mallard drake climbing shortly after take-off.*

5-43 *Mallard hen gliding.*

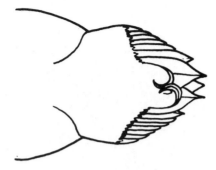

5-44 *Straight and level flight, tail feathers fully compressed.*

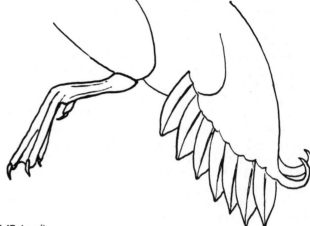

5-47 *Landing.*

5-45 *Tail feathers fully extended.*

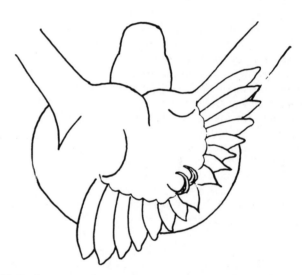

5-48 *Turning.*

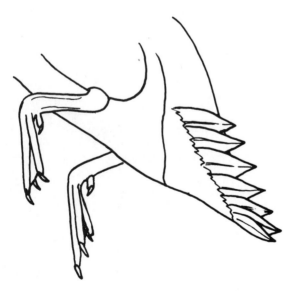

5-46 *Take-off.*

The position and the extension of the tail is another very important detail to be considered when drawing the bird in its various flight forms. Some of the more common tail configurations are:

Straight and level flight: tail is fully compressed (Fig. 5-44).

Take-off: tail is fully fanned out; it is also convex and raised (Fig. 5-46).

Landing: tail is fully fanned out; it is also concave and lowered (Fig. 5-47).

Turning: tail is fully fanned out; it is also twisted so that one side is much higher than the other side and acts as a rudder (Fig. 5-48).

PART III

Advanced Game Bird Carving

The projects and text in Part I took the beginner from his first carving and painting attempts to slightly more complicated carvings. Parts II, III, and IV will help the serious carver to achieve advanced amateur and professional work. Here, in Part III, the carver will not only progress into more complex carvings, he will also be introduced to some of the carving and finishing techniques used by professional bird carvers to add realism to their carvings.

CHAPTER

6
Advanced Carving Techniques

The accurate and painstaking duplication of important features such as body detail, head and bill, tarsi and feet, outstretched wings, crossed primaries and other feather groups, and individual feathers is one of the distinctive qualities that separate a professional from an amateur carving.

POWER TOOLS

Several power tools are almost a necessity for life-size, or nearly life-size, professional carvings. The carver of miniature birds will also find these tools useful, but considerably less important owing to the much smaller amount of wood removal involved.

Without much doubt, the band saw is the most useful laborsaving tool for the carver. There are many band saws available. In selecting a band saw, an important consideration is the capacity of the machine, i.e., maximum depth and — of lesser importance — width of cut (the distance from the band saw frame to the blade). Most home workshop band saws have a maximum depth of cut of six inches or less, completely inadequate for cutting out the body blocks of life-size geese and some of the larger ducks. If the carver can afford the expenditure, the Rockwell 14-inch wood cutting band saw is the best available. For a relatively small additional cost, a height attachment for this saw can be obtained that increases the depth of cut from 6½ inches to 12¼ inches, a capacity of cut found only on the very large, industrial band saws.

For most carvers, the next most useful power tool is the electric hand drill. In addition to drilling holes for eyes, legs, etc., it is also suitable for disc-sanding, grinding, wire-brushing, buffing, and other operations (Figs. 6-3, 4).

The high-speed grinder is the author's most-used power hand tool. It is used exclusively with rotary files and is very effective in removing both wood and metal. It is especially good for removing wood from hard-to-get-to places, such as underneath the crossed primaries. Practically all of the carving of the brass legs and the feet shown in this chapter was done with this tool. A large and powerful tool, the hand grinder must be handled with both hands. To gain the

necessary confidence for using it on a carving, a certain amount of practice is required (Fig. 6-5). Small hand grinders and flexible shaft tools such as the Foredom are fine for small, detailed work, but they just do not have the power for removing appreciable amounts of wood (Fig. 6-6).

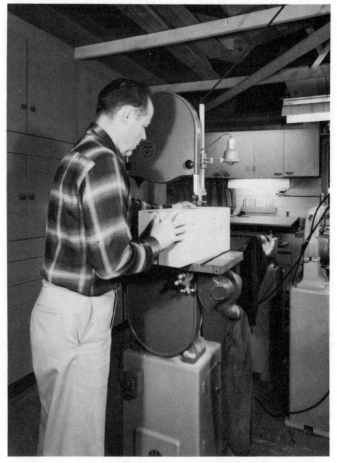

6-1 *The band saw is the carver's most useful power tool.*

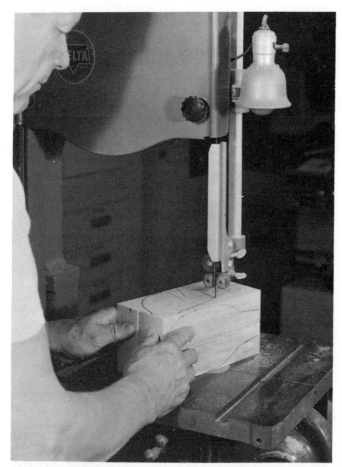

6-2 Sawing out the body for a mountain quail carving.

6-3 The wire brush is useful for removing extraneous material from bases.

6-4 Disc sanders are available in several sizes.

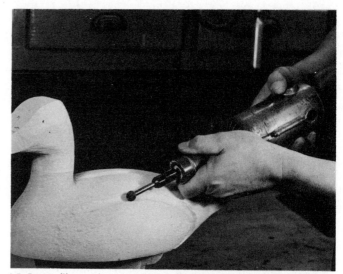

6-5 Rotary files used in a high-speed grinder remove both wood and metal efficiently.

6-6 The Foredom flexible shaft tool works well for small, detailed work.

Power sanders utilizing sanding belts and contour wheels are very useful in shaping both the upper and lower surfaces of outstretched wings. Some carvers use oscillating hand sanders for smoothing the body of the carving, but the author prefers to sand by hand, except in shaping the wing.

6-7 *Accurate joints are easy to make on the power jointer.*

6-8 *Hand-joining requires careful removal of wood.*

GLUING UP THE BLOCK

In many cases, the size of the carving and the thickness of the wood available make it necessary to laminate two or more pieces of wood in order to obtain a block of sufficient size. If possible, machine the pieces flat and true on a power jointer (Fig. 6-7). If a jointer is not readily available, have them joined for a nominal charge at a lumberyard or a cabinet shop. If this cannot be done, the only alternative is to join them by hand.

Accurate hand-joining is not easy. It can be facilitated considerably, however, by the use of a joiner plane or any plane with a long planing surface (Fig. 6-8). Check the block in both directions with a straightedge and start removing the high spots (Fig. 6-9). Take plenty of time, and after every few cuts check the block along its full length and width with a straightedge. As the block becomes flat, reduce the depth of cut on the plane and work even more carefully until an accurate surface is obtained. Small inaccuracies can be corrected by moving the block back and forth on a piece of sandpaper attached to a perfectly flat surface. Sanding is not normally recommended if the glue joint is to develop its maximum strength; however, if fairly coarse sandpaper is used, sanding causes less trouble than a thick glue line. Try to remove all of the sanding dust prior to applying the glue.

If an accurate joint has been made, one of the best glues to use is Weldwood's plastic resin glue. This glue comes in powder form and is easily mixed with cold water. Carefully read and follow the directions on the can, especially those regarding temperature and curing time. Brush on the glue evenly to both mating surfaces and allow the glue to set for approximately five minutes before closing the joint (Fig. 6-10). Toenail the blocks together on the ends to prevent slippage and apply sufficient pressure with clamps to squeeze out the excess glue and bring the parts closely together, forming a thin glue line (Fig. 6-11).

If an accurate joint between the two parts has not been made, it is much better to use an epoxy adhesive, which

6-9 *Check the block with a straightedge every few cuts.*

gives a strong joint even if the glue line is thick. Minnesota Mining and Manufacturing (3M) makes a number of epoxies, and their Scotch-Weld No. 2158 B/A is an excellent adhesive for wood-to-wood and also wood-to-metal joints.

The importance of this procedure should not be minimized for nothing is more discouraging than to spend many hours on a good carving and then find that a poor glue joint was originally made on the block. Usually a bad glue joint is apparent after the glued-up block has been sawed to shape. If the glue joint is open for an appreciable length, it is much better to saw the block in two at the glue line, rejoin, and reglue. If the open joint is not extensive, it can be repaired without too much effort. Proceed with the carving until the bird is near its final shape. Then, make a saw cut into the glue line, cutting into the carving until the area of the bad joint is completely opened and the glue has been removed, leaving clean wood. Completely fill the saw cut with epoxy adhesive and cover the area with masking tape to prevent the adhesive from running out.

6-10 *Brush on the glue evenly to both mating surfaces.*

6-12 *Add an insert to provide strength for the green-winged teal's crest feathers.*

INSERTS

To provide sufficient strength for parts of certain carvings, it is sometimes necessary to insert a separate piece of wood whose grain runs at an angle to the grain of the body or head block. The crested head of a green-winged teal or a wood duck requires inserts of this type (Fig. 6-12). An insert of a stronger, and usually harder, wood may be required in some cases. The long and delicate tail feathers on male pintails (Figs. 6-13, 14) and old squaw ducks are good examples of features requiring hardwood inserts. For certain parts, such as the fanned-out tail of most birds, it is desirable to make the insert of two or more pieces with the grain of each piece running at an angle to the other, paralleling the feathers as closely as possible (Figs. 6-15, 16).

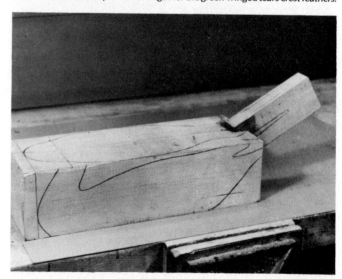

6-13 *A hardwood insert has been added to supply strength for the pintail's long tail feathers.*

6-11 *Apply sufficient pressure with clamps to squeeze out excess glue.*

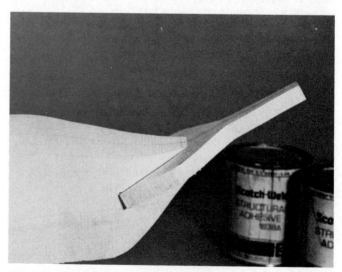

6-14 *Alternate method for making a tail insert.*

A-1 *California quail, 1981 (Collection of Ward Bros. Foundation Museum, Salisbury, Maryland)*

B-1 *Wood ducks, 1980. (Collection of author)*

B-2 *White-fronted goose family, 1978. (Collection of Carroll L. Wainwright, Jr., New York)*

C-1 *Preening Ross's goose, 1978. (Collection of Dr. J. Lynwood Herrington, Jr., Tennessee)*

C-2 *Life-size Canada goose, 1981. (Collection of Paul F. O'Brien, Jr., Louisiana)*

D-1 *Greater prairie chickens, 1980. (Collection of author)*

D-2 *Ring-necked pheasant, 1968. (Collection of Jon Chaney, California)*

E-1 *Stretching hooded merganser drake, 1981. (Collection of Dr. and Mrs. J. L. Silagi, Texas)*

E-2 *Common snipe, 1981. (Collection of Mrs. Mary Halbert, California)*

F-1 *Preening blue goose, 1976.*

G-1 *Scaled quail, 1978. (Collection of Dr. Ray Zeigler, Texas)*

G-2 *Bobwhite quail, 1979. (Collection of Mrs. Lillian Wright, Florida)*

G-3 *Chukar partridge, 1980. (Collection of Julie and Mike Kaplan, California)*

H-1 *Band-tailed pigeons, 1970. (Collection of Doug Miller, Colorado)*

6-15 *Inserts have been installed for the band-tailed pigeon's tail.*

6-18 *In some cases, it is simpler to make the whole part of hardwood.*

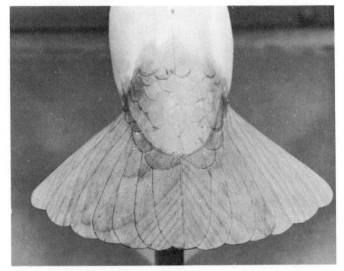

6-16 *The band-tailed pigeon's tail insert has been made from two pieces.*

Sometimes it is simpler to make the whole part of hardwood rather than to make a separate insert. In Figure 6-18 the entire head of the mountain quail is made of alder instead of making a hardwood insert for the bill. Woodcock and snipe are other examples of where it may be easier to make the whole head and bill of hardwood. For the feeding mountail quail shown in Figure 6-17, a hardwood insert was used for the bill only, instead of making the entire head of hardwood. This was done because a separate head would have necessitated a glue joint between the head and the end grain of the body block: end-grain gluing should be avoided where possible.

An insert should be made for any fairly thin section where the grain of the wood runs at an angle of 20 degrees or more across the section. On extremely thin sections, the accept-

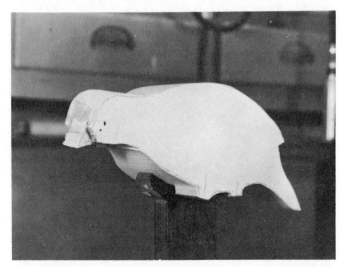

6-17 *A hardwood insert was added for the bill of this mountain quail carving.*

6-19 *For some parts, it is necessary to use metal for the insert.*

6-20 *Making cutout for tail insert on a wood duck carving.*

able angle of the grain across the section would be much smaller than 20 degrees.

For some parts – the topknot feathers on valley, Gambel's, and mountain quail, for instance – even hardwood does not provide sufficient strength. When duplicating these and other delicate, vulnerable parts, brass or some other fairly easily worked metal should be used (Fig. 6-19).

If the band saw is available, it is always easier to make the cut-out for the insert before the block has been sawed to shape (Fig. 6-20). If the carver does not have access to a band saw, it is probably easier to make the cut-out after the body block has been sawed, as the removal of considerably less wood is involved. In this case, two parallel cuts are made with a stiff-backed saw, such as a dovetail saw, and the wood in between is removed with a chisel.

REPAIRS

Sometimes, after the block has been sawed out or after the rough shaping has been partially accomplished, a check in the wood is uncovered (Fig. 6-21). If the check is not extensive, the wood can be quite easily salvaged. Proceed with the rough carving until the bird is near its final shape in the

area of the check. Then, make a single saw cut into the check, cutting into the carving until the check is no longer visible (Fig. 6-22). Completely fill the saw cut with epoxy adhesive and cover the area with masking tape to prevent the adhesive from running out (Fig. 6-23).

If the check is quite wide, it may be desirable to remove the checked area by making a wedged-shaped cut. Then, fit a wedge of the same material and with the grain in the same direction in place and secure with epoxy.

Quite often, some of the more fragile parts of the carving (bills, wing primaries, tail feathers, etc.) are accidently broken. If the broken-off piece can be found, it can be easily cemented back in place with epoxy. When the epoxy has set, sand off the excess cement and retouch the area with matching paint. The epoxy recommended for gluing up the block is quite thick and sticky and will normally, by its own

6-21 *A check has been uncovered in the tail area.*

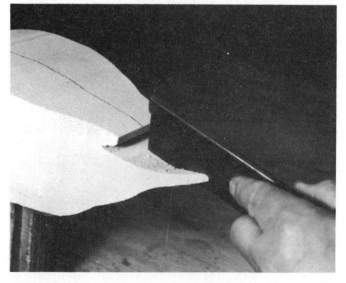

6-22 *Cut into the block until the check is no longer visible.*

6-23 *Completely fill the saw cut with epoxy.*

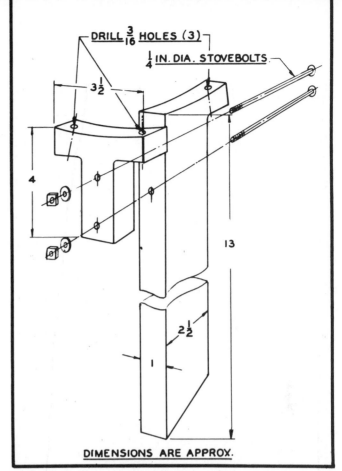

DIMENSIONS ARE APPROX.

6-24 *A holding fixture capable of supporting larger carvings.*

wet adhesive force, hold the broken-off piece in place until it has set. If some support is required to maintain alignment, cover the area with waxed paper and apply a clamp. Another easy way to hold the parts together is to wrap masking tape around the joint.

If the broken-off piece cannot be found, cut off the broken area on a bevel, and fit and cement a new piece of wood, cut to the same bevel angle, in place. Here again, masking tape will usually hold the parts in place until the epoxy sets.

The amount of time required for epoxy to set can be reduced drastically (from approximately three hours, depending on room temperature, to fifteen or twenty minutes) by applying heat, using a heat lamp or an ordinary lightbulb. Take care not to burn or scorch the wood.

Quick-setting epoxy is convenient to use and is strong enough (after it has set approximately one hour) for some repair jobs. However, on breaks where the gluing area is small, the use of a stronger epoxy, such as 3M's Scotch-Weld, is recommended.

MORE HOLDING FIXTURES

The importance of holding fixtures in reducing carving time and effort, and improving the quality of the carving by permitting the use of both hands to guide the wood-removing tool, has already been discussed in Chapter 1. Figure 6-24 shows how to construct a holding fixture capable of supporting larger, life-size carvings. Additional holding fixtures are shown in Figure 6-28.

A fixture, similar in design to the ones already covered, can be attached on the upper side of the carving to provide access to the underside of the carving. For some operations (the carving of the bill is a good example) it is very practical

6-25 *Attach the holding fixture by means of three woodscrews.*

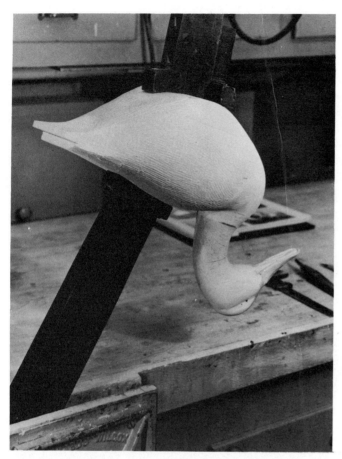

6-26 *It is often practical to use both holding fixtures simultaneously.*

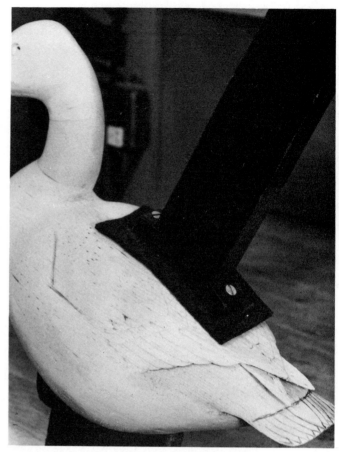

6-27 *Use heavy felt to protect carving details.*

6-28 *Various holding fixtures used by the author.*

to use both fixtures at the same time so that the surfaces of the whole bill can be worked upon with a minimum of effort (Fig. 6-26). Where it is necessary to attach the holding fixture after detailed feather carving has been done, insert a piece of heavy felt between the fixture and the carving to protect the work (Fig. 6-27).

At times, other simple holding fixtures can facilitate the execution of the carving considerably. Figures 6-29 and 30 show fixtures used during the carving of the head and wing of a preening wood duck (an advanced project covered in Chapter 8). While being carved, the head was temporarily screwed and glued to the holding fixture.

6-29 *Simple fixture for holding preening wood duck head for carving.*

6-30 *A piece has been glued to the wing block for support during carving.*

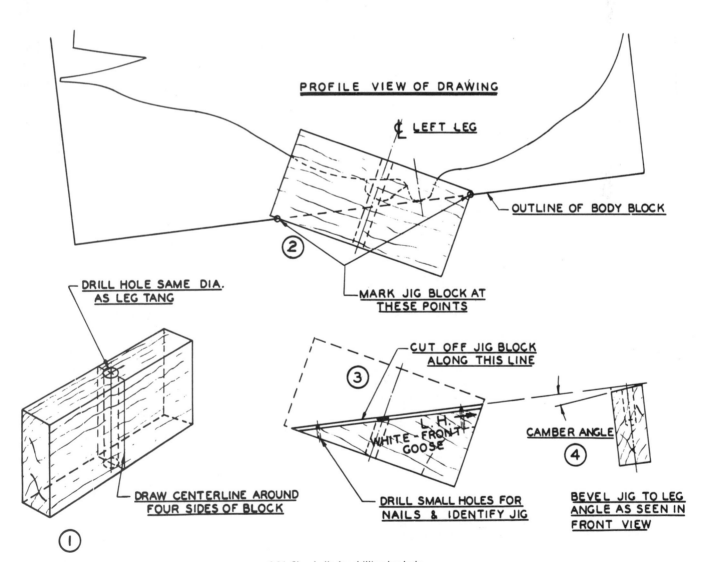

PROFILE VIEW OF DRAWING

₵ LEFT LEG

OUTLINE OF BODY BLOCK

② MARK JIG BLOCK AT THESE POINTS

DRILL HOLE SAME DIA. AS LEG TANG

DRAW CENTERLINE AROUND FOUR SIDES OF BLOCK

①

③ CUT OFF JIG BLOCK ALONG THIS LINE

L.H. WHITE-FRONT GOOSE

DRILL SMALL HOLES FOR NAILS & IDENTIFY JIG

CAMBER ANGLE

④ BEVEL JIG TO LEG ANGLE AS SEEN IN FRONT VIEW

6-31 *Simple jig for drilling leg hole.*

DRILLING FOR LEGS

If the compound angle of each leg, as determined on the drawing, is to be accurately duplicated, simple jigs for the drilling of the body holes are a necessity (Fig. 6-31).

These jigs are quite easy to construct from scrap pieces of wood (preferably hardwood) approximately 1 inch thick, 2 to 3 inches wide, and 6 inches long. First, near the midpoint of each block, locate the hole centerline and drill holes of the proper diameter through the blocks at this point. By means of a square, continue this centerline around on all four sides of the block. Add the outline of the body block to the profile view of the drawing, lay the jig block on one of the leg centerlines, and make a mark at each end so that the jig block can be cut off at the proper angle. Cut the jig block along this line and bevel the edge to an angle equal to the camber angle of the leg (the leg angle as seen in the front view). Make the drill jig for the other leg in the same manner. Identify the left and right jigs, show the direction they are to be installed by an arrow, and further identify the jigs by species for future use.

Transfer the leg centerlines to the body block at the same time the profile view is transferred. Using a square, extend the intersections of the leg centerlines with the edge of the body block on across the bottom of the body block. Locate the legs symmetrically on either side of the body block centerline. Nail the drill jigs in place at these locations (be sure that they are parallel to the body block centerline) and drill holes to the proper depth (Fig. 6-32).

6-32 *Drilling the leg holes.*

CARVING THE BODY

The extent to which the wings, legs, and certain feather groups modify the bird's exterior shape depends on the actual position of the wings and legs and also upon muscular control of the feathers. This can only be learned by careful study of photographs and live birds. As the serious carver progresses to more complicated, professional carvings, he must devote more time and give additional consideration not only to these fine details of body form but also to faithfully duplicating other equally important details such as the crossed primaries, feather groups and individual feathers, head and bill details, tail details, and others.

6-33 *The head of this coot carving is an integral part of the body.*

When the drawing has been transferred to the block, the body is normally sawed out in the manner described in Chapter 1. One exception to this procedure occurs when sawing blocks for birds in the flight position or any other position where the neck and head are extended forward and turned to one side. In a situation of this kind, the sequence of sawing out the block becomes important and the plan view should always be cut out first. After the plan view has been sawed, attach the two loose pieces in the usual manner and make the profile cut, extending it only to the point where the neck starts to curve in the lateral direction. Remove all the loose pieces at this point, and retransfer the profile head and neck layout to the actual curved surface. Then, lay the neck and head part of the body block flat on the saw table (holding the body up off the table) and saw to shape. With this procedure, the head and neck layout will be true, and the saw cuts in this area will be made perpendicular to these parts (Fig. 6-33).

After the body block has been sawed to shape (except when the head is an integral part of the body block), make the head and neck. Select wood of the correct thickness and transfer the head drawing onto it, positioning the head so the bill is parallel to the grain. Mark the eye location and drill a small hole completely through the head block at that point. (If desired, a hole large enough to receive the eyes may be drilled through the head at this time.) On larger carvings, it is often necessary to make the head and neck from two or more pieces. If the head of the carving is to be turned to one side, at least one of the head-neck-body joints should be made parallel to the waterline or the ground, depending on whether the carving is a decoy or standing type. The head can then be rotated on this plane without changing the predetermined angle of the bill relative to the ground.

Depending on the head position, it is sometimes easier to carve the bill (especially its underside) before the head is attached to the body. In this case, the head is joined with epoxy (the quick-setting variety works fine) to the holding fixture, and the bill and the forward part of the head are then carved to shape (Fig. 6-35). When this work is completed, the head is sawed from the holding fixture and is sanded flat and true again, ready to be attached to the body (or neck).

Although dowelling the head, neck, and body adds some complications, it increases the strength of the joints. However, since decorative carvings are normally not subjected to rough handling, the carver may decide not to use dowels. For those who wish to use dowels for joining the head, neck, and body, the procedure is described below.

Drill the head, neck, and body for dowels. The accuracy of the drilled dowel holes can be improved greatly by the use of a simple drill jig (Fig. 6-34). This drill jig is nothing more than a scrap piece of wood (preferably hardwood)

6-35 Holding fixture for carving bill.

6-36 Press parts firmly together to squeeze out excess adhesive.

6-34 Use a simple jig to drill the dowel holes.

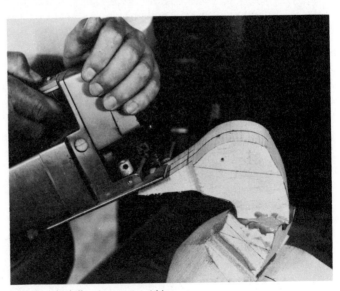

6-37 Cut the bill to its proper width.

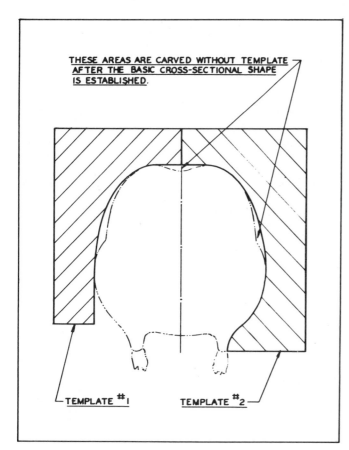

THESE AREAS ARE CARVED WITHOUT TEMPLATE
AFTER THE BASIC CROSS-SECTIONAL SHAPE
IS ESTABLISHED.

TEMPLATE #1   TEMPLATE #2

6-38 Cross-sectional templates.

6-39 Shape lower part of body to match template two.

6-40 Remove lower holding fixture and complete overall shaping of the bird.

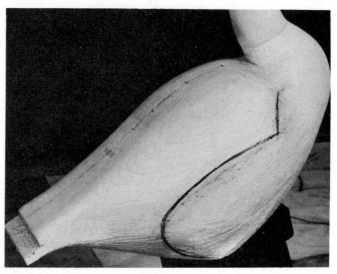

6-41 Draw in the outline of the side feathers.

with a hole drilled through it at right angles. Make the dowel holes slightly larger than the dowels themselves to accommodate for small errors in drilling and to permit the mating surfaces to fit accurately together. Apply epoxy adhesive to all mating surfaces, including the dowels and dowel holes, and press the parts firmly together to squeeze out excess adhesive (Fig. 6-36). Turn the head to the desired position and use small nails toenailed in the edges of the parts to hold them in place while the adhesive is curing.

Next, after the epoxy has cured, attach the holding fixture to the body. Before starting any wood removal, draw a centerline on the top of the body and also on the head and bill. If desired, the plan view of the bill can be drawn in and sawed to its proper width at this time (Fig. 6-37).

For standing carvings, it is a good idea to use a second body template, in addition to the one described in Chapter 1, to check the contour of the lower body and to obtain symmetry (Fig. 6-38). First rough out the body to match template #1 and continue the roughing operation until the cross-sectional shape matches template #2 (Figure 6-39). At this point, it is advisable to attach a holding fixture to the top side of the body, remove the lower holding fixture, and rough out the lower chest, breast, and belly so that the shape of the entire bird can be viewed critically (Fig. 6-40). Then, reinstall the lower fixture and remove the upper fix-

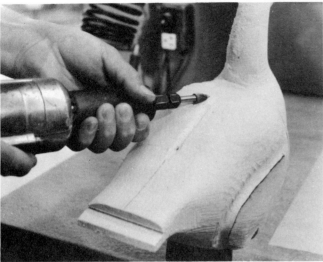

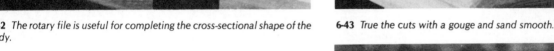

6-42 *The rotary file is useful for completing the cross-sectional shape of the body.*

6-43 *True the cuts with a gouge and sand smooth.*

ture to permit additional shaping on the upper side of the carving.

When the general overall shape of the body has been established, sand the rough-carved areas fairly smooth to facilitate the drawing of pencil layouts on the wood surface. Now, draw the outline of the side feathers on both sides of the carving (Fig. 6-41), and complete the cross-sectional shape of the body by carving the intersection of the side feathers with the scapulars, wing secondaries, and flanks and by carving the v-shaped depression (usually rounded at the bottom) on the centerline of the body where the scapulars meet. A grinder equipped with rotary files may be used for roughing out these areas, followed by gouges and sandpaper to true up and blend in the cuts (Figs. 6-42, 43).

6-44 *The cross-sectional shape of most birds is not a true oval.*

6-45 *The scapulars are quite prominent on geese (lesser Canada goose).*

INDIVIDUAL FEATHER CARVING

A great deal of realism can be added without too much effort to the overall bird carving by carving individual feathers. This delineation of the feathers also tends to soften the normally hard, smooth lines of the carving and provides some of the texture needed to obtain a realistic-looking bird carving. With the exception of the flight and tail feathers, the edges of most feathers are very delicate and lacy. It is very difficult, if not impossible, to duplicate this soft edge in painting the edges of individually carved feathers. However, the edges of the carved feathers can be softened somewhat and made more realistic by burning in feather detail, a technique described in Chapter 7 (see page 158).

Because feathers are not flat but are curved in both directions, forming a convex bulge, the carving around the individual feather can be quite deep, provided the feather is rounded off and sanded, giving a curved-outward appearance. On the sides, breast, chest, belly, rump, and tail coverts, individual feather carving can add a feeling of softness by breaking up the smooth surface into one that undulates as it appears to do on the real bird. The edges of these feathers should be sanded down to practically nothing so that all harsh lines are eliminated. Large feathers, including the primaries, secondaries, tertials, some of the scapulars, and the tail feathers should be carved in a more prominent manner. Their surfaces should be convex but their edges must be retained. There is a strong tendency nowadays to accentuate the parting of barbs, which causes v-shaped splits in the feather vane. On a well-groomed bird, few of the large feathers mentioned above have splits in their vanes; therefore, a certain amount of judgment should be exercised in deciding how far to go with this practice. On other feathers such as the side feathers, the barbs are often separated.

One of the most difficult phases of bird carving is getting an accurate layout of the feather patterns drawn on the carving. The feathers on fresh and mounted specimens are often disarranged, making it difficult to distinguish the various feathers and to locate them in their correct positions. In addition to referring to actual specimens, study photographs, which often show the feather pattern quite clearly. There is no substitute for studying the feather patterns on live birds, and those carvers who have access to the real thing are the most fortunate.

In the case of some prominent feather groups, it is advisable to carve the overall shape of the group before laying out and carving the individual feathers. The wing primary groups (when folded), the tertials, the scapulars, the tail feathers, and the side feathers are good examples of where this treatment can be used to advantage. (The side feather groups have already been partially carved. See Figures 6-42 and 43.)

First, lay out the overall shape of the scapulars and remove wood until these feathers stand out as a group (Figs. 6-46 through 6-50). Next, lay out the crossed primaries, the tertials, the secondaries, the wing coverts (if exposed), and the rear scapulars on one side of the carving (Fig. 6-51). When this layout has been completed satisfactorily, copy

6-46 *Lay out the overall shape of the scapulars (white-fronted goose).*

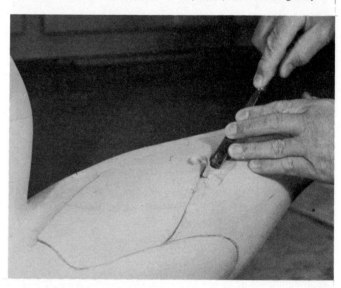

6-47 *Remove wood so that the scapulars stand out as a feather group.*

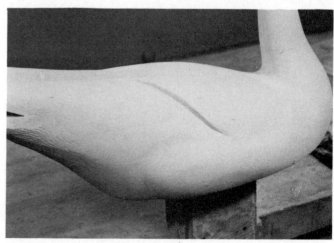

6-48 *Showing the amount of wood removed from behind the scapulars.*

6-49 *Layout of the scapulars on a canvasback decoy.*

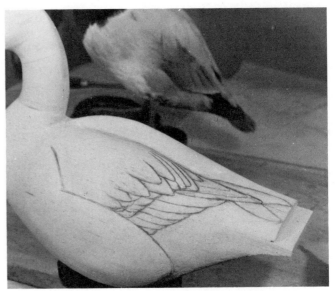

6-52 *Trace layout onto thin paper and transfer it to the other side.*

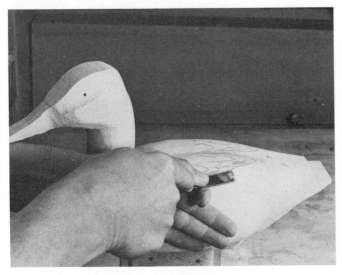

6-50 *Remove wood from around the scapulars.*

6-53 *Showing completed feather-pattern layout.*

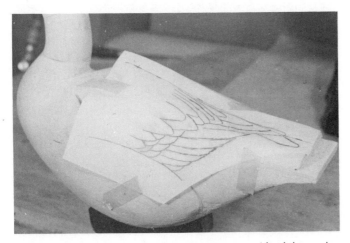

6-51 *Make an accurate feather-pattern layout on one side of the carving.*

it on tracing paper and transfer it, by means of carbon paper, to the other side (Figs. 6-52, 53). It is a good practice to save these layouts for future use and file them with the other drawings used on a particular carving.

Now, carve the crossed primaries, tertials, and secondaries. This area is probably the most difficult part of the bird to carve; it is even more difficult to describe the procedure accurately. First, remove the wood forming the V behind the crossed primaries by making deep cuts with a sharp knife along the outline of the primaries and removing the wood in steps by means of a chisel. Then, make cuts around the outer sides of the primaries and along the rear of the exposed secondaries and remove the wood adjacent to these cuts from the flank and upper tail covert areas (Figs. 6-54, 55). Next, cut in the outline of the tertials where they overlap the primaries. For this discussion, it will be assumed that the primaries of the left wing overlap the primaries of the right wing.

Remember that the primary feathers are curved and conform neatly to the contour of the bird's body in the flank

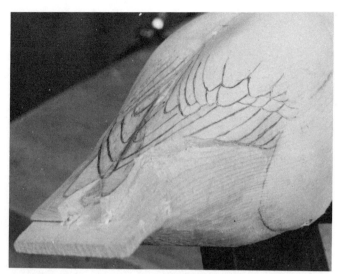

6-54 *Start removing the wood next to the secondaries and crossed primaries.*

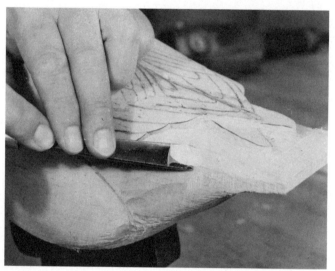

6-55 *Remove wood from the upper side of the primaries and the flank area.*

6-56 *Crossed primaries on a male baldpate.*

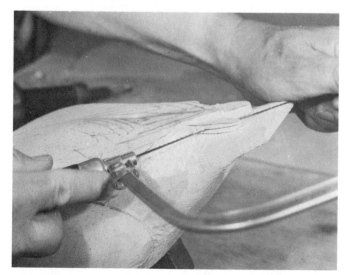

6-57 *Carefully saw out the wood from under the primaries.*

areas. This, in turn, means that the two groups of primaries, at their points of intersection, do not rest flatly one upon the other, but are actually slightly on edge (Fig. 6-56).

The upper side of the left-wing primary group, which protrudes from under the tertials, is now carved to its final depth and shape, taking into account the curvature of the primaries and the angle at which they lie. Also, carve the upper side of the protruding primaries of the right wing to their final shape and depth. This requires removing wood not only to a greater depth than that required for the left group, but also at an opposite bevel.

Next, remove the wood lying under the primary groups. This can be expedited by using a coping saw to cut a wedge-shaped piece of wood from under each primary group (Fig. 6-57). Continue removing wood from this area until the primary groups stand out and the general shape of the rump, flanks, and upper tail covert area, as they blend into the tail, is established. Now, carefully reduce the thickness of the two primary groups until they are from $1/16$ to $3/32$ inch thick. Further carve the intersection area, on both the upper and lower sides, until the primary groups are clearly defined and appear to cross each other realistically (Fig. 6-60). In some situations, the primary groups must be carved beyond the intersection area (further forward) to a point where they are covered by the secondary feathers.

The carving of this general area, including the tail, can be simplified by attaching both the lower and upper holding fixtures at the same time so that the position of the carving can be quickly changed for easier access. On very thin sections, such as the crossed primaries, or any area that requires detailed carving, thoroughly soak the wood with thinned-down lacquer sanding sealer and allow the wood to dry completely before carving further. This makes carving easier because the sealer adds considerable strength to the wood, helps eliminate splitting, and generally makes the wood more homogeneous.

Needless to say, considerable care, patience, and ingenuity must be exercised in carving the crossed primaries and the other overlapping feathers in this area. Removal of the wood is difficult in spots and requires the use of various chisels and gouges. A small, tapered rotary file used in a high-speed grinder is good for removing wood from some of these tight areas (Fig. 6-58). However, until the carver becomes proficient in handling this tool, he should use it only for less critical areas.

After the feathers have been individually drawn on the carving, the outline of each feather is cut in with the tip of a sharp knife (Fig. 6-59). Starting with the rearmost feather, wood is removed on a fairly sharp bevel to the outline of the adjacent overlapping feather (or feathers) by means of a sharp knife or chisel. Now, round off the feather, giving it a curved-outward appearance and reduce the exposed rear edge to practically nothing. Sand the feather smooth. Continue working forward until all of the feathers in the group have been individually carved (Fig. 6-60). Because the exposed wing coverts, especially on geese, lie in prominent rows, each row should be carved as a group before carving the individual feathers (Fig. 6-62).

6-60 *Individually carve all the feathers in this area.*

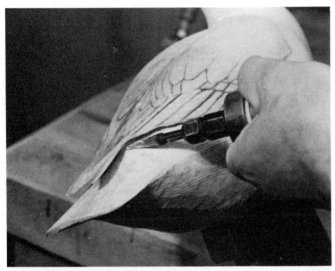

6-58 *Removing wood from under the primaries with a tapered rotary file.*

6-61 *After the scapulars are carved, lay out and carve the other feather groups.*

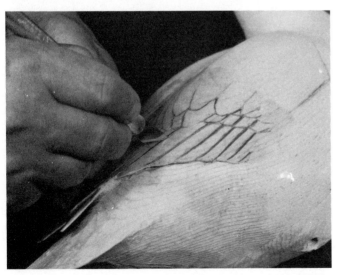

6-59 *Outline the individual tertial and secondary feathers with a sharp knife.*

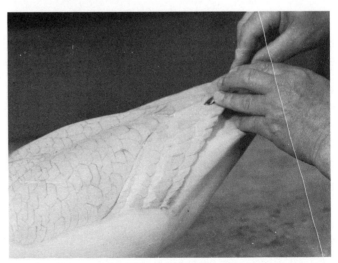

6-62 *The wing coverts should be carved as a row prior to individual feather carving.*

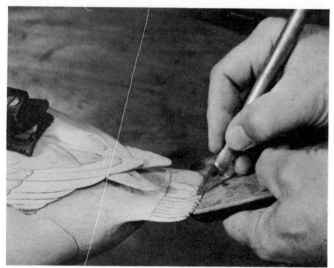

6-63 *Lay out the tail feathers next.*

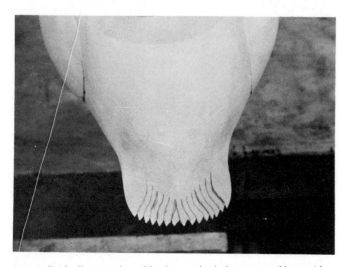

6-64 *Cut the tips of the tail feathers to shape.*

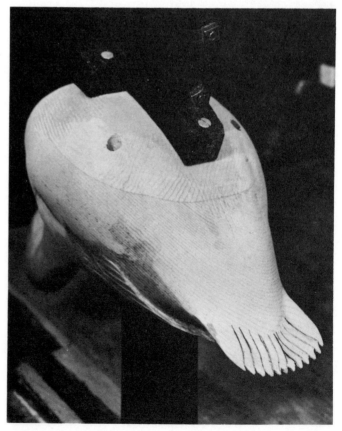

6-65 *Individually carve the tail feathers on both the upper and lower sides.*
6-66 *The use of both holding fixtures will facilitate the carving of the tail.*

TAIL CARVING

The next step in carving the body is to complete the tail. As pointed out in Chapter 5, the shape of the tail can be flat, concave, or convex, depending on the bird's activity. This overall shape must be established first. Next, lay out the rearmost extent of the tail covert feathers, both upper and lower. Except in the area of the tail coverts, the thickness of the bird's tail is determined by the overlapping tail feathers and is quite thin. Carve the tail in the area of the exposed tail feathers to the proper thickness. The tail covert feathers may be demarcated by either carving or painting (or both), depending on the preference of the carver, but in either case, the upper and lower tail covert feathers must be blended into the tail feather area.

Lay out the individual tail feathers properly. On both the tail and the wing, the leading edges of the feathers on the upper side are visible, while on the lower side, the trailing edges of the feathers can be seen. After the individual feathers are drawn in, cut the tips of these feathers to shape. Back up the thin feathers with a scrap block of wood (Fig. 6-64). Proceed with the carving of the individual feathers (Figs. 6-65, 66).

HEAD CARVING

The head and bill constitute two of the more conspicuous parts of the carving; their accurate duplication is essential for an advanced or professional carving. The bill is one of the few parts of the bird's exterior with a fixed size and shape; there is absolutely no acceptable reason for artistic license in depicting it. For those carvers who do not have actual specimens, life-size photographs showing the profile, plan, and bottom views of all the game bird bills have been included in Chapter 13.

On most game birds, the size and shape of the feathered head for a particular bird remain fairly constant. Ducks are one exception: the size and shape of their heads can vary considerably, especially the heads of the long-crested male ducks (wood duck, green-winged teal, hooded merganser, red-breasted merganser, American and Barrow's golden-eyes, and bufflehead). This variation of the shape and size

6-68 *Greater scaup male.*

6-67 *The shape of some ducks' heads can vary considerably.*

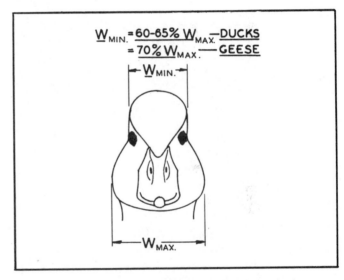

$$W_{MIN.} = 60\text{-}65\% \ W_{MAX.} \underline{\text{—DUCKS}}$$
$$= 70\% \ W_{MAX.} \underline{\text{—GEESE}}$$

6-69 *Crown width compared to overall head width of waterfowl.*

of the head is due primarily to the muscular control of the feathers, although some of the puffiness in the cheek area possibly is due to direct muscular control in addition to the enlargement caused by feather erection (Fig. 6-67).

In carving the head and bill on a duck, first reduce the thickness of the head in the general area above the upper cheek (Fig. 6-69). Also reduce the thickness of the neck behind the cheeks to the approximate thickness of the upper head. This dimension will vary depending on the amount of neck extension; if the head is in a low position, the thickness of the neck will approach the maximum thickness of the head. On high-crowned ducks, such as the Barrow's golden-eye, bufflehead, and others, the crown is rounded (Fig. 5-11); on other ducks and geese, the top of the head is more nearly flat (Figs. 6-68, 6-70).

6-70 *Head and neck of common Canada goose.*

Proceed by roughly shaping the chin, lower cheek, and foreneck areas. Lay out the culmen of the bill and the intersection of the upper bill with the forehead. Next, draw a vertical line on both sides of the head at the rearmost part of the lower mandible and reduce the width of the bill at this point to its actual width (Fig. 6-71). Be careful not to cut into the cheek itself. Lay out the bill-cheek intersection line on both sides of the head. Carefully carve the bill and cheek to these lines (Fig. 6-72). Now, carve the bill down on either side of the forehead until the proper height of the bill is obtained and the bill-forehead area is clearly defined (Fig. 6-73). Continue by carving the bill to proper shape and thickness on out to its tip. Accurately duplicate the edges of the upper mandible by making a cut with a sharp knife along this line and remove the wood below this line down

6-73 Carve bill so that the bill-forehead area is clearly defined.

6-71 Lay out the culmen and reduce width of bill back to its rearmost extent.

6-74 Lay out the lower mandible and carve to its correct width.

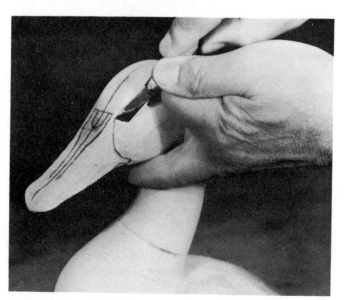

6-72 Carefuly carve cheek down to the bill-cheek intersection line.

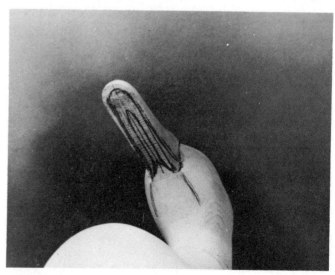

6-75 Lay out the detail on the lower side of the lower mandible.

to the actual width of the lower mandible (Fig. 6-74). Sketch in the intersection of the lower mandible with the chin and carve to shape. Lay out the nail at the tip of the bill and carve down the surrounding wood until the nail is slightly prominent.

Now, turn the carving upside down so that the lower side of the bill is exposed and lay out the edge of the lower mandible and the tapered recessed area on the bottom of the lower mandible (Fig. 6-75). Carve this lower area carefully, incorporating as much detail as possible, including the lower nail (Fig. 6-76). Turn the carving right side up and locate the nostrils by drilling two small holes at their extremities. Lay out the concave area surrounding the nostrils and remove the wood in this area with a small gouge. Outline the shape of the actual nostril and carve to a depth of about $\frac{1}{16}$ inch. Study the fine grooves near the edges of the mandibles on waterfowl and duplicate them using a small V gouge or burning tool as will be discussed later. This carving procedure for the head and bill of a duck applies generally to the other game birds.

Complete the head by drilling holes of the correct diameter for the eyes, if this has not already been done. Absolute symmetry is essential. Add a small amount of filler in the hole and insert the eye to its proper depth and partially cover the eye around its periphery with filler. Although wood dough, plastic wood, Tuf-Carv, caulking compound, and other materials can be used as filler, the author prefers talcum powder mixed into Hyplar modeling paste. This mixture does not become hard or brittle, it carves well, and sands fairly well. If low heat and pressure are used, this mixture also burns quite cleanly for feather detailing. It does, however, shrink some when drying, so that more than one application may be necessary to get the desired results. After the mixture has dried thoroughly, remove excess material until the natural shape of the eye has been established

(Fig. 6-78). Finish the eye installation by carving the eyelid to shape. When sanding adjacent to the eyes, be careful not to scratch the glass surface with the sandpaper. Scratches can usually be prevented by placing the thumb and nail of one hand over the eye while sanding.

6-77 Note eye detail on this female blue-winged teal.

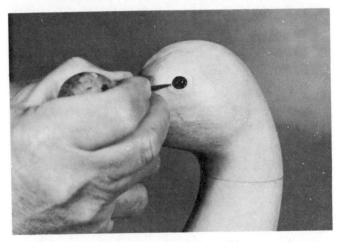
6-78 Accurately shape the eyes and carve the eyelids.

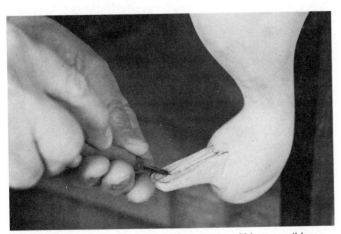
6-76 Incorporate as much detail on the lower mandible as possible.

6-79 Completed head of a canvasback drake.

OPEN BILL CARVING

To duplicate a bird in an aggressive or feeding position or to make the bird appear to be calling or talking, it is necessary to carve the bill in the open position. Carving the upper and lower mandibles and the tongue in detail is very difficult to accomplish accurately due to their very limited accessibility. It can be done in a relatively easy manner, however, if the head is cut in two on a line roughly bisecting the angle formed by the upper and lower mandibles.

First make an accurate drawing of the head profile with the lower mandible opened the desired amount and with the tongue in its correct position. (See Figure 8-47.) Draw in the cut-off line, located as mentioned above. Now, make a new drawing with the upper part of the head raised ⅛ inch as shown. (Adding the ⅛ inch will provide extra material, so that when the two parts are cut and are accurately sanded and glued together, the head will conform to the original profile drawing.) Although the tongue can be carved as an integral part of the lower mandible, it is easier to carve it as a separate piece and attach it with epoxy.

Proceed with the carving of the upper mandible in the usual manner, roughly shaping the forward part of the head at the same time. Do not attempt to carve the lower mandible at this point. When the upper mandible (Fig. 6-80) is completed, saw the head in two along the line shown (Fig. 6-81). Clamp the upper part of the head in a vise and hollow out the inside of the bill and continue the hollowing into the throat area. To accurately duplicate the inner sides of the mandibles and the tongue most carvers need to refer to a fresh or thawed specimen.

Next, cut the lower mandible to its proper width and shape and carve the side and underside details. Hollow out the inside to receive the tongue. The lamellae (the comblike

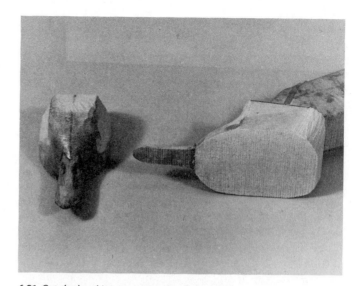

6-81 *Cut the head into two parts on the band saw.*

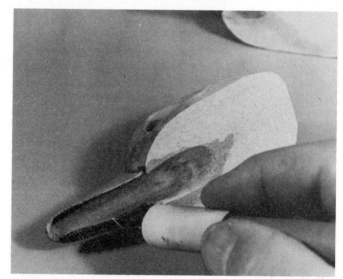

6-82 *After hollowing the bill, burn in the lamellae.*

6-80 *Carve the upper mandible and draw in the cut-off line.*

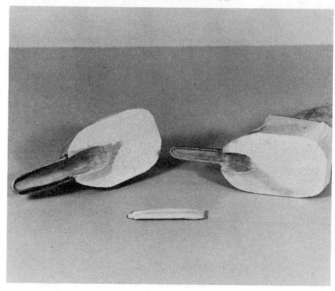

6-83 *The parts are now ready to be assembled.*

serrations on the inside of the upper mandible and the outside of the lower mandible are duplicated by burning in short parallel lines with the feather-detail burning tool described in Chapter 7 (Fig. 6-82). Cut out the tongue from a small piece of wood and carve it to shape, making it fit the inside of the lower mandible (Figs. 8-47 and 6-83). Attach it with epoxy.

Now, sand the mating surfaces of the two head parts accurately. Apply epoxy to these surfaces and accurately position them so that the mandibles are in proper alignment (Fig. 6-84). After the epoxy has set, the head can be attached to the body, or neck, and carved to its final shape (Fig. 6-85).

WING CARVING

Prior to actual carving, make an accurate full-size drawing showing the planform shape and feather detail on both the upper and lower surfaces; a front view; and usually at least one cross-sectional view (see Chapter 5).

After the drawing has been completed, ascertain the size of the rough wing block. The plan view provides the length and width dimensions. The thickness of the block must be sufficient to accommodate both the curvature of the wing as seen in the front view and the maximum cross-sectional thickness, which occurs at the wing's root. When the overall wing block size has been established, consideration must be given to grain direction so that adequate strength of the entire finished wing is assured.

The bird's wings become very thin (actually one feather thick) in the areas where the primaries, secondaries, and tertials are not overlapped by the wing covert feathers. To duplicate the wing with any degree of realism, these thin areas must be approximated.

When the wing is fully extended, the angle between the outermost primary feather and the secondary feathers (also the tertials) approaches 90 degrees. As the amount of wing extension decreases, this angle also decreases and approaches zero degrees when the wing is folded or almost folded. In duplicating most wing positions, therefore, it is necessary to make the wing block from two or more pieces in order to obtain the proper grain direction for maximum strength. If the carved wing in the areas of the primaries, secondaries, and tertials is to be quite thin (approaching the thickness of the actual wing), it is also advisable to make the wing block in the manner described above but from a stronger wood. The author uses alder, a hardwood species that carves quite well, for all wing carvings.

As shown in Figure 6-86, the block for the outstretched wings of a band-tailed pigeon was made from three pieces, whereas in Figure 6-87 the partially extended wing of a wood

6-84 Epoxy the parts together. Be sure mandibles are properly aligned.

6-85 Finished widgeon head.

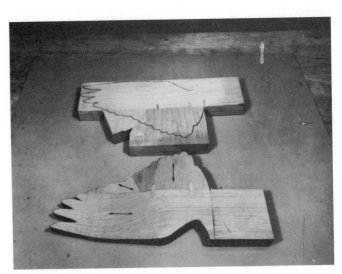

6-86 Each wing for the band-tailed pigeon was made from three pieces.

duck was made from one piece. Figure 6-88 shows still another situation, where the wing for a preening mallard was in an intermediate position and two pieces of wood were required for the wing block.

When duplicating a fully extended wing, it is necessary to glue the end grain of the block that forms the secondaries and tertial to the main spanwise block. End-grain gluing is generally considered unacceptable; however, the advent of epoxy adhesives makes possible a much stronger end-grain joint. It is still advisable to add splines, with their grain running in a fore-and-aft direction, to reinforce the end-grain joint (Fig. 6-86). On wings with considerable camber, or chordwise curvature (the wings of a band-tailed pigeon are excellent examples), the block forming the secondaries and tertials should be cut at an angle so that the resulting grain direction will be more or less parallel to these feathers (Fig. 6-89).

Some means of holding the wing block during the shaping and carving operations must be provided. In most cases, sufficient material can be left on the inboard section of the wing to permit clamping in a vise. In the case of the block for the preening wood duck wing, the board from which the block was cut was not of sufficient width to provide a holding point, so it was necessary to attach by means of epoxy a temporary scrap piece of wood for holding purposes (Fig. 6-90).

After the wing block has been assembled and the adhesive cured, transfer the plan-view layout of the wing to the block and cut to shape (Fig. 6-86). It is usually possible, especially on outstretched wings, to approximate some of the spanwise wing curvature (as seen from the front view) by removing wood with the band saw in a manner similar to that of sawing out the body block.

6-88 *The wing for a preening mallard was made from two pieces.*

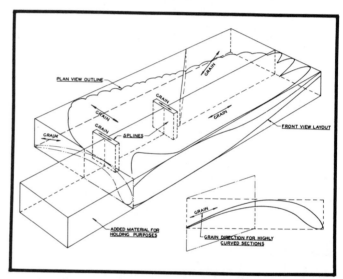

6-89 *Showing the construction of the wing block for a band-tailed pigeon.*

6-87 *The wing for a preening wood duck was made from one piece.*

6-90 *This wing was attached to a scrap piece of wood for support while being carved.*

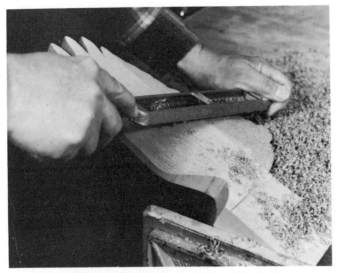

6-91 *Remove wood from the top side of the wing with a Surform rasp.*

6-94 *Further shaping of the upper surface with a Surform rasp.*

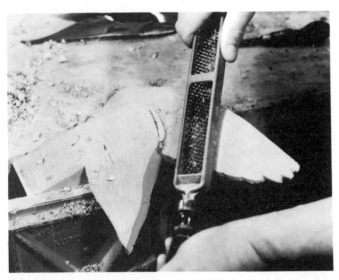

6-92 *The Surform rasp is being pulled to remove the wood from the primaries.*

6-95 *Removing wood from the lower wing surface with a gouge.*

6-93 *The round Surform rasp is also useful for shaping the upper surface.*

6-96 *Wood can be removed from concave areas with a large rotary file.*

When as much wood as possible has been removed with the band saw, start shaping the upper side of the wing (Figs. 6-91 through 94). Most of the chordwise curvature exists in the inboard section of the bird's wing, with maximum curvature near the root of the wing and practically none near the tip. Completely shape the upper surface and sand smooth.

Now, turn the wing over and start removing wood on the lower surface. Figures 6-95, 96, and 97 show some of the ways to accomplish this wood removal.

After the wing has been shaped to its final thickness (except in the root area, where wood is retained for holding or attaching purposes), transfer the feather-pattern layout to both the upper and lower surfaces (Fig. 6-98). Proceed with individual feather carving as described earlier (Fig. 6-99). The primary feathers have heavy, prominent shafts. Con-

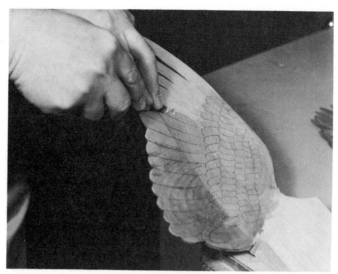

6-99 Carve the wing feathers individually.

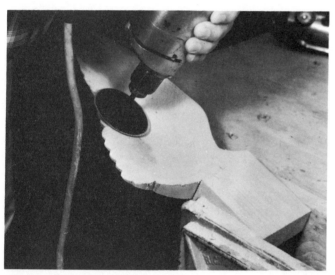

6-97 The disc sander is useful for removing wood from the under surface.

6-100 The shaft of each primary feather has been carved in on this wing.

6-98 Lay out the feather pattern on both surfaces of the wing.

6-101 Feather detail burning is easier to do before rather than after the wing is attached to the body.

siderable realism can be obtained by carving in these feather members (Fig. 6-100). Burning in further feather detail (see Chapter 7) is much easier before the wing is attached to the body (Fig. 6-101).

When all carving and other detail work has been completed, cut off the excess wood at the root, leaving enough material to make the wing-body joint — usually one half inch is sufficient — and shape the wing in this area. Locate the wing (or wings) accurately and gouge out the body to receive the wing stub (Fig. 6-102). Now, attach the wing with epoxy adhesive and hold in place with one or more nails until the epoxy cures. When the epoxy has cured, complete the wing joint by filling all openings around the wing butt with Plastic Wood or wood dough and sand smooth. The remaining feather carving in this area can now be completed.

6-102 *Gouge out the body to receive the wing stubs.*

6-103 *Showing completed wing installation (band-tailed pigeon.)*

CARVING LEGS AND FEET

Contemporary bird carvers use more different methods in duplicating the legs (tarsi) and feet than on any other part of the carving. These techniques vary from legs and feet carved from wood to complicated castings of metal, or plastic with metal inserts, made from molds of the actual foot and leg of a bird. Some of the more popular ways of constructing these parts will be covered here. The carver can then select the method or combination of methods that appeals to him. In most cases, his decision will be based not only on his mechanical ability but also on the available tools. Like all other phases of bird carving, there are many ways to get the job done; possibly some of the best ways are yet to be discovered. Regardless of which method of duplicating the legs and feet is used, an actual specimen from which to work is essential for a professional result.

The author has not used castings for legs and feet for two reasons. The first is the large number of patterns and molds required to duplicate not only the many game bird species, but also the different leg and foot positions of each species. The second is the difficulty involved, using the limited materials that lend themselves to home foundry work, in obtaining the strength required for shipping life-size birds. However, carvers should not be discouraged from experimenting with this fabrication process and taking advantage of its possible savings in time.

Because of the difficulty in obtaining the very high temperatures required to melt most stronger metals, home castings usually are done with lead or a lead alloy that can be melted fairly easily. For larger carvings, cast lead legs do not provide sufficient strength, and it is usually necessary to cast around a reinforcing steel or brass rod. Because the strength requirements of feet are less, they lend themselves to the casting method of fabrication better than legs. However, there are problems in casting the toe nails (if they are duplicated realistically) as it is often difficult to make the molten metal flow into these parts.

Molds can be made from several materials. One of the more popular mold materials is hardwood, such as maple, which will resist the melted lead for some time. Plaster is also used but its life is short. Flexible molds made from silicon rubber (RTV) are best but are rather expensive to make.

Some commercially produced legs and feet are now available (see Appendix) for those who are unable to make their own or wish to save time and effort. These legs are usually cast from molds that were made using actual bird parts as patterns. The use of commercial legs and feet, or homemade ones, made in this manner is discouraged in most competitive shows. Points may be lost and an otherwise winning carving may lose because of this. The author is definitely opposed to using actual bird parts as patterns for molds for he believes this practice violates the ethics of realistic bird carving. There is nothing unethical about using cast parts provided the patterns and molds are made by the carver himself. Carving feet and legs, like other parts of the bird, is a challenge — the serious carver should face this challenge rather than take the easy way out.

Probably the simplest way to depict the legs and webbed feet (and the method requiring fewest tools) is to carve them from wood (Fig. 6-104). The legs of some birds, however, are so small that wood does not supply sufficient strength for normal handling. If wood is used, make the tarsi from hardwood; maple dowel stock is readily available and a good choice. The feet for waterfowl carvings can be made from a small flat piece of the same kind of wood used for the body of the carving; but, again, making them from hardwood will help reduce the possibility of accidental breakage. The detailed carving on both tarsi and feet can be performed with a knife and small gouges, although small rotary files, powered by the Foredom flexible shaft tool, or small hand grinders are very useful in carving the rather complicated details. Make the small hind toe from an individual piece of wood and cement it into a hole after the leg is carved to shape. When constructing the legs completely

from wood, locate both legs at approximately the same angle so that they can be inserted into the holes drilled in the body and also in the mounting base.

A variation of this method is shown in Figure 6-105. Greater strength and the necessary flexibility for different leg positions are provided by the use of a small metal rod or wire running through the wood leg. The leg rod must extend sufficiently above and below the leg to provide attachment to the body and to the mounting base. Drill the holes for the legs in the body in the manner described on page 110. Where the rods extend below the feet, bend them at angles to make them parallel to each other and at approximate right angles to the mounting surface (Fig. 6-106). Then, drill holes in the base to match the leg rods. After the leg rods have been fitted by temporarily installing them in the body and mount-

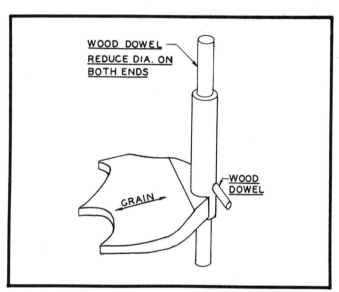

6-104 Simple wood leg and foot.

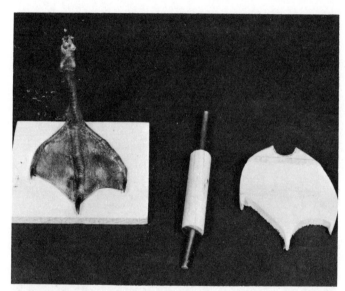

6-106 Leg and foot parts ready for assembly.

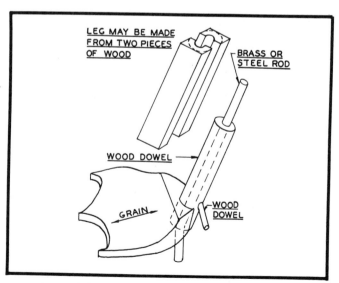

6-105 The use of a brass or steel rod permits greater flexibility of leg positions.

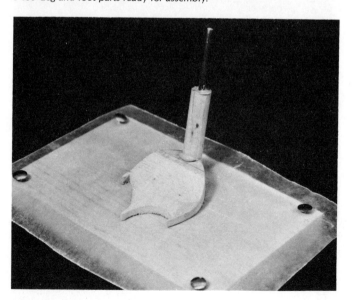

6-107 Attach foot to the leg with epoxy.

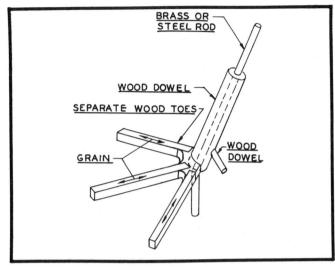

6-108 *Unwebbed feet may also be made of wood.*

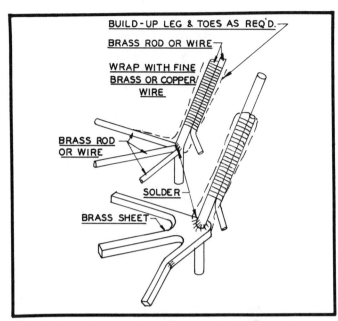

6-109 *The leg and foot can be made from metal and built up with plastics.*

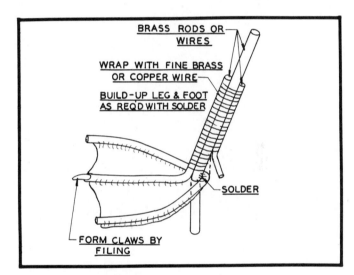

6-110 *Making foot and leg from small rods or wires.*

ing base, the drilled wood dowel, which will be carved to the leg's shape, can be slipped on and attached by means of epoxy adhesive. If drilling the dowel presents a problem, make the wood part of the leg from two pieces, gouge it out to receive the metal rod, assemble on the rod, and attach with epoxy. Relieve the wood foot at the proper angle to fit the leg and then affix with epoxy (Fig. 6-107).

This method can also be used to duplicate the legs and feet of game birds with unwebbed feet (Fig. 6-108). For unwebbed feet, it is usually easier to make the toes from individual pieces of wood.

Unfortunately, wood does not provide enough strength for the legs and feet of professional bird carvings. The toes and claws are especially vulnerable to breakage when the carving is handled or dusted. Also, it is most difficult to make wooden feet conform accurately to an irregularly shaped mounting base, such as a piece of driftwood. As soon as the beginner acquires some experience shaping feet and legs, he should start experimenting with the use of metal.

One of the more popular methods of simulating legs and feet is to make the legs from small rods and the toes from wire and build them up to the approximate shape by means of a plastic (Fig. 6-109). Many different materials such as Plastic Wood, liquid metal, automotive body fillers, and fiberglass are used. In almost all cases, the building-up process must be done in layers so that the material will properly cure in place, a procedure requiring considerable time. The built-up legs and feet are then carved to shape. A disadvantage of this method is that cracks sometimes develop in the plastic when the legs are inadvertently flexed. As Figure 6-109 shows, the foot can be made of one piece, cut from brass sheet of sufficient thickness, instead of brass rods. In this case, the toes are carved to shape without being built up with plastic.

Another popular method, which gives more durable results, is to use three small brass rods or wires for the leg and to make the toes from two wires of the proper diameter (Fig. 6-110). Build up both the legs and feet with solder, and then carve or file to the required shape. Make the heavier main leg wire and bend to the proper angle in the manner described for the wood-covered metal leg. Bend the smaller forward leg rod to form the middle toe, and shape the even smaller rear rod to form the small hind toe. Then, make the inner and outer toes from a common wire bent in a rough V shape and solder it to the main leg rod. All of the parts can be secured in place for soldering by means of fine brass wire wrapped around the parts (Fig. 6-111). Fuse the three leg wires and attach the inner and outer toe wire with a solder of a higher melting point, such as silver solder, so that the lower-melting-point soft solder can be used for building up the leg and toes without affecting these main joints. Silver solder requires the use of an acetylene or Presto-Lite torch in order to bring the parts up to the correct temperature (Figs. 6-112, 113). On larger legs, where more metal mass is

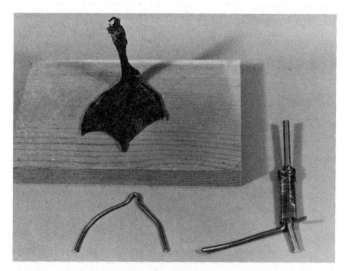

6-111 *Parts for built-up wire foot and leg ready for assembly.*

6-112 *Drill a hole in a concrete block to support the leg and foot while soft soldering.*

6-113 *Attach the parts and build up leg with soft solder.*

involved, an oxyacetylene torch is much more desirable, if not mandatory. If the carver does not possess this type of equipment, it is often possible to take the leg and foot parts to a repair shop and have them either brazed or silver soldered. After the parts have been attached together and built up the desired amount, carve the leg and toes to shape. This can be accomplished by hand files or, more easily, with rotary files powered by a high-speed grinder.

Whenever it becomes necessary to bend the metal toes to conform to the mounting surface, make bends only at the joint locations of the toes. As previously mentioned in Chapter 3, the outer toe has four, the middle toe three, and the inner toe two joints, counting the attachment joint. To bend down the toe, make a v-shaped cut with a file or other tool on the bottom of the toe at the joint location. This cut will permit the toe to bend in a realistic manner. Close the joints with soft solder after all of the bends have been made.

The webs of waterfowl feet can be made from soft brass, copper, lead, or any thin material that can be formed in two directions to fit the toes. Some carvers use fabric, or chamois skin. The metal webs are usually attached to the toes with soft solder; however, epoxy not only can be used for webs made from fabric or other nonmetallic materials, but also can be substituted for the soft solder when metal webs are used.

The writer prefers to carve the legs and feet from solid brass. This method provides excellent strength and durability but is not simple and requires tools and equipment that may not be available to some carvers. The legs are carved from brass rods, and the toes from brass sheet. In some cases, the three toes are cut out as one piece; in other instances, they are cut out individually. The procedure normally followed by the author is described below.

The diameter of the leg rod is determined from an actual specimen. If a specimen is not available, this dimension, as well as the length of the leg, or tarsus, and the size and shape of the foot, can be approximated from the data given in chapters 13 and 14. The length of the rod is determined by the length of the tarsus plus the length of the tang (the part of the rod that inserts into the body). The length of the tang should be at least six times its diameter, which is turned on a metal lathe to the diameter of the holes drilled in the body block. When the lower part of the tibia (drumstick) is exposed and is at a pronounced angle to the tarsus, the upper tang is made from a separate brass rod, silver soldered in place (Figs. 6-118, 122). The attachment of the lower tang, by which the standing carving is secured to the mounting base, is somewhat more difficult to make. It is very important that the lower tangs of the two feet be parallel to each other and, to facilitate drilling the mounting holes in the base, perpendicular to the ground.

Set the miter gauge on a disc sander to match the angle of the leg as seen in the profile view, and tilt the sander table to match the camber angle of the leg as seen from the front view. The bottom of the leg rod is then sanded off at this compound angle. The body, with the legs inserted, is now placed on a flat surface. If the above procedure has been properly carried out, the legs can be rotated until both of their bottoms are flat against the surface and the angle of the body relative to the ground, as seen in the profile view, will be correct. The centerline of the leg rods, as seen from the front, are now marked.

The lower tangs are cut from a brass rod (their length, again, should be at least six times their diameter). These rods are located on the leg centerlines, as far forward as possible, and are silver soldered in place (Fig. 6-114).

After the lower tangs are silver soldered, the legs are again inserted into the body and are rotated until the bottom of each tang rests against a flat surface. The front centerlines are re-marked, using a felt tip pen. The rough shape of the tarsi, as seen from the front, is drawn on the rods and as much excess material as possible is removed using a band saw with a metal cutting blade.

In the past the author cut out the foot as one piece from brass sheet (Fig. 6-115). But now he usually cuts the toes out separately because this requires less material, makes the cutting out and carving easier, and permits a more realistic placement of the toes relative to the tarsi. Silver soldering the individual toes to the leg rod, however, is more difficult than attaching an entire foot and requires a holding fixture of some sort (Fig. 6-116).

It is easier to carve toes in pairs than individually. This is done by cutting out and shaping the corresponding toes of each foot as one piece. This method makes it possible to securely hold one toe in a vise, while leaving the other toe completely exposed and unrestricted for carving (Fig. 6-117). After the two toes are almost completely shaped, they are cut in two and are bent to the desired configuration. The attaching ends are filed or sanded to the correct angles and the toes are then silver soldered to the leg rod (Fig. 6-116).

Whenever more than two parts are to be soldered together, the author either attaches the parts together mechanically (Fig. 6-118) or devises a holding fixture. If the lower tang is not mechanically attached before being soldered, its joint will be lost when the toes are silver soldered in place unless the tang is somehow held in its proper loca-

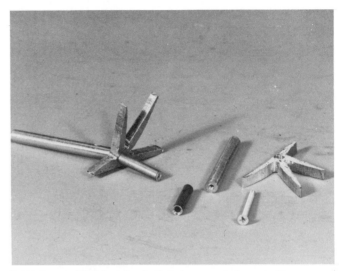

6-115 *Legs and feet for a band-tailed pigeon ready for assembly.*

6-116 *Jury rig for holding leg rod while attaching toes with silver solder.*

6-114 *The lower tang is silver soldered to the leg rod.*

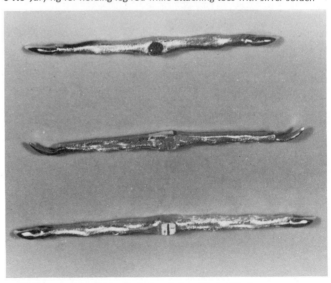

6-117 *Toes are carved in pairs before being attached to leg.*

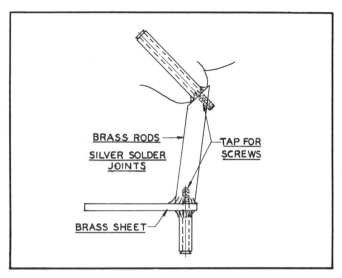

6-118 *Parts are held together mechanically on this foot-leg assembly.*

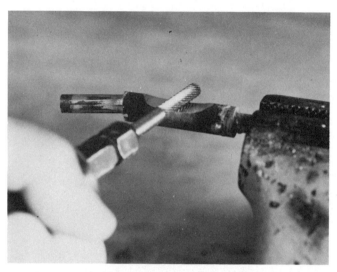

6-119 *Removing metal from side of leg with a rotary file.*

tion and position. The author drills a hole in a concrete block, or brick, of the proper diameter and to such a depth that the tang will just hit bottom. The leg rod is then restrained by a holding fixture to prevent its movement. Although the tang joint will probably melt during soldering of the toes, its alignment will remain unaffected after the joint has cooled (Fig. 6-116).

Practically all the carving of the legs and toes is done with rotary files (there are many shapes and sizes from which to choose) used in a high-speed grinder (Fig. 6-119). The Foredom flexible shaft tool with small, rotary files is also useful for some of the fine detail. Almost all the shaping of the claws is done by hand, using diemaker's files (Fig. 6-121). The final smoothing is also done by hand, using riffler files. The claws are polished smooth on a buffing wheel.

The procedure involved in carving a part from brass is not unlike that in carving a part from wood, although removal of metal is, of course, more difficult and slower. The harder brass is, the easier it is machined. Because soft brass tends to clog the teeth of the rotary files, they will require frequent and rather difficult cleaning. The overall shape of the leg is first established and then the details — tendons, joints, and wrinkles — are carved in. If too much material is removed, the part can be built up with either soft solder or silver solder. If silver solder is used, care must be exercised to prevent melting and losing some, or all, of the previously made joints. For example, silver solder can be added to the upper part of the leg provided the lower part and toes are wrapped with a wet cloth.

The hind toe is made from a separate piece of brass sheet or a rod sanded flat on both sides. The leg is drilled at the proper location and the toe is soft soldered (to prevent melting the other joints) in place and is then carved to shape (Figs. 6-120, 121).

Because the heel of the rear foot of a striding bird is usually off the ground, the lower mounting tang can not be attached to the leg rod. In this case, a small tang can be silver soldered to the middle toe (Fig. 6-122).

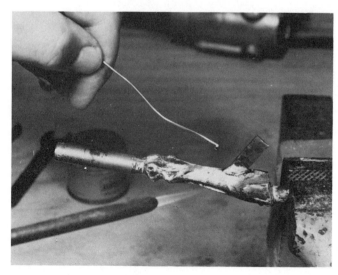

6-120 *Soft soldering small hind toe to leg.*

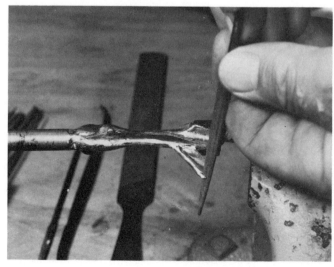

6-121 *The small hind toe is carved with diemaker's files.*

The author uses lead sheet, hammered thin and sanded clean, for the web of the feet of waterfowl (Fig. 6-124). After cutting a hole in the lead sheet, slip the lead over the tang and form the web to the bottom of the foot. Once the lead sheet is in its proper place, draw lines around the toes and between the toes. Then remove the sheet and cut it to shape with a pair of scissors. Scale detail is added with a thin, dull instrument, and the small V-shaped notches on the front edge of the web are either cut or filed. The smaller webs on upland game birds, including the pectinations (the comb-like membranes along the edges of the toes), can also be duplicated in this manner.

After all the detailing is finished, the mating surfaces are sanded clean and wiped with acetone or some other grease remover. The Scotch-Weld epoxy mentioned earlier is excellent for adhering metal to metal and is applied sparingly on the underside of the toes. The web is clamped in place using wood clothespins (Fig. 6-125). The setting of this

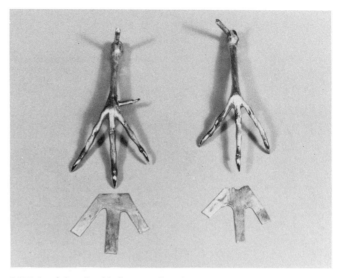

6-124 Lead sheet is added to provide webs at the intersection of the toes and to build up toe pads.

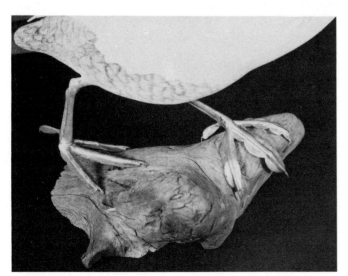

6-122 Note small tang on center toe (coot feet).

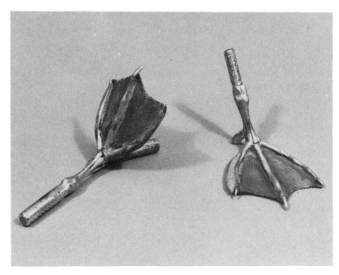

6-125 Clothespins are used to hold lead webs in place while epoxy sets.

6-123 Completed feet and legs for a coot carving.

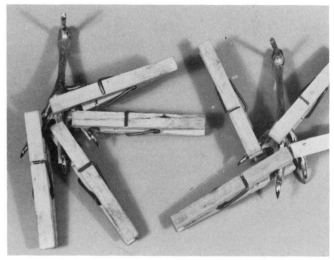

6-126 The lead webs have been assembled to these hooded merganser's feet.

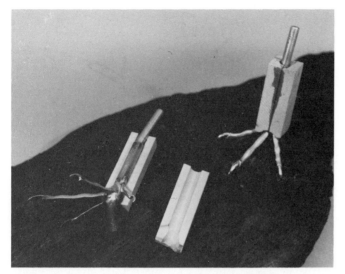

6-127 *Add wood to build up leg for some upland game birds.*

epoxy can be greatly accelerated by placing the part into an oven for about 15 minutes at 160 degrees Fahrenheit.

On some upland game birds (prairie chickens, grouse, and ptarmigans) the tarsi are covered with feathers. This can be duplicated by drilling two pieces of wood clamped together to fit the leg rod (Fig. 6-127). The lower ends of the wood pieces are carved to fit the toes and are then assembled to the leg with epoxy. After the epoxy has set, the feathered leg is then carved to shape (Fig. 6-128).

The feet of full-bodied birds that are resting or crouching are not attached to the base (Fig. 6-129). The carved bird is attached by means of a dowel extending from the base into the body of the carving. The legs and feet are made in the normal manner except the lower mounting tangs are eliminated. Figure 6-131 shows a simple holding fixture consisting of a piece of aluminum sheet bent to the proper angle (aluminum sheet is used to prevent the silver solder from adhering).

Complete the feet and legs by spraying them with primer.

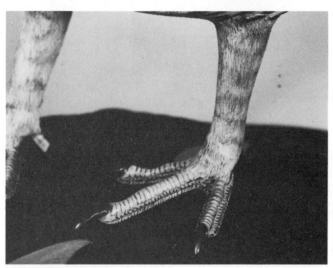

6-128 *Carve to shape and burn in feather detail.*

6-130 *Finished feet and legs on a white-fronted goose carving.*

6-129 *Finished leg and foot on a chukar partridge carving.*

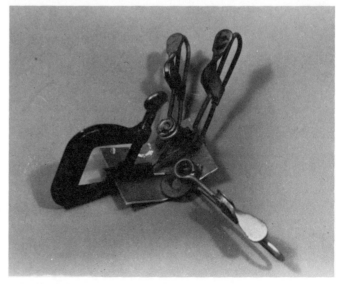

6-131 *Simple holding fixture for silver soldering toes to leg rod.*

INDIVIDUAL FEATHERING TECHNIQUE

Great improvements in the carving and painting of birds were made during the 1960's, primarily as a result of formal and informal competitions. In a continual effort to more closely duplicate the actual bird, carvers added more detail, refined existing methods, and originated new techniques.

Probably the most dramatic change in the art of bird carving was brought about by the introduction of the individual feathering technique, which basically consists of making many of the feathers (primaries, secondaries, coverts, tail feathers, and others) individually and assembling them to the wing and body structures in a manner very similar to that of the real bird's. Although used to a very limited degree much earlier, this technique became prominent in the early 1970's when a number of carvings were displayed that not only featured this method of construction to its fullest extent but also incorporated positions and actions that had rarely been attempted before.

These *super-carvings*, now being produced by a number of top carvers, have been very well received and are viewed with awe and admiration by almost everyone who sees them. There are a few carvers and collectors, however, who think that a beautiful piece made in this manner is no longer a carving – possibly more like a piecemeal sculpture – and tend to criticize and belittle the artistry, planning, skill, and patience that went into it. These individuals further believe that the techniques of the early working decoy maker should remain relatively unchanged, and they stubbornly resist using many of the newer methods that were responsible for the emergence of fine, realistic bird carvings from the craft category into an original American art form.

The author believes that the individual carver should plan and carve birds in a manner that pleases him, but if he wishes to sell his work consistently, he may (at least on occasions) have to conform to the desires of collectors. Also, if he wishes to enter his carvings in competitive shows, and win, he may have to make changes and incorporate techniques that he does not particularly like. The individually feathered carvings have been criticized most severely in relation to competitions. Eventually, contest committees will probably develop new judging categories so that the super-type carving is not judged against the more conventionally constructed carving. Hard and fast rules that can distinguish these carvings properly will not be easy to devise, and it remains to be seen whether making these distinctions will be a benefit or detriment to American bird carving art as a whole.

Although many carvers may not have the ability to conceive a super-carving or the energy, skill, and patience to execute such a complicated project, they can learn much from this relatively new technique that can be applied directly to simpler types of carvings.

About the only way to accurately determine the shape, contour, and location of individual feathers and their attachment to the basic structure is by reference to an actual bird. Therefore, a fresh or thawed specimen is almost a necessity if individually made feathers are to be used to any great extent.

To make individual feathers, the carver must have thin wood strips, of even thickness, approximately $\frac{1}{32}$ inch thick and of sufficient width to accommodate the widest feather he plans to make. Basswood is generally preferred, although other woods can be substituted successfully. The author has used alder (a wood similar to maple, but softer), which is stronger than basswood, with good results. If precut veneer is not available, probably the easiest way to make your own is to rip the thin strips on a table saw. A smooth-cutting, hollow ground blade works well and leaves few saw marks. If a table saw is not available, a band saw can be used, although it will not produce strips as thin or even as those possible with a table saw. A portable belt sander is useful for reducing the thickness and/or removing saw marks (Fig. 6-132).

Although making individual feathers is tedious and very time-consuming, the procedure is quite simple. First, a drawing of the feather that is to be reproduced, showing its shape and shaft location, must be transferred to the thin piece of material. The feather is then cut out using a sharp knife; if the material is quite thin, a pair of sharp scissors may be used. The edges are reduced in thickness by further sanding.

Shaft detail can be added in three different ways. Except on strongly shafted feathers, such as the primaries on most birds and the tail feathers on large birds, the shaft is usually burned in by making two accurately converging lines with the burning tool (Figs. 7-36, 37). When the shaft is quite prominent, it can either be carved as part of the feather (a very difficult and time-consuming job) or added as two separate pieces. When individual pieces are used, a tapered piece of material whose length is equal to that of the shaft and whose thickness on one end is equal to slightly more than one half of the total shaft thickness and tapered to practically nothing on the other end must be made. This can be done by hand, or more easily with a portable belt sander. A strip whose width equals the maximum width of the shaft on one end and tapers to practically nothing on the other end is then cut off this piece with a straight edge and a very

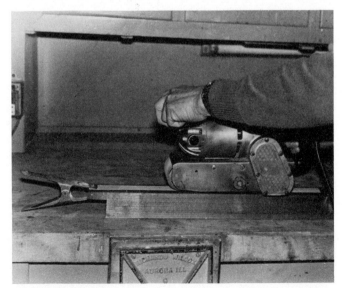

6-132 *The portable belt sander quickly reduces the thickness and smooths the thin feather material.*

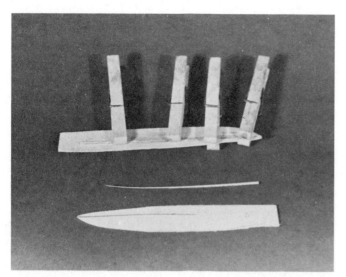

6-133 *The shaft of the feather can be added as two separate pieces.*

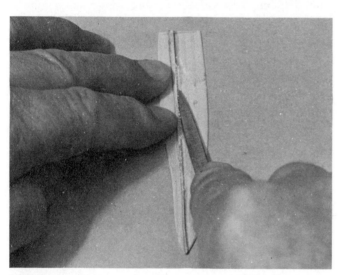

6-134 *The excess epoxy can be easily removed with a riffler file.*

6-135 *Burned surfaces must be cleaned thoroughly before painting.*

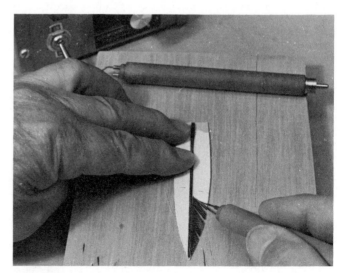

6-136 *Barb separation can be accomplished with a hot burning tool.*

sharp knife or razor blade. This small, tapered strip is then dragged through some epoxy spread thinly on a flat surface (care must be taken that the epoxy is applied evenly to the entire length of the shaft piece). The shaft is then laid on the feather shaft line and is held in place by small clamps, such as clothespins (Fig. 6-133). After the epoxy has set fairly well, the same procedure is followed on the other side of the feather.

When the epoxy has hardened thoroughly, the surplus can be removed quite easily from the feather vane with a riffler type file (Fig. 6-134). The shaft should then be sanded to its final cross-sectional shape, which is oval or elliptical on the upper side and rectangular with the edges rounded over on the lower side.

The carver must be careful when burning in barb detail to make sure that the tip of the iron, though placed next to the shaft, is not so close as to burn into it. See Chapter 7 for instructions on feather-detail burning.

It is most important that all burned surfaces be cleaned thoroughly before they are painted. The products of combustion and other particles can be removed or loosened quite effectively and easily by brushing vigorously with a stainless steel brush. If compressed air is available, the loose particles can be removed with a high velocity stream of air; if not, brushing with a soft bristle brush while blowing with the mouth will usually do the job. Rubbing the surface with a tack rag (an impregnated cloth obtainable at a paint store) also helps to remove loose particles (Fig. 6-135).

As was mentioned previously, many carvers accentuate the parting of barbs, which causes the v-shaped gaps in feather vanes. Although this practice can be carried to an extreme, a certain amount of barb parting adds realism and texture. Separation of barbs can be duplicated easily and effectively with a burning tool, such as The Detailer whose tip can be made very hot. The barb lines are burned in a normal manner up to where the part in the barb lines is desired. The v-shaped piece is removed by making two deep burns. The barb lines are then continued but are made parallel to the other side of the v-cut (Fig. 6-136).

Because feathers are not flat, but are curved along their length and cross section, some means of forming the simulated feather must be used to duplicate the natural curve. One of the easiest ways to permanently bend wood is to apply heat, water, and pressure. This can be done in many ways: holding the feather in the steam from a tea kettle or applying a household steam iron directly, for example. The author uses a large, old-fashioned electric soldering iron as the heat source and lays a wet rag on the tip to provide steam. The feather is then placed directly on the wet rag and pressure is applied to both sides to obtain simple lengthwise curvature (Fig. 6-137). To obtain curvature in both the lengthwise and crosswise directions, a female form (made from a piece of scrap wood gouged to the proper shape) is used. The simulated feather is wrapped in a wet cloth and placed over the form. Heat and pressure are then supplied with the tip of a hot soldering iron (Fig. 6-138).

Several ways in which the individual feathering technique can be applied to improve conventional carvings are described in the following sections.

Crest Feathers

Duplicating the raised crest feathers on such birds as the prairie chicken (Figs. 6-139, 140), ruffed grouse, sharp-tailed grouse, scaled quail, and others is one of the simplest applications of the individual feathering technique.

If a specimen is available, either remove one of the crest feathers or lift one up with a needle or the point of a knife. Note the length, width, and shape of the feather. When it is not possible to check a real feather, try to determine its length from a photograph (since the length of the bill is known, the feather length can be estimated by ratio and proportion). The width of these feathers is usually about one fifth or one sixth of their length, and they are generally

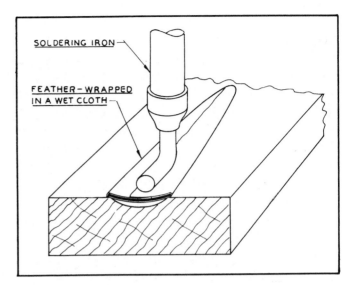

6-138 One way that feathers can be bent along their cross section.

6-139, 140 Crest feathers on a prairie chicken carving.

6-137 Bending a feather lengthwise using a soldering iron.

6-141 *Place the feathers on the layout to determine their overlaps.*

6-142 *Attach the tail feathers to each other in their proper sequence and position.*

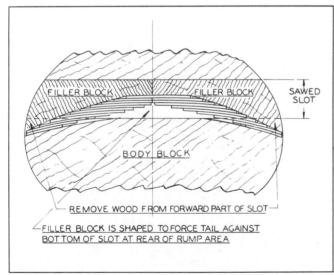

6-143 *Cross section of rump area near the forward part of the tail.*

tapered with rounded ends. Lay out seven or eight feathers, making them somewhat longer than the actual feather, on one of the thin strips of wood. Because crest feathers are small and hard to hold, it is easier to burn in the shaft and barbs before cutting out the feathers. Next, using one of the methods described earlier, bend each of the feathers until their curved shape (lengthwise) corresponds to the real thing.

Now, hold the feathers individually on the head of the carving and determine their locations. Cut the feathers to their proper length and trace around each of them so that the wood can be mortised out to receive them. Attach the feathers with epoxy, starting with the rearmost and working forward. Tiny pins, the type used for attaching sequins, are useful for holding the feathers in place while the epoxy is setting.

Tail Feathers

The making of an accurate layout of the shape and the arrangement of the tail feathers is the most important phase of this procedure. Changes are infinitely easier to make on paper than on the final tail; therefore, do not attempt any shortcuts or minimize the importance of this step.

The tail of a bird is divided into a right group and a left group, each group often acting separately (Fig. 5-45). The hooded merganser's tail used here as an example has twenty feathers (Fig. 6-141). Most birds have fewer tail feathers, usually from twelve to eighteen. Except when viewed from below, all of the feathers can be seen only when the tail is fanned out.

After the layout is completed, trace off the individual feathers onto the thin material, numbering them so that their proper location can be easily determined later. Now, cut them out and place them, two adjacent feathers at a time, on the layout and mark their upper and lower overlaps. This is done to define the area which is to be burned as it is usually not necessary to burn barb detail over the entire feather on both sides (Fig. 6-141).

The tail feathers are quite strongly shafted. However, only the shafts on the lower side of the two outermost feathers and the upper side of one center feather are exposed along most of their lengths. At the carver's discretion, the shafts on these three feathers may be added as separate pieces (Fig. 6-133) or burned in along with the rest of the tail feather shafts.

After the barb detail is burned, steam the feathers and bend them, so they are slightly convex along their cross section (Fig. 6-138). Attach the finished feathers together with epoxy, starting with the outermost and working toward the center (Fig. 6-142). Use epoxy sparingly so as to avoid forcing any onto the exposed part of the feather. If this does occur, the excess epoxy can be removed later by carefully placing the tip of the hot burning tool in the previously burned barb lines. After the epoxy has set, accurately trim or sand the forward edge of the assembly.

The tail feather assembly must now be attached to the body. The slot to receive the tail should be made before cutting out the original body block and can be accomplished with a band saw or, more accurately, by making a series of cuts on a table saw. The tail used in this example was for a stretching (wing and leg) hooded merganser. In this case, the tail would be convex (as viewed from above). In other instances, such as when the bird is taking off, the tail would be concave.

The forward part of the slot's lower surface is now shaped to conform to the convex shape (Fig. 6-143). A filler block, or blocks, must be carved next to fill the void between the tail feathers and the body. In the example shown, the filler was made from two pieces (Figs. 6-143, 144). It is most important that these filler blocks be made to fit accurately and tightly. After they have been fitted, remove the tail assembly and replace the filler blocks, holding them securely in place with temporary wedges (Fig. 6-145). The upper and lower tail covert area and the rump can now be carved to their final shapes without damaging the fragile tail feathers. When this is finished, install the tail and filler blocks with

6-146 *Install the tail and carve and burn the upper tail coverts.*

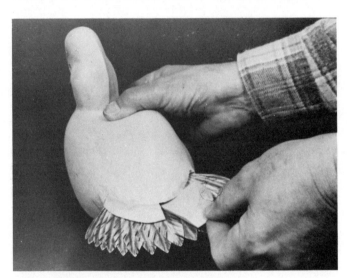

6-144 *The filler is made from two pieces of wood.*

6-147 *Rough out the body in the normal manner.*

6-145 *Hold the filler blocks in place with wedges.*

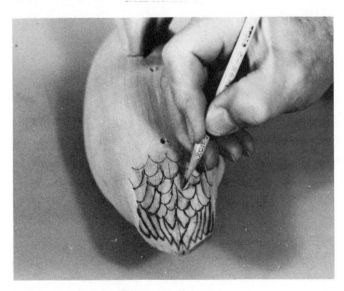

6-148 *Lay out the tail and the upper tail coverts.*

epoxy. After the epoxy has set, carefully carve and burn the individual tail covert feathers (Fig. 6-146).

Insertion of Crossed Primaries and Tertials

It is usually very difficult, if not impossible, to accurately carve the tail, upper tail coverts, rump, the crossed primary groups, and the tertials from the body block because of the very limited access to at least some of these parts. A better job can be done and much more detail and realism can be gotten if the folded primary groups and the tertials are made and inserted separately.

To describe and illustrate this procedure, the carving of a green-winged teal decorative decoy is used as an example. (See Figure 8-53 for drawing.) This general method, with slight variations can be applied to other waterfowl species.

The body block is cut out and carved in the normal manner except no wood is left from which to carve the crossed primaries and the tertials (Fig. 6-147). The tail feathers, upper tail coverts, and rump feathers are drawn in and carved (Fig. 6-148). The primary groups are located next and the exposed secondaries, tertials, and scapular feathers are sketched on one side of the carved surface and are transferred to the other side as previously described. A drawing of one set of the folded primaries is made and is traced on to a piece of soft metal. Lead sheet works very well, but if it is not available soft aluminum or galvanized sheet can be used. At this point, the carver must decide where to terminate the primary group. In this example, it was terminated just above the wing secondary group. The metal template representing the primary group is cut off at that point and bent to match the curvature and twist of an actual duck's wing. It is formed to match the curvature of the body where the folded primary group will attach to the body block (Fig. 6-149). This template is now used as a form for checking the shape of the carved primary group (Fig. 6-150).

Additional realism can be obtained with very little more work by making the folded primary groups from individual

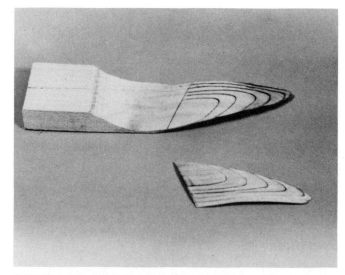

6-150 *The primary groups are carved to match the template.*

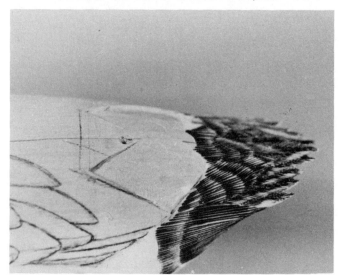

6-151 *Relieve the body block to receive the primary groups.*

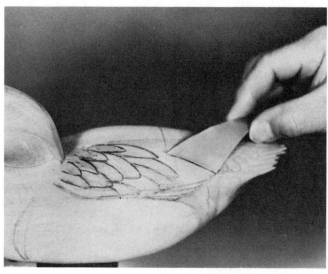

6-149 *Use a metal template to check the curvature of the primary groups.*

6-152 *Remove wood from the rear of the scapular groups.*

feathers. The method described above is followed except that instead of carving the folded primary group from a single piece, the feathers are made and bent individually. It is usually necessary to make only the outermost six or seven feathers as the secondaries and tertials cover the others. Also, as only the tips and the trailing edges of these feathers are exposed, it is not necessary to burn barb detail over the entire feather. Except for the lower side of the outermost primary, very little of the shafts are exposed; therefore, they may be effectively burned in rather than added as separate pieces (see Figure 8-17).

The body block is now relieved to receive the folded primary groups (Fig. 6-151). Before attaching the primary groups to the body block, barb detail is burned in on the tail, coverts, and rump.

Wood is removed from the body block at the rear of the scapular group (Fig. 6-152) to a depth that will allow for the installation of the individual tertial feathers, which are made at this time (Fig. 6-153). The outline of the lowermost tertial feather is traced on a piece of transparent paper and is cut out. This paper template is then placed in its proper position on the carving and its cut-off line is marked and carefully trimmed (Fig. 6-154). If the paper template does not fit perfectly, the procedure is repeated until an accurately fitting template is obtained. The paper template is then placed on the back side of the simulated tertial feather, the cut-off line is transferred to the wood, and the excess wood is trimmed off cleanly with a sharp knife.

An alternative method for installing the tertials, which probably gives more consistent results with no more effort, is to undercut the scapulars to a depth of $\frac{1}{32}$ to $\frac{1}{16}$ inch and then slip the tertial into this slot. Undercutting can be performed with a hook-bladed knife (Fig. 6-167), with a small pointed saw (such as made by Exacto), or with a small cutting wheel used in the Foredom.

After a little epoxy is applied to the underside of the feather, it is placed on the carving and held in its proper place by means of masking tape and tiny pins (Fig. 6-155).

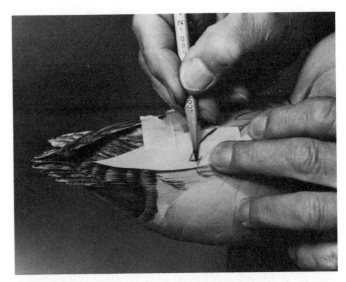
6-154 A paper template is used to mark the feather cut off.

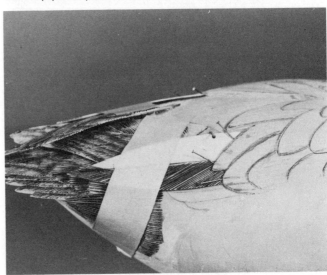
6-155 The feather is held in place by means of masking tape and small pins.

6-153 Tertial feathers for a green-winged teal carving.

6-156 The individual tertials have all been installed.

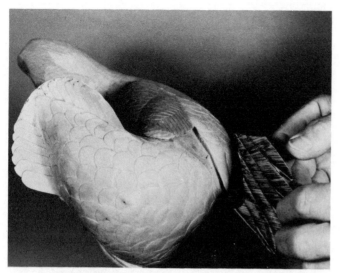

6-157 *The secondaries and side feathers of this prairie chicken carving have been relieved to receive the primaries.*

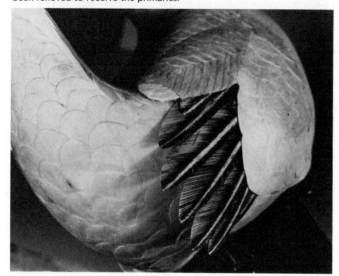

6-158 *The inserted primaries are epoxied in place.*

After the epoxy has set, the thickness of the unexposed part of the feather is reduced to practically nothing in order to keep the overlap areas from becoming too thick. Repeat this process for the remaining tertials (Fig. 6-156). After the tertials are all in place, the individual scapular feathers are carved.

The extended primaries of displaying upland game birds can be made individually and inserted. After the individual feathers are made and detailed, they are joined together with epoxy, as previously described for the tail group. Figures 6-157 and 6-158 show the inserted primaries of a displaying prairie chicken.

The Complete Wing

Besides being unbelievably light, splendidly functional, and extremely durable, a bird's wing is beautiful and complex almost beyond description — it is certainly one of nature's masterpieces. Although man can never come close

to duplicating the superb construction of a wing, the individual feathering technique makes it possible to attain a delicate realism that is almost impossible to achieve by carving from a solid block. Also, the use of very thin, but strong, and completely separated flight feathers greatly enhances the feeling of motion. The individual feathering technique is definitely shown to its very best advantage when used on wings, especially those in the flight configuration.

Before attempting to duplicate the wing of a bird in great detail, the serious carver should do as much research as he possibly can and study live birds at every opportunity. Some wing movements are too fast to be discerned by the unaided eye, but fortunately many fine photographs are available for close study. Edgar Queeny's fine book, *Prairie Wings*, for example, contains an excellent collection of photographs of waterfowl in flight.

The wing is capable of assuming many positions and shapes. The very flexible flight feathers dramatically reflect the air loads imposed on them which in turn help impart the feeling of movement. During the downstroke and in gliding flight, the flight feathers are pressed closely together. In these conditions, the pressure on the lower side is positive, causing the covert feathers on the underside to conform smoothly to the wing's surface, while the coverts on the upper side lie more loosely, being subjected to a negative pressure. During the upstroke, the flight feathers are separated to permit the flow of air between them. When there is no air load, such as when the bird is stretching its wing, the lower coverts lie quite loosely and extend from the sur-

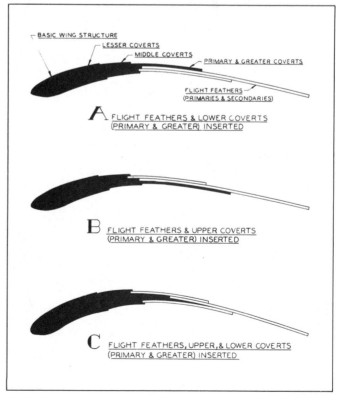

6-159 *The wing can be constructed in at least three different ways.*

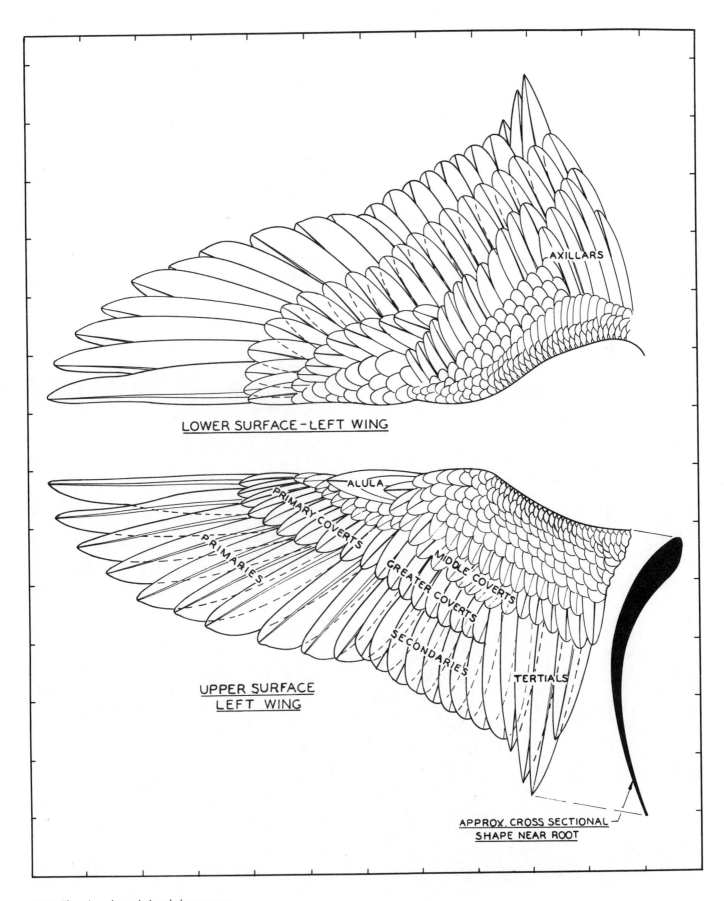

LOWER SURFACE—LEFT WING

UPPER SURFACE
LEFT WING

AXILLARS

ALULA

PRIMARY COVERTS

PRIMARIES

GREATER COVERTS

MIDDLE COVERTS

SECONDARIES

TERTIALS

APPROX. CROSS SECTIONAL
SHAPE NEAR ROOT

6-160 *The wing of a male hooded merganser.*

face of the wing. These are but a few of the details that a carver who wishes to attain realism must consider.

The individual feathering technique can be used in at least three different ways in the construction of the wing:

1. The upper coverts are carved on the basic wing structure and the flight feathers and lower coverts are individually made and inserted (Fig. 6-159A).
2. The lower coverts are carved on the basic wing structure and the flight feathers and upper coverts are individually made and inserted (Fig. 6-159B).
3. The flight feathers are attached to a tang carved from the basic wing structure and both the upper and lower coverts are individually made and inserted (Fig. 6-159C).

Usually the insertion of individual feathers on a wing is limited to the flight feathers, tertials, and the upper and lower primary and greater coverts. The upper and lower middle coverts may also be inserted individually. However, if feather insertion is carried too far, an artificial, shingled effect often results. When birds are portrayed in flight, a good effect is obtained by individually making and inserting the alula feathers and the axillars.

As before, an accurate drawing of the upper and lower surfaces of the wing is *mandatory*. Mistakes on the actual wing are very difficult to correct. It is, therefore, most important that the drawing show the exact location of each feather that is to be inserted and also the ones that are to be carved (Fig. 6-160).

First, the shape and grain direction of the basic wing structure must be determined. It is essential that at least some of this structure have grain running in the spanwise direction. If either the upper or lower coverts are to be carved from the wing structure, the grain in this area should be generally fore and aft. Figure 6-161 shows one way this can be achieved. When end-grain gluing is involved, as shown in Figure 6-161, epoxy should be used.

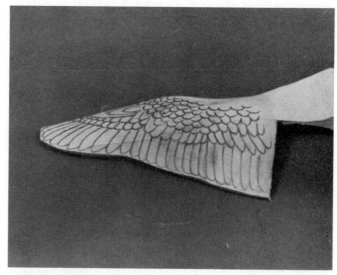

6-162 *Transfer the layout of the wing's upper surface for the drawing to the basic wing structure.*

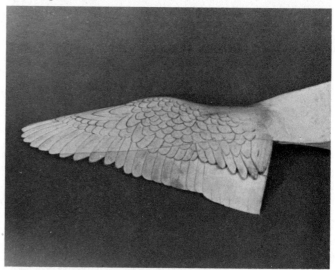

6-163 *Carve the upper primary and greater coverts.*

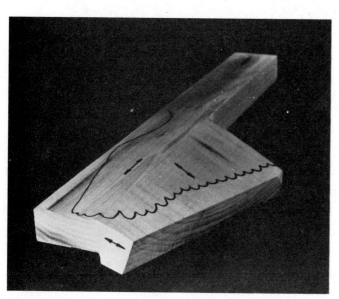

6-161 *Showing the build-up and grain direction of the basic wing structure.*

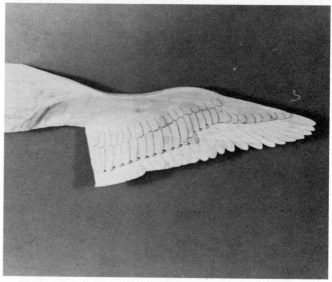

6-164 *Relieve the lower wing surface to the rear of the coverts.*

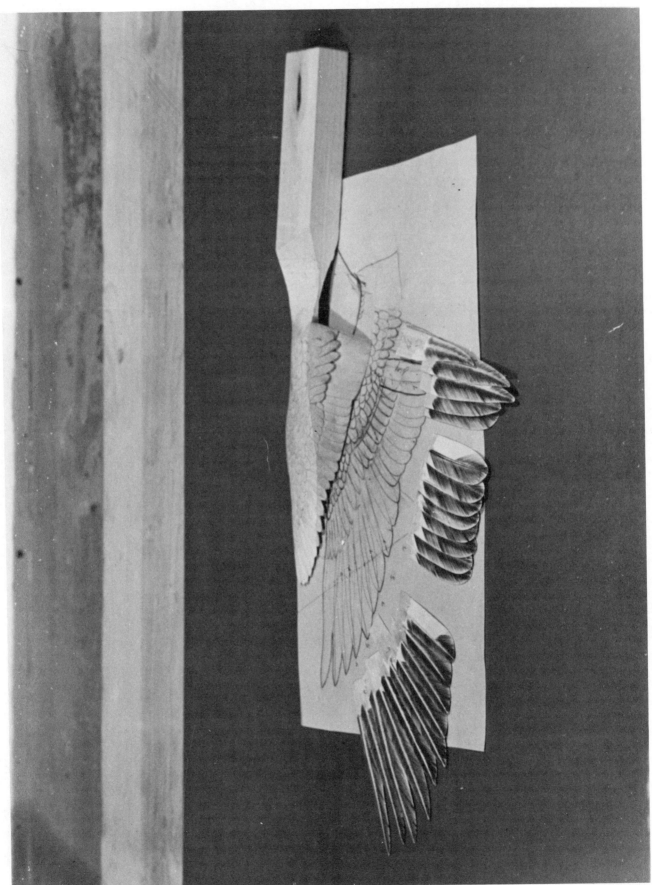

6-165 *Showing the wing drawing, the basic wing structure, and the individual flight feathers.*

In this example of a male hooded merganser stretching his wing, carving the upper coverts and inserting the lower ones works best because the lower coverts lie loosely in this configuration – a condition ideal for feather insertion.

After the epoxy has set, the basic wing structure is carved to its final shape, as described earlier in this chapter. The upper covert feather layout is then transferred from the drawing to the wing (Fig. 6-162), and these feathers are individually carved on the upper surface (Fig. 6-163). Note how the coverts in the tertial area are carved quite deeply (about 3/32 inch) in order to receive the inserted tertials.

Now, transfer the lower covert layout to the lower surface and carefully remove wood aft of this area to a depth of approximately 3/32 inch at the rear of the lower coverts tapering to approximately 1/32 inch thick at the trailing edge of the upper coverts. After this has been accomplished, lay out the lower side of the upper coverts and individually carve them. It is necessary to carve only about the rear one third of each covert as they will be covered by the flight feathers (Fig. 6-164).

Make the individual flight feathers (Fig. 6-165), as described previously. In order to seal effectively on the downstroke, the flight feathers have the cross-sectional shape shown in Figure 6-166. If the carved feathers are to nest realistically, this S-shaped bend must be duplicated as closely as possible, using the bending methods described earlier. The secondary feathers are further "cupped" on their tips, which also should be duplicated. After this bending, or forming, is accomplished, the flight feathers must also be bent along their length. Under conditions of no load, these feathers have a permanent downward bend to offset deflections from air loads and also, possibly, to conform to the shape of the body when they are folded. This amount of downward bend can be determined from a specimen. For wings in the flight configuration, the lengthwise bend of the flight feathers can be determined from photographs.

6-167 *Undercut the coverts to receive the inserted tertials.*

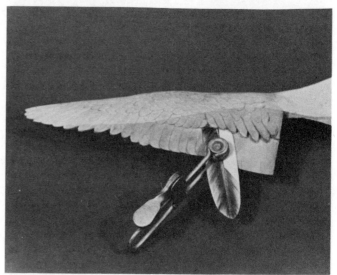

6-168 *Install the outermost tertial.*

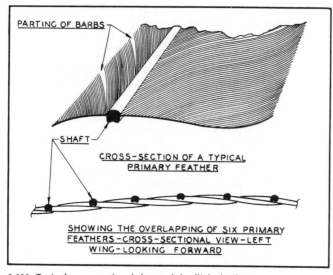

6-166 *Typical cross-sectional shape of the flight feathers.*

6-169 *Reduce the thickness of the inserted feather in the unexposed area.*

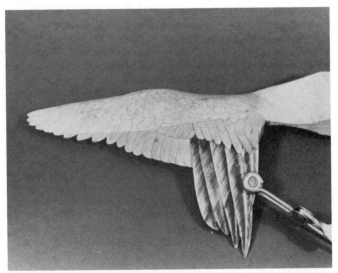

6-170 *Showing the last tertial clamped in place.*

The actual feather insertion is started with the outermost tertial. As described earlier, a paper template of the feather is made to determine the cut-off line, and then the deeply carved covert feathers are undercut to receive the tertials (Fig. 6-167). Apply epoxy sparingly and clamp the tertial in place (Fig. 6-168). Before the epoxy sets, double check to be sure the feather is in its proper location. After the epoxy has set, reduce the thickness of the feather in the unexposed area to practically nothing so that an excessive build-up will not occur, especially in the primary area (Fig. 6-169). Now, undercut the coverts for the second tertial and continue this procedure for the remaining tertials (Fig. 6-170). Although not shown in this example, it is a good practice to burn the coverts before inserting any feathers. This elimi-

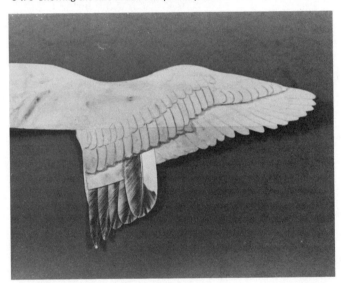

6-171 *First secondary feather is epoxied in place.*

6-173 *Continue inserting the primaries, proceeding outward.*

6-172 *All of the secondaries have now been inserted.*

6-174 *All of the primaries have now been inserted.*

nates the possibility of getting burn marks on the already detailed feathers.

Now, turn the wing over and insert the flight feathers, starting with the innermost secondary feather (Fig. 6-171) and continuing outward until all the flight feathers have been installed (Figs. 6-172, 173, 174).

Make the individual lower covert feathers next and insert them, starting with the innermost and proceeding on out (Figs. 6-175, 176). In the example shown, some of the middle coverts were also inserted. The insertion of these feathers is optional.

After all the feathers have been inserted, individually carve the remaining coverts and burn them (Fig. 6-177). On the wing shown in Figure 6-177, the alula feathers were carved, not inserted, which also is optional. However, on wings depicting a flight configuration, it is easier and more effective to insert the alula feathers. Because they would

have been completely hidden, the axillars were not made, but in most flight configurations, they would be visible and should be individually made and inserted.

Other Uses

Although the individual feathering techniques also may be used for body feathers, it generally produces an artificial, shingled effect because of the difficulty in making body feathers thin enough to lay as flat as they do on the real bird. In some instances, as when the scapulars or other body feathers are raised, individually inserted feathers add realism and produce results that would be extremely difficult to obtain with feathers carved from a solid block. Leg coverts on long-shinned birds such as hawks can also be effectively inserted.

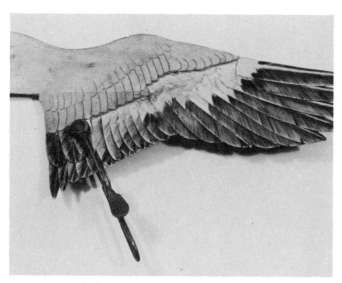

6-175 *Start inserting the lower greater coverts and proceed outward.*

6-176 *A few of the middle coverts were inserted on this wing.*

6-178 *The finished wing of a male hooded merganser carving (Collection of Dr. and Mrs. J. L. Silagi, Texas).*

◄ **6-177** *Complete the wing by carving and burning the rest of the under and upper covert feathers.*

CHAPTER

7

Advanced Finishing Techniques

The plumage of even the drabbest bird is incredibly complex and beautiful. No one appreciates this more than the carver-artist who tries to simulate with paint and brush the elusive colors and infinitely detailed texture of these winged marvels. Chapter 2, "Painting for Beginners," dealt mainly with the novice's first attempts at applying color to the carving. Chapter 7 will be devoted primarily to some of the ways the carver-artist can attempt to duplicate the texture and some of the detail of the bird's plumage. The word "attempt" is used, for no one will ever come very close to actually copying either the texture or color of the bird's plumage.

Strive for two important goals in painting and texturing a bird carving. First, duplicate, as authentically as possible, the bird's coloring; second, make the finished carving appear "soft." Although this elusive quality of softness in the finished bird carving is somewhat easier to obtain on birds with distinctive feather patterns than on birds of largely the same color, it is certainly not a simple accomplishment in either case. The techniques described below will help produce this very desirable soft appearance on the finished carving.

Most carvers use one or a combination of any or all of the following methods in trying to simulate the bird's feathers and other parts:

Painting Individual Feathers
Further Use of Brushmarks
Carving Individual Feathers
Gouge Carving
Burning In Feather Detail
Painting Feathers With Burned-In Detail
Adding Vermiculations
Other Possible Techniques
Duplicating Iridescence
Painting Legs and Feet

PAINTING INDIVIDUAL FEATHERS

Painting individual feathers is one of the better ways of obtaining the "soft" effect and is essential for good, realistically finished bird carvings. In addition to a great deal of patience and painting skill, individual feather painting requires an accurate layout of the feather pattern, duplicating not only the location of each feather but also its shape and markings. An excellent way to learn the individual feather-painting technique is to practice on a flat surface.

7-1 *A tertial feather from the wing of a lesser Canada goose.*

7-2 *Apply paint evenly and fairly thickly over the sketched feather.*

7-3 *Duplicate the barb lines on one side of the shaft.*

7-5 *Add barb lines to the other side of the feather starting at the shaft.*

7-4 *Locate the shaft with a single stroke of the brush.*

7-6 *Complete the feather by painting in the shaft.*

The novice should start out by attempting to duplicate a single, solid-color feather. A wing primary or a tail feather makes a good subject. Actual specimens should be obtained, if possible.

Sketch or trace the feather outline onto a piece of wood or paper sealed by a single coat of Hyplar, mixed to the approximate color of the feather. Now, mix oil paints to duplicate the color of the feather as closely as possible. Medium may be added, but the consistency of the paint should be quite heavy. Using a flat sable brush, apply the mixed paint evenly and fairly thickly over the sketched feather (Fig. 7-2). Next, using a flat bristle brush and parallel brushstrokes, duplicate the barb lines on one side of the shaft, running from the other side of the approximate shaft location to the feather's edge (Fig. 7-3). Locate the shaft by a single stroke of a fine brush (Fig. 7-4). Now, add the barb lines on the other side of the feather, but this time start each of the parallel brushstrokes exactly at the shaft (Fig. 7-5). (Cutting

off the bristles of a flat brush at an angle about the same as the angle between the barbs and the shaft will help considerably in mastering this technique.)

Mix paint to match the color of the shaft. Complete the feather by carefully painting in the tapered shaft over the wet feather paint (Fig. 7-6). The shaft will appear more realistic if a highlight is added along one of its edges or on its centerline.

Next, try to duplicate a single feather edged or striped with a second color. The pintail drake's tertial feathers are a basic grayish-beige color with a black stripe running the length of the exposed vane. One of these feathers makes an excellent subject for this exercise.

Sketch the outline of the feather and also the outline of the black stripe on a piece of wood or paper that has been sealed by a coat of gray Hyplar (Fig. 7-7). Note how the black stripe starts out on one side of the shaft but soon crosses over and extends on both sides of the shaft. Also note that

7-7 *Sketch in the outline of the feather, including the black area.*

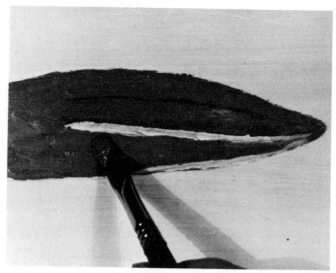

7-9 *Apply the basic feather paint to the rest of the feather.*

7-8 *Apply white paint below the black area and on the lower edge.*

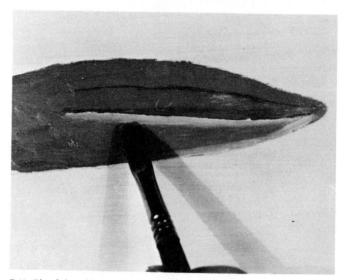

7-10 *Blend the white into the basic feather paint.*

the basic feather color is somewhat lighter in shade next to the lower side of the black stripe, as is the lower edge of the feather. First, apply stripes of pure white paint along the lower edge of the black stripe area and on the lower edge of the feather (Fig. 7-8). Now, mix a small amount of black and burnt umber into white oil paint and apply between the white stripes and also on the upper side of the feathers (Fig. 7-9).

Using a flat sable brush, blend the white along the black stripe area and on the lower edge of the feather into the basic feather paint (Fig. 7-10). Next, duplicate the barb lines on both sides of the feather in the manner previously described (Fig. 7-11). Mix a small amount of burnt umber into black and carefully paint in the black stripe (Fig. 7-12). Using a clean, flat bristle brush, add the barb lines across the approximate shaft location to the lower edge of the black stripe (Fig. 7-13), this time dragging the black paint just barely into the lighter, basic color. (Wipe the brush clean after

7-11 *Add barb lines to both sides of the feather.*

7-12 *Carefully paint in the black area.*

7-15 *Add barb lines to the other side of the black area starting at the shaft.*

7-13 *Add barb lines to the lower part of the black area.*

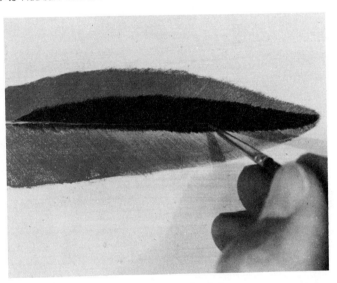

7-16 *Complete the feather by painting in the shaft.*

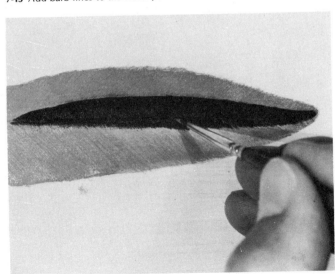

7-14 *Locate the shaft of the feather.*

each stroke.) Locate the shaft with a stroke of a fine brush (Fig. 7-14) and add the barb lines on the upper side of the shaft, starting from the shaft line and extending slightly into the basic color (Fig. 7-15). Complete the feather by painting in the shaft (Fig. 7-16).

Next, attempt to duplicate a group of feathers. The side feathers of a female green-winged teal will be used for this exercise (Fig. 7-17).

First, sketch in six or so of the side feathers on a surface to which an undercoat of the approximate basic color (tan) has been applied. Next, using burnt umber, paint in the dark areas of each feather (Fig. 7-18). Add a small amount of raw sienna into white paint and paint in the edges of each feather. Add a little more raw sienna into a separate portion of this mixture and paint in the light areas on the inner parts of the feathers (Fig. 7-19). Now, with very light strokes of a badger-hair fan brush, drag the dark paint back into the lighter paint and proceed on forward and drag the lighter

7-17 Side feathers on a female green-winged teal.

7-19 Paint in the light-colored areas of the feathers.

7-18 Sketch several side feathers and paint in the dark areas.

7-20 Blend colors very lightly with a badger-hair fan blender.

paint back into the dark paint (Fig. 7-20). (If this procedure seems difficult at first, practice on a single feather.) Clean the bristles after each stroke. If too much of one color is dragged back into the other color, it may be necessary to touch up these areas.

Note how the barbs are separated at the feather edges and terminate in fine lines. Paint in these lines, starting in the wet feather paint and moving rearward, with individual strokes of a fine, pointed brush — a round 00 or 000 sable brush will do nicely (Fig. 7-21). (The author saves his old, small sable brushes. Some of these brushes, whose remaining bristles are all spread out, work very well in making several fine lines with a single stroke.) The paint should be thinned considerably with medium and turpentine to achieve these fine, separate lines.

Now, do the same with the next feather, but this time drag the paint of the second feather into the wet paint of the first, keeping the brush fairly clean (Fig. 7-22). These hun-

7-21 Paint in the fine barb lines with individual strokes.

7-22 *Continue working on forward with the individual barb lines.*

7-24 *Practicing painting the side feathers of a Canada goose.*

dreds of fine lines contribute greatly to imparting softness to the finished carving. The feather group can be made to appear even more realistic by dragging the dry badger-hair fan blender *ever* so lightly over the feathers (Fig. 7-23). In some cases, it may be advisable to let the paint dry partially before attempting this. It is very important to keep the brush clean and dry and to make short, rearward strokes, again, *very, very* lightly!

Figure 7-24 shows another exercise. In this case, the side feathers of a Canada goose are used as the example. The duplication of these feathers is accomplished in a manner similar to that described above.

The novice should not expect to master the techniques involved in these exercises on the first attempt, for the realistic blending of the edges of two different colors while they are both wet requires very careful brushwork. If the first try

is not satisfactory, the oil paint can be easily wiped off for a second attempt.

FURTHER USE OF BRUSHMARKS

Brushmarks can not only duplicate the barbs on individual feathers, they also can effectively give texture to areas where the feather pattern is quite indistinct. A good example would be the breast and chest of a Canada goose (Fig. 7-25).

Apply the darker of the two colors first in crescent-shaped stripes, representing a part of each feather (Fig. 7-26). Next, add the lighter basic color between the dark stripes (Fig. 7-27). The consistency of the two paints should be fairly thick, and they should be applied quite heavily. Starting

7-23 *Drag the dry fan blender very, very lightly over the finished feather pattern.*

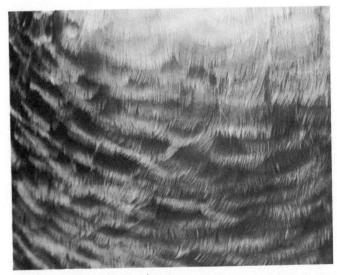

7-25 *Chest feathers of a Canada goose.*

7-26 *Apply the darker of the two colors first.*

7-28 *Starting from the rear, drag the lighter color into the darker color.*

from the rearmost feather, pull each of the lighter-colored areas individually very gently into the adjacent darker area, using a dry, badger-hair fan brush, kept as clean as possible (Fig. 7-28). The rearward strokes should be angled first one way and then the other. This angling enhances the effect of individual feathers.

A variation of this method can also be used to produce natural effects in the areas of the same general color, such as the white belly and undertail coverts of a Canada goose. Paint the basic white color over the whole area; then add irregular stripes or blotches of white mixed with a small amount of raw umber. Starting from the rear, make brushstrokes in the manner described above.

Brushmarks provide an excellent means of reducing the harsh line of demarcation between the areas of different colors. A good example would be the white patch on the black head and neck of a Canada goose. An actual speci-

men should be studied if possible; if not, see Figure 7-29 and note how the very fine black feathers on the front of the throat patch extend over the white feathers, while on the rear of the patch, the fine white feathers extend over the black head and neck feathers.

In painting the head and neck of a Canada goose, first draw in and paint the white patch, being careful to feather out the edges so no ridges of paint are left. Using a fan brush, start from the rear of the throat patch and add brushmarks. Allow the white paint to dry; then paint the surrounding black area. Using a fine, pointed sable brush or a fan brush, lightly drag the wet black paint in fine, irregular lines back over the white on the forward edge of the throat patch. On the rear edge, drag the black paint forward slightly to eliminate any ridges of paint. When the black has dried, add some more white paint to the rearward part of the throat patch and drag it lightly back over the black.

7-27 *Paint in the lighter color between the dark stripes.*

7-29 *The head of a common Canada goose.*

All of this can be done at one time, but considerable care and practice is required when there is such a difference in the two colors.

Notice the intersection of areas of different colors on other birds. Except between prominent feathers, there is never a harsh line – so often seen on painted carvings – separating the two colors.

CARVING INDIVIDUAL FEATHERS

Some individual feather carving, if properly done, will add texture and improve the appearance of almost all realistic bird carvings. Feather carving has already been discussed in Chapters 1 and 6.

GOUGE CARVING

If expertly executed, fairly realistic texture can be added by means of toolmarks. The V-gouge is the tool most often used to obtain this effect, although regular gouges, rasps, rotary files, fine-threaded taps used as scrapers, and other tools are also used by some carvers. In most cases, texture added in this manner is an exaggeration of the real thing; therefore, considerable practice is required, and in some cases, a great deal of care and restraint must be exercised.

Gouge carving is especially effective on the birds' long side feathers, whose barbs tend to separate. It is also effective on the neck feathers of most geese. These feathers are long and narrow and tend to lie one on top of the other, forming ridges and valleys in a somewhat irregular pattern (Figs. 7-32, 33). Gouge carving can also be used to simulate the feathers covering the legs of most birds just above the tarsi; for the long upper tail coverts of a wood duck; the crested heads on some ducks; and other places where the hairlike barbs of the feathers are noticeably separated.

7-31 Gouge carving was used on the crest of this male wood duck.

7-32 Gouge carving can be used effectively on the necks of most geese, such as this blue goose.

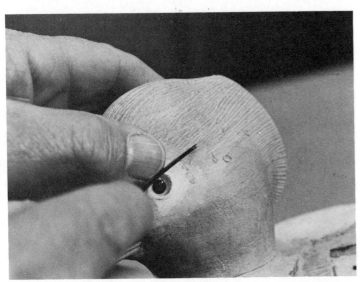
7-30 Gouging feather detail on the head of a male hooded merganser.

7-33 The neck feathers were gouge-carved on this blue goose carving.

BURNING IN FEATHER DETAIL

Although time-consuming and tedious, burning is the most effective way of adding texture and feather detail. Until recently, feather-detail burning was done either with a small soldering iron, whose tip was sharpened to a knife edge, or with a similar type tool sold in wood burning kits. The shape and sharpness of the point are very important in obtaining fine, accurate lines. The shape of the tip also determines the position of the user's hand. A double-bevel skew point works well. It fits into small corners, and the hand can be held in a comfortable position, away from most of the heat. For comfort and accuracy, the carving should be placed in the most convenient position, and if necessary, a support for the hand should be provided.

A much more sophisticated burning tool, called The Detailer (see Appendix), has been developed that features a heat control and readily interchangeable handpieces incorporating differently shaped tips (Figs. 7-34, 35). The metal tip on the old soldering-type burning tool was heated by an element inside it. On The Detailer, the tip is made from very hard wire bent and/or welded to the desired shape, ground flat, and sharpened. It is heated within a few seconds by its own resistance to the voltage-controlled electric current that passes through it. The tip can be used for long periods before requiring a light honing to bring back the sharp edge. Furthermore, unlike the old types of tools, little or no carbon builds up on The Detailer, and practically no tip cleaning is required. Although the tip is located close to the fingers, giving excellent control, there is very little heat radiated to the fingers, again in contrast to the older tools. The handle, or handpiece, remains quite cool, even when maximum heat is used. The Detailer is more expensive than the simple wood-burning tools, but it is well worth the extra expense.

The wood burning tool is held like a pencil, and the shaft of the feather is first burned in as two converging lines (Fig. 7-36). One of The Detailer's tips, a long skew called the "spear", is excellent for freehand burning of long shafts;

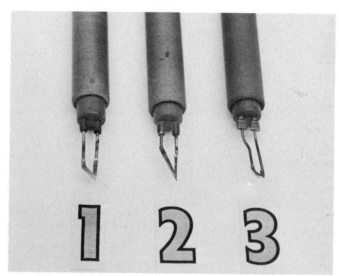

7-35 Three tips most used by the author: (1) for general feather-detail burning; (2) for freehand burning in of long shaft lines; (3) for burning hard-to-get-at places.

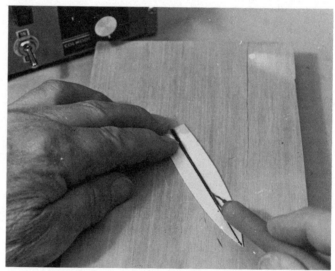

7-36 Burning in the shaft of a tertial feather freehand.

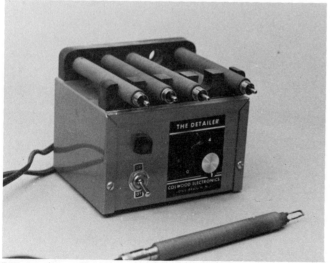

7-34 An advanced burning tool. Rack for storing extra handpieces was made by author.

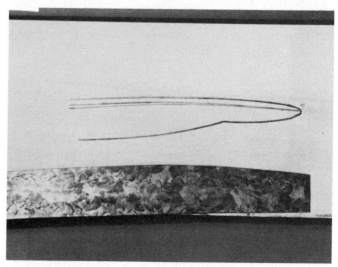

7-37 A simple template can facilitate burning in of long shaft lines.

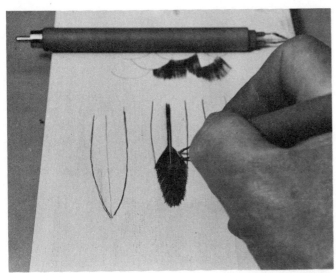

7-38 *Practicing burning feather detail.*

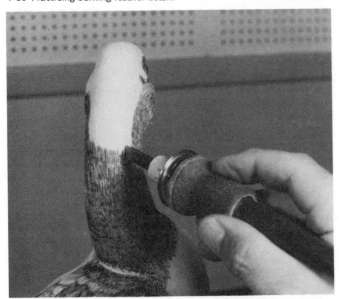

7-39 *Where the feathers are small, burn in short, fine lines.*

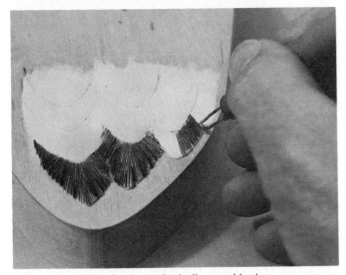

7-40 *Burning feather detail on individually carved feathers.*

however, when using old type burning tools, it is often desirable to use a metal template to guide the tip when burning these long lines (Fig. 7-37). After the shaft is burned in, parallel lines representing the barbs are burned in at an angle from the shaft to the feather's edge, as fine and as close together as possible. The barb lines can be made either by moving the fingers or by moving the entire arm.

It is strongly recommended that the beginner spend some time practicing the burning technique on scrap pieces of wood before he attempts to work on the actual carving (Fig. 7-38). He will soon find that a certain knack is required to make straight, closely spaced lines, and will experience some difficulty at first in accurately making the two converging shaft lines.

For cleaner, sharper burn lines, the wood should be coated with gesso before burning. After burning, the carving should be thoroughly cleaned before any painting is done. As mentioned in Chapter 6, combustion products and other particles can be removed or loosened by brushing the carving vigorously with a stainless steel brush (Fig. 7-42). Remaining loose particles can be blown away with a stream of air or wiped off with a tack rag.

Burning works especially well on carved feathers (Fig. 7-40), not only to add detail and texture but also to soften the carved edge of the feather. On large feathers, such as the wing primaries, greater realism is attained when the shaft is carved in or added as a separate piece (see Chapter 6), rather than burned in, before burning the barb lines. The burning technique also can be used on uncarved feathers. In this case, first outline the feathers in pencil, and then burn in the shaft and barbs as described above.

In areas where the feathers are very small, actually more like hairs, such as on the head and neck of most birds, burning short, fine lines will add realistic texture. This is accomplished by starting from the rear and working forward, varying the angle of the short lines relative to each other (Fig. 7-39).

The burning tool also is effective for duplicating barb separation on individually made feathers (see Chapter 6). The v-shaped piece can be easily removed by making two deep burns with The Detailer whose tip is red hot (Fig. 6-136).

PAINTING FEATHERS WITH BURNED-IN DETAIL

Detail is much easier to obtain when painting feathers if the shaft and barbs have been burned in. The side feathers of a female green-winged teal will be used again as an example to demonstrate this painting technique.

Sketch seven or eight feathers on a scrap piece of wood. Follow the instructions on individual feather carving in Chapter 6 to carve these feathers as shown in Figure 7-40, and then sand them smooth. Since the barbs on large side feathers are often parted, this exercise also will include duplication of these separations. It is best to make these separations at the time the barb detail is burned in rather than before. Start burning the barbs as described above. Wherever a parting of the barbs is desired, leave a small triangular area unburned, and continue the barb burning on the other side of this unburned triangle. After burning in detail on the entire feather, make two cuts with the point of a sharp knife along the two sides of each of the unburned triangles. Remove the small triangular-shaped pieces of wood down to a depth equal to the feather thickness. This can be done with a long-pointed knife, such as an Exacto (Fig. 1-1), but a specially ground chisel is easier to use and gives better results (Fig. 7-41).

After the feathers have all been burned, clean them thoroughly with a stainless steel brush and remove all of the loose particles (Fig. 7-42). Apply an undercoat of Hyplar about the same color (burnt umber) as the darkest brown marking on the feather. Mix the paint as described in the previous side feather painting exercise. Add very little painting medium. Now, using the burnt umber, paint in the dark areas of each feather. Apply paint sparingly (in this case, it is not necessary to duplicate the barb lines with brushstrokes) with light brushstrokes *across* the burned barb lines. Do *not* attempt to fill the burned lines with paint. Next, paint the inner light areas of the feather in a similar manner. Now, using the light-colored paint, brush very lightly across the outer barb lines (Fig. 7-43). Blend the colors by dragging a dry fan blender, ever so lightly, from the front to the rear of the feather pattern. With a little practice, the soft, lacy feeling of the actual side feathers can be approximated.

The shafts of some of the more prominent feathers, such as primaries, secondaries, tertials, some scapulars, and tail feathers, are often colored differently than the feather vane. These feathers can be painted more easily and accurately when the shafts have been burned in (or added as separate pieces). The shaft has considerably more gloss than the surrounding feather. The gloss can be gotten by mixing the paint with linseed oil, copal medium, or some other high gloss medium. Paint in the shaft lines very carefully. If the paint inadvertently extends onto the feather barbs, retouch the feather vane, trying to keep the shaft as straight edged as possible. On larger feathers, the shaft can be highlighted along most of its length for added effectiveness.

7-42 *Thoroughly clean burned areas by brushing.*

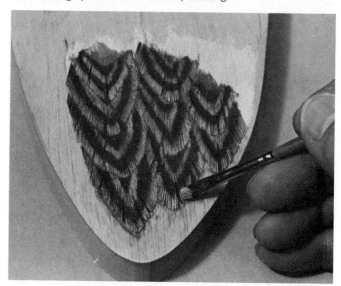

7-43 *Paint feather lightly across the burned barb lines.*

7-41 *The small v-shaped barb separation piece is cut out with a specially ground chisel.*

7-44 *The bufflehead drake painted in Chapter 2 has been stripped, additional carving detail has been added, and it has been re-painted. (Collection of Jack Brackney, El Cajon, California).*

7-45 *Vermiculation detail on a green-winged teal drake.*

ADDING VERMICULATIONS

Many male ducks and, to a lesser degree, female canvas-backs and greater scaups have fine, irregular, wavy lines called vermiculations on at least some of their feathers. These feather markings, probably incorrectly classified as texture, are a very important plumage detail. For true realism, the vermiculations on these ducks must somehow be duplicated.

7-46 *Vermiculation detail on the scapulars and tertials of a male greater scaup.*

Many different techniques have been used to copy these difficult markings, with varying degrees of success. Making irregular, parallel lines with a comb in wet, dark paint applied over a dry, lighter-colored base coat can give a somewhat natural effect. A much better job can be done, with a great deal of work, by painting each of these lines in with a fine sable brush.

A better and easier way is to add the vermiculations with a drawing fountain pen. India ink works well, and black ink can be mixed with white and/or brown India ink to match the vermiculations on most ducks and mergansers (Fig. 7-47). Ink does have one drawback: it is not completely waterproof and must be covered with a protective coating. The author has recently used Grumbacher's Hyplar, thinned with water to about the consistency of ink, with very good results. This acrylic paint is, of course, permanent and does not require a protective coating. If ink is used for the vermiculations, a protective coating should be sprayed — rather than brushed — on, as the brushing probably will smear the ink. The author uses Krylon Satin Varnish. If desired, a wash of thinned Hyplar can be applied over the protected ink vermiculations or directly on the Hyplar vermiculations to tone them down or create the effect, to some degree, of individual feathers.

Oil paint, thinned with turpentine to the consistency of ink, can also be applied successfully with a fountain pen and, like Hyplar, needs no protective coating. Rather than filling the reservoir, the fountain pen should be dipped lightly into the thinned material used for the vermiculations for

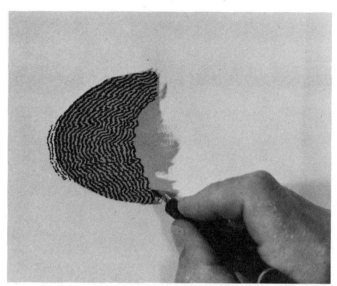

7-47 *Practicing vermiculations with a pen and India ink.*

better results. It is also advisable to immerse the point occasionally into clean water (if ink or Hyplar is used) or turpentine (if thinned oil paint is used) to prevent the vermiculation material from drying and clogging the point.

When making the vermiculations, move the pen back and forth at right angles to the direction of the vermiculation line. This lateral movement will produce a line that will vary in width and will have irregular edges. Practice and careful study of the real thing can produce some very realistic results.

First paint the area of the vermiculations to match the basic color of the feathers and let dry thoroughly. Acrylic paint, such as Hyplar, will generally receive either the ink or the thinned-down Hyplar better than oil paint; however, if there is any blending of colors, as on the female canvasback, the very fast-drying Hyplar is much more difficult to handle. If oil paint is used (and allowed to dry thoroughly) and will not take the ink or thinned-down Hyplar, the trouble is probably caused by an oily film, which can be removed by a light rubbing with steel wool and by further cleaning the surface with paint thinner applied lightly with a clean cloth.

OTHER POSSIBLE TECHNIQUES

The carver-artist should be constantly on the lookout for newer, better ways of creating the illusion of softness and realistically duplicating the texture of the plumage.

Two other procedures for obtaining texture warrant some experimentation. One involves the use of Grumbacher's Hyplar Modeling Paste applied directly with a brush to the primed carving. Texture can be added in the wet paste by means of brushmarks, with a very fine comb, or by other means. The other method is to add some of the fine, terminating barb lines in oil paint that is not quite dry, using a thin instrument such as a palette knife. This technique can also be used effectively in conjunction with the brushmarks method described earlier.

DUPLICATING IRIDESCENCE

Of all the problems involved in painting a carving, duplicating iridescence is the most difficult and frustrating. The coloring of bird feathers is of two types: pigmentary and structural. The blue in a tie or the red in a shirt are pigmentary colors; the colors in a rainbow or a drop of oil on water are structural colors. The brilliant iridescent colors seen on parts of certain birds are structural. Some of a bird's colors are structural but not iridescent; however, the carver-artist should consider all feather colors, except the iridescent colors, as pigmentary.

Iridescent colors on bird feathers result from the interference of light waves by the thousands of overlapping and twisted barbules in conjunction with pigment granules located just under the surface of the barbules. Under certain conditions the light waves are refracted so that a particular color of the spectrum is seen; all other colors are absorbed by the pigment granules. A mallard drake's head is a good example. Under many light conditions only the pigmented color, a dark blackish-blue, is seen. When the direct light comes from behind the observer, a very brilliant iridescent green highlights parts of the head. As the bird moves his head, or the observer his position, the areas of iridescence will move to different locations or disappear completely.

This brief discussion of iridescence on bird feathers is oversimplified, but it does point out some of the problems facing the carver-artist when trying to duplicate iridescence on a three-dimensional object usually illuminated from a variable light source. It is much simpler to achieve the effect of iridescence on canvas than on a carving, because the light source is always from a fixed point.

Most carvers attempt to duplicate iridescence by one of two methods, or a combination of the two. Both techniques involve duplicating the iridescence that would normally be seen when the light source is from a predetermined location relative to the carving. Here, again, there is no substitute for an actual specimen, preferably a mounted bird, from which to determine not only the iridescent colors but also their location.

The first method utilizes different colors or shades of pigmented paint to duplicate the iridescence. Some carver-artists apply all the colors wet on wet; others allow one color to dry before adding additional colors; still other carver-artists apply the different colors in the form of washes (colors thinned with medium until they are translucent).

The other popular method of duplicating iridescence is to utilize bronze powders, metallic flakes, or materials iridescent in themselves. Bronze powders are generally mixed into a vehicle such as varnish, painting medium, or some other liquid, which allows the metal flakes to float to the surface. This mixture, applied over a pigmented surface, creates a metallic effect that appears iridescent. The biggest objection to the use of these metallic materials is their apparent lack of color permanence when exposed to sunlight. However, if the carving is always located in areas with only subdued indirect light, the bronze powders will retain their color over fairly long periods. The author has several carvings done more than ten years ago on which the bronze powders used still retain their colors.

The author has tried a number of different methods in attempting to duplicate iridescence. The procedure he used for a number of years is described below. As this method involves the use of bronze powders, there can be a problem of color permanence.

Using as a model a mallard drake's head, feather detail is first burned in over the entire head and neck. This added texture, which duplicates the fine, hairlike feathers, tends to break up the reflected light and adds a great deal of realism to both the pigmented and the iridescent areas. The head and neck are then painted with oil paints, mixed and applied to duplicate as closely as possible the pigmented and iridescent colors. In locating the areas of iridescence, there must be some theoretical location of the light source relative to the carving. The writer uses two imaginary light sources, one from the right rear and the other from the left rear, which highlight both sides of the head. After the oil paint dries, a small amount of green bronze powder, mixed with turpentine, is applied sparingly as a highlight to the iridescent areas. When this is dry, a very light protective coating of Krylon Satin Varnish is sprayed on.

The author has now discarded the use of bronze powder completely and uses only oil paints in attempting to duplicate iridescent colors. This change was made after he had gained considerable experience in mixing, locating, and applying the colors normally seen as iridescent on the actual bird under a given lighting condition.

All methods of simulating iridescence with which the author is familiar leave much to be desired. There is probably more room for improvement in this phase of the finishing of realistic bird carvings than in any other area. The carver-artist should use all of his ingenuity to try to improve upon existing methods or, better still, to develop a new technique of simulating this beautiful marvel of plumage coloring.

PAINTING LEGS AND FEET

Feet and tarsi are two of the most difficult parts of the bird to paint, largely because they are covered with small, intricate scales that are extremely difficult to duplicate.

One method of representing these scales is to apply an undercoat that is darker than the basic foot color, allow this to dry thoroughly, and then paint the feet and tarsi to match their actual colors as closely as possible. (If the feet are very dark, such as on Canada geese, the undercoat should be somewhat lighter than the basic color.) A small pointed tool, such as a small dowel sharpened at one end, is then used to scratch, very carefully, the scale detail through the wet paint so that darker undercolor shows through.

After this has been done, the larger scales, such as those on the toes and the forward part of the tarsi, are highlighted, using paint thinned with a medium that will give a slight sheen. Then, being careful not to smear the scale detail, apply more of this painting medium onto the wet, painted surface. The medium will run into the scratched lines and make them appear more realistic.

The web adjacent to the toes on the feet of most ducks is a lighter color than the rest of the web. Also, the joints of the toes are slightly darker than the toes themselves. Making the entire web on ducks one color is one of the more common errors in painting feet.

Finding a reference for the actual color of the feet is very difficult. Probably the best reference for waterfowl is F.H. Kortright's *The Ducks, Geese, and Swans of North America.* However, true colors can only be observed in the live bird as the feet and bills lose their natural colors rapidly once the bird is dead. Anyone having access to fresh specimens should make color sketches of these parts before the colors start to change.

7-48 *The webs of some ducks, such as this pintail drake, are a lighter color near the toes. Note the darker toe joints.*

7-49 *The feet of a male wood duck.*

8
Advanced Carving Projects

Some of the techniques required for executing advanced realistic bird carvings were covered in Chapters 6 and 7. Several projects, increasing in complexity, have been included in this chapter to provide incentive for the serious amateur to progress. As we have stressed before, and covered in detail in Chapter 5, the carver should attempt to introduce changes to drawings and pictured carvings rather than copy them directly.

PAINTING INSTRUCTIONS

Throughout this chapter, information is included to help the serious amateur who has trouble duplicating colors. The presentation of these painting instructions follows, in general, the description for a given species used by F.H. Kortright in his excellent book *The Ducks, Geese, and Swans of North America*. The beginning carver-artist is strongly urged to refer to Kortright's fine descriptions and to the color plates by T.M. Shortt.

Specifying the exact proportions of two or more colors required to produce a given color is most difficult. The method used in this chapter gives a fair approximation. When the coloring of a particular part of the bird is described as "burnt umber, black," the two colors should be mixed in approximately equal amounts. When the coloring of a part is described as "white, ••black, •Thalo blue," white is the basic color to which a small amount of black and an even smaller amount of Thalo blue is added, i.e., "••" means to add a small amount, "•" means to add an even smaller amount.

8-1 *Rough carve the head and body.*

8-2 *Lay out the scapulars, tertials, primaries, and side feathers.*

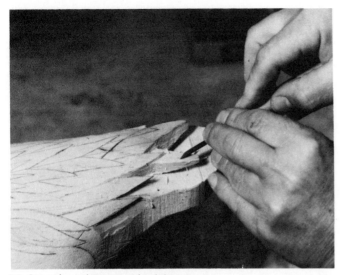

8-3 *Carve down the upper side of the primaries.*

8-4 *Carve the individual primary feathers.*

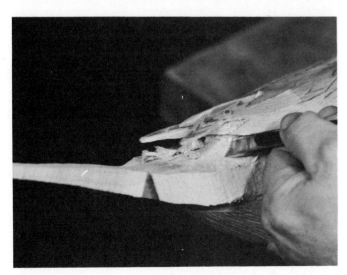

8-5 *Remove the wood from under the primaries and shape the rump.*

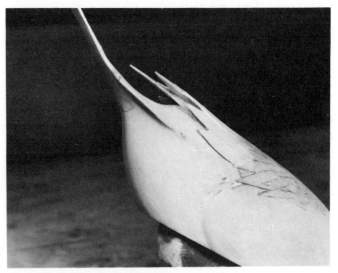

8-6 *Carefully carve the long tail feathers.*

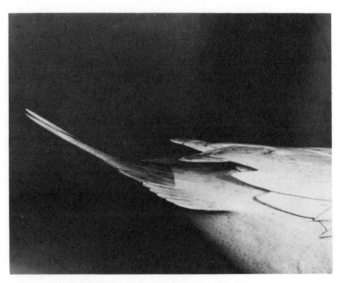

8-7 *Completed tail and carved primaries.*

PINTAIL DRAKE DECOY
(See Figure L-1, page 236)

The pintail drake, with his long, graceful neck and tail and his strikingly marked scapulars and tertials, is an interesting and beautiful subject for carving (Fig. 5-1).

A block 4 inches thick, 6 inches wide, and approximately 15 inches long is required for the body. To obtain sufficient strength for the long and delicate tail feathers, make a hardwood insert, attached with epoxy adhesive (Fig. 6-13). When the epoxy has cured, saw out the block in the normal manner. Cut out the head from a piece of wood 1¾ inches thick and attach it to the body by means of a dowel and epoxy.

After the body has been roughed out, sand smooth and lay out the primaries, tertials, and scapulars (Figs. 8-1, 2). Carve the crossed primary groups as described in Chapter 6. It is sometimes easier to carve the individual primary feathers before removing the wood that lies directly under them

(Fig. 8-4). This eliminates the danger of breaking these rather fragile projections during the detailed feather carving.

Continue by shaping the flanks and upper and lower tail covert areas (Fig. 8-5). Carefully reduce the thickness of the hardwood insert for the long tail feathers (Fig. 8-6). Next, lay out the individual tail feathers and carve them on both upper and lower sides (Fig. 8-7). Complete the body by individually carving all of the tertial and scapular feathers.

Carve the head and bill next. The pintail has a fairly long and narrow bill. Check the life-size pictures in Chapter 13 to determine these dimensions. Note how the bill does not widen at its base, but actually narrows slightly. Making the bill too wide at the base is a common error. Drill for the glass eyes and install them with Plastic Wood or a similar material. When the Plastic Wood has thoroughly dried, carefully shape the eyes and carve the eyelids.

Sand the entire carving smooth and seal with thinned-down lacquer sanding sealer or brushing lacquer. If desired,

8-10 Scapulars are inserted next, covering the forward ends of the tertials.

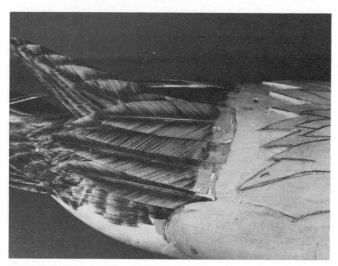

8-8 Body is mortised to receive the carved primary groups.

8-11 Front view of pintail drake showing head and neck and body shape.

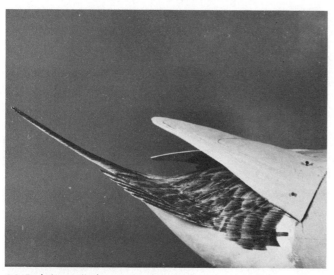

8-9 Tertials epoxied in place and body carved to receive inserted scapulars.

8-12 Good profile view of pintail drake.

8-13 *Pintail drake carving (Collection of Paul F. O'Brien, Jr., Louisiana).*

additional feather detail may be added by the burning technique described in Chapter 7. Before burning, paint the entire carving with gesso for cleaner burning.

An alternate method of making the tail insert is shown in Figure 6-14. Although a little more difficult to make, this method will generally produce better results than the one described at the start of this project.

The crossed primaries, tertials, and some of the scapulars may be added individually, rather than carved. This method is described in Chapter 6 (see Figures 6-149 through 6-156). As shown in Figures 8-9, 10, and 13, the crossed primaries are inserted and attached first. The tertials are then added, covering the mortises for the primaries. A few of the scapulars are inserted next to cover the forward ends of the tertials.

Head
Bill culmen and lower mandible: black, ••burnt umber.
Bill sides: white, ••black, •Thalo blue.
Forehead, crown, chin, throat, and cheek: burnt umber, raw sienna, ••white.
Back of head: burnt umber, black.

Neck
Hindneck: burnt umber, black, shading gradually into the body color at base of neck; vermiculated with black, burnt umber near base.
Foreneck: white, •raw umber; extends into sides of neck.

Body
Back, inner scapulars, and sides: white, ••black, •raw umber; vermiculated with black, burnt umber.
Outer scapulars, outer web: black, ••burnt umber, ••Thalo blue; edged with white, •raw sienna, •black.
Rump: white, ••burnt umber, •black; vermiculated with black, burnt umber.
Upper tail coverts: black, ••burnt umber, ••Thalo blue. Inner web – white, •black, •burnt umber.
Lower tail coverts: black, •burnt umber. Outer webs edged with white, •raw umber.

Flanks: white, •raw sienna.
Breast and chest: white •raw umber.

Tail
Two center feathers: black, ••burnt umber, ••Thalo blue.
Other feathers: black, •burnt umber, •white; lighter on edges.

Wing
Primaries: black, burnt umber, •white; lighter on edges. Shafts: black.
Tertials: white, ••burnt umber, •black. Center stripe – black, ••burnt umber, ••Thalo blue.

PINTAIL HEN DECOY
(See Figure L-2, page 236)

Although not as flashy as their male counterparts, female ducks have their own subtle beauty and make very pleasing carvings. Most amateur carvers are inhibited about painting these birds and prefer to stick with the more colorful males. Without doubt, female ducks, due to their more intricate feather markings, are more difficult to paint than males. However, the feeling of softness is much easier to obtain and much more realism can usually be achieved in carvings of females than of males in various duck species.

Figures 7-17 through 7-23 show the basic procedure for painting the side feathers of a green-winged teal hen, using brushstrokes to duplicate feather barbs and barb separation. When feather detail is burned in, the painting of female ducks is greatly simplified (see page 159). The pintail hen is almost as graceful as her mate and makes a fine carving subject.

Head and Neck
Bill: white, ••black, •Thalo blue. Darker near tip and along culmen.

8-14 *Pintail hen feeding.*

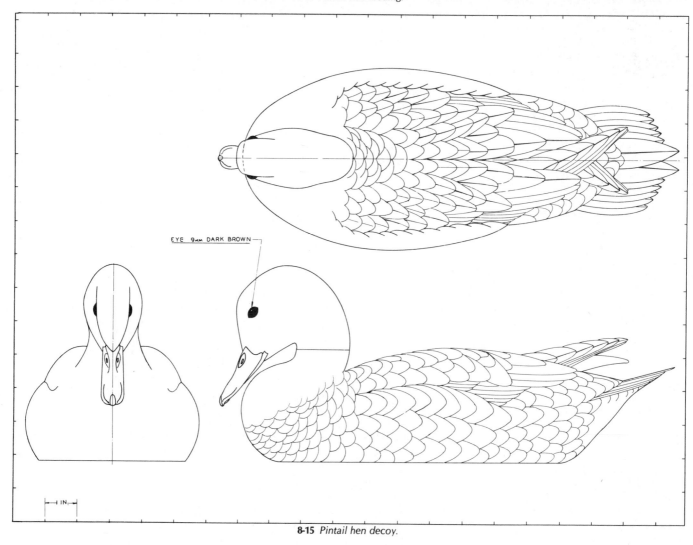

EYE 9mm DARK BROWN

IN.

8-15 *Pintail hen decoy.*

8-16 *Carve bill and head before attaching to body.*

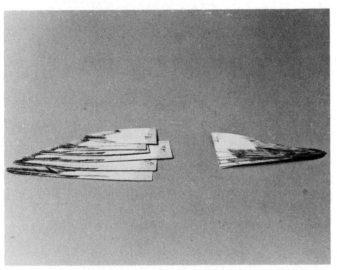

8-17 *The folded primaries have been made up with individual feathers.*

8-18 *Carve and burn tail, upper tail coverts, and rump before attaching folded primaries permanently.*

8-19 *The inserted individual tertials cover the mortises for the folded primaries.*

8-20 *Pintail hen decorative decoy from above.*

8-21 *Pintail hen decorative decoy (Collection of Tim Egan, California).*

Forehead, crown, back of head, and neck: white, raw sienna, •raw umber. Streaked with burnt umber.

Cheeks and side of neck: white, •raw sienna, •raw umber. Streaked with burnt umber.

Chin, throat, and foreneck: somewhat lighter than cheeks, streaked with burnt umber, white, raw sienna.

Body

Back and scapulars: burnt umber, ••raw sienna. V-shaped markings — white, raw sienna, •raw umber, •burnt sienna. Feathers edged with white, •raw sienna, •raw umber.

Rump: burnt umber, ••raw sienna. V-shaped markings — white, •raw sienna. Feathers edged with white, •raw umber.

Sides: burnt umber, ••raw sienna. V-shaped markings — white, ••raw sienna. Feathers edged with white, •raw sienna.

Chest: burnt umber, white, raw sienna. V-shaped markings — white, raw sienna. Feathers edged with white, •raw sienna. Feathers becoming smaller with edging about the same width as the larger, side feathers to give a lighter overall effect.

Breast and belly: white, •raw umber. Spotted with white, •burnt umber, •raw sienna.

Flanks: burnt umber, white, raw sienna. Large edgings — white, •raw umber.

Upper tail coverts: burnt umber, ••raw sienna. Marked and edged with white, raw sienna, •raw umber, •burnt sienna.

Lower tail coverts: burnt umber, white, raw sienna. Edged with white, •raw umber.

Tail

Upper side: burnt umber, ••raw sienna. Barred with white, raw sienna, •burnt sienna, •raw umber.

Lower side: white, ••raw umber. Edged and barred with white, •raw sienna, •raw umber.

Wing

Primaries: burnt umber, •white, •raw sienna. Lighter inner webs faintly edged with white, •raw sienna, •raw umber.

Secondaries (speculum): raw sienna, ••burnt umber, ••white. Rear edging — white, •raw umber.

Greater coverts: burnt umber, white, raw sienna. Rear edging — raw umber, ••white.

Tertials: burnt umber, ••raw sienna, ••white. Barred with white, raw sienna, •raw umber, •burnt sienna. Edged with white, •raw sienna, •raw umber.

CANVASBACK DECOY
(See Figure J-1, page 234)

The regal canvasback drake, with his thick, richly covered neck and distinctively sloped head and bill, is a favorite with both hunters and carvers.

The stepwise carving of a canvasback decoy and standing canvasback drake was illustrated in Chapter 6 (see "Carving the Body," page 110, and "Head Carving," page 119). Painting a half-body canvasback drake decoy was described in Chapter 2 (see pages 47-50). For the addition of vermiculations, refer to pages 161-162 and Figure 8-23.

8-22 *Carve the scapulars as a group before individual feather carving.*

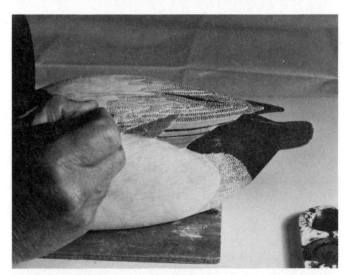

8-23 *Adding vermiculations with a drawing type fountain pen.*

8-24 *The kingly canvasback drake.*

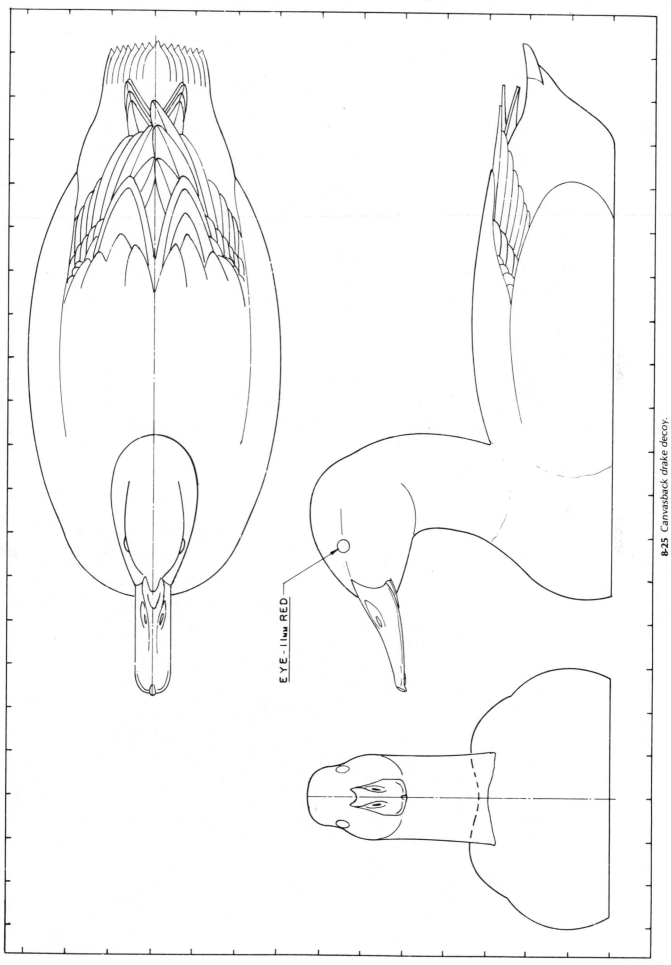

EYE-11mm RED

8-25 Canvasback drake decoy.

8-26 *Finished canvasback drake decoys (Collections of Jack Campbell and Paul Johnsgard, Nebraska).*

8-27 *Male wood duck.*

WOOD DUCK DECOY

(See Figure B-1, page 98, and Figure K-2, page 235)

The male wood duck is undisputed as the most beautiful of all waterfowl. No words can accurately describe his rich, iridescent plumage, ever changing in the sunlight. Obviously, the wood duck drake is a most difficult subject to paint, but while it is impossible to duplicate his illusive coloring exactly, the carver-artist can achieve some gratifying results and, in so doing, gain invaluable painting experience.

Except for the addition of a hardwood insert to strengthen his long crest (Fig. 8-28), the carving of the wood duck presents no unusual problems.

8-30 *Note body shape, extent of side feathers, and crossed primaries.*

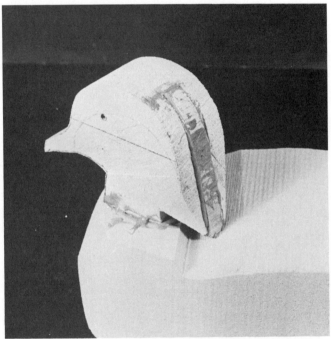

8-28 *Add a hardwood insert to provide strength for the crest feathers.*

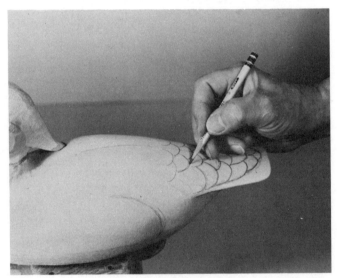

8-31 *Lay out the upper tail coverts and rump feathers.*

8-29 *Rough carve the head and body.*

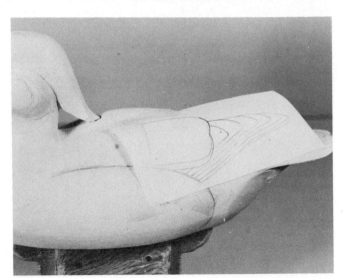

8-32 *Make a layout of the tertials and primaries on a transparent piece of paper and transfer it to the body block.*

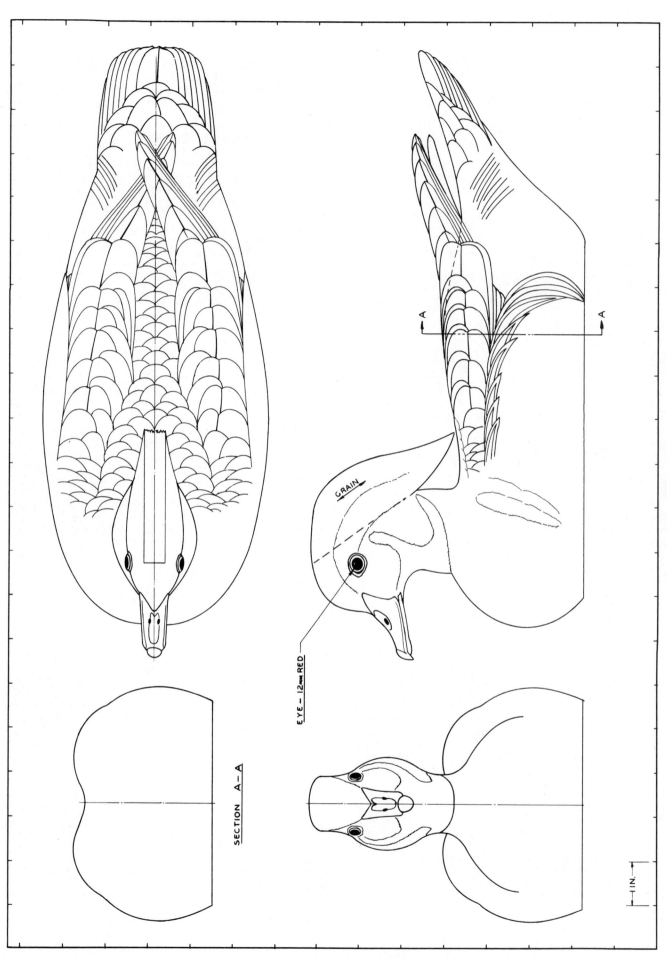

SECTION A—A

GRAIN

EYE — 12mm RED

A

A

1 IN.

8-33 *Wood duck drake decoy.*

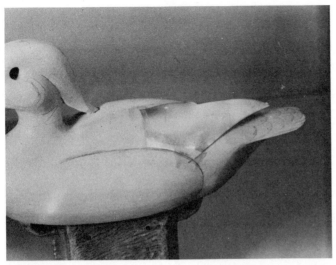

8-34 *A soft aluminum template is useful in determining the contour of the carved tertials and primaries.*

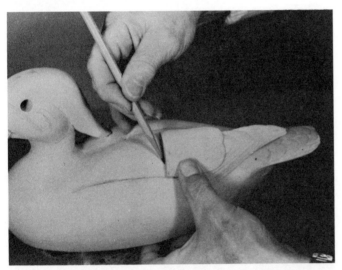

8-35 *After tertials and primaries are carved from a separate piece, locate them on the body and mark for mortises.*

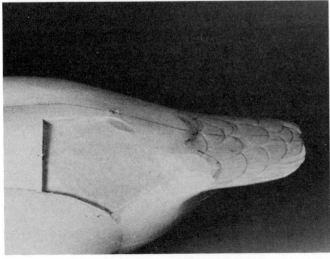

8-36 *Mortise the body to receive the tertials and primaries.*

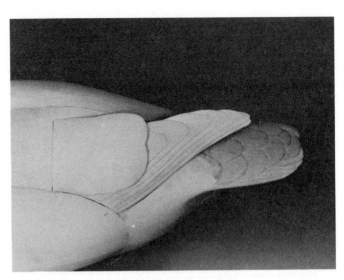

8-37 *Tertials and primaries are temporarily in place.*

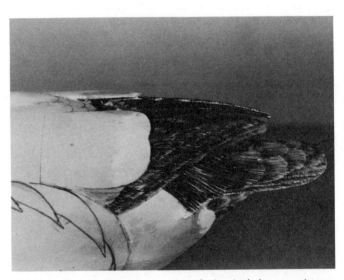

8-38 *Burn tail, upper tail coverts, rump, and primaries before epoxying tertials and primaries to body.*

8-39 *Lay out remaining tertials and other feathers on body.*

Head

Bill culmen, tip, and lower mandible: black, ••burnt umber.

Bill base: cadmium red (medium). Border edging on cheek – cadmium yellow (medium).

Bill sides: white, •raw umber, blend into base.

Refer to figure 8-41A for the approximate location of the following head and neck colors:

Violet: alizarin crimson, Thalo blue, ••white.

Greenish-violet: add cadmium yellow (medium) to violet mixture.

Reddish-violet: add more alizarin crimson to violet mixture.

Green: Thalo blue, cadmium yellow (medium).

Bluish-green: add more blue to the green mixture.

Body

Back: Thalo blue, cadmium yellow (medium), burnt umber; add yellow-green highlights to the feathers near the middle and rear of the back.

Scapulars: black, ••burnt umber, ••Thalo blue; highlight feathers with greenish-violet.

Sides: yellow ochre (light), •raw umber; vermiculated with black, burnt umber; upper feathers edged with black, ••burnt umber, ••Thalo blue. White stripes between black edgings.

Rump: similar to back.

Upper tail coverts: black, ••burnt umber, ••Thalo blue; highlight feathers with greenish-violet.

Lower tail coverts: burnt umber, ••black, •white.

Flank patch: cadmium red (deep), cobalt blue; highlight feathers with streaks of cadmium orange, burnt umber. Blend into patch.

Belly: white, •raw umber.

Chest: cadmium red (deep), cobalt blue, •black. Triangular chest markings – white, •raw umber.

8-40 *Study of a wood duck drake.*

8-41 *Close-up of the chest markings on a wood duck drake.*

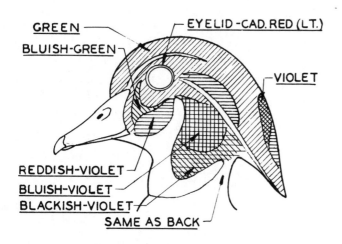

8-41A *Approximate location of the head colors.*

Tail

Upper side: black, ••burnt umber, ••Thalo blue; highlight feathers with greenish-violet and Thalo blue.

Lower side: burnt umber, •white.

Wing

Primaries, outer webs: white, •black, •raw umber.

Primaries, inner webs: burnt umber, •white; highlight tips with bluish-violet.

Tertials: black, ••burnt umber, ••Thalo blue; highlight feathers with violet. Inner tertials have white tips.

Speculum: bluish-green.

8-42 *Finished decorative wood duck drake (Collection of Paul F. O'Brien, Jr., Louisiana).*

8-43 *American widgeon drake. Photos of standing birds can be useful in planning a decoy carving. Note added imaginary waterline.*

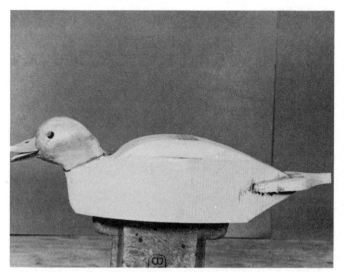

8-44 *A tail insert is used for added strength.*

8-45 *Showing carved tail feathers and coverts.*

AMERICAN WIDGEON DECOY
(See Figure M-1, page 237)

The colorful and graceful American widgeon drake makes a fine carving subject. This saucy and feisty character is best represented in an aggressive position, a pose that will give the amateur carver a chance to try his hand at open bill carving. The carving of the open bill is described and illustrated in Chapter 6 (see Figures 6-80 through 6-85).

Figure 8-43 shows how a photo of a standing bird can be used in the planning of a decoy carving. The primaries, tertials, and some of the scapulars can either be carved from the body block or added individually, as shown in Figures 8-48, 49, and 50. See Chapter 6 for individual feather insertion. A tail insert was added to gain additional strength (Fig. 8-44).

Head
Upper mandible: white, ••black, •Thalo blue.
Lower mandible, tip, and base of bill: black, ••burnt umber.
Tongue: white, ••cadmium red (light), •black.
Forehead and crown: white, •raw umber, •raw sienna.
Eye patch: cadmium yellow (medium), ••Thalo blue. Darker around eye and hindneck (add black).
Rest of head: white, •raw sienna, •raw umber. Speckled with black, burnt umber.

Body
Back, scapulars, and side feathers: white, burnt sienna, ••burnt umber, •black. Vermiculated with black, burnt umber.
Chest: white, burnt sienna, ••burnt umber, •black. Feathers edged with white, black, alizarin.
Rump: white, •black, •raw umber. Vermiculated with burnt umber, •white, •raw sienna.
Flank: white, •raw umber.

Tail
Upper side: Middle feathers — burnt umber, ••raw sienna, •white. Others — white, ••raw umber, •black. Edged with white, •raw sienna.
Lower side: white, ••raw sienna, •black.
Upper coverts: black, ••burnt umber. Inner edges bordered with white, •raw umber.
Lower coverts: black, ••burnt umber.

Wing
Primaries: burnt umber, •white, •raw sienna.
Tertials: Outer webs — black, ••burnt umber, •white, •raw umber. Inner webs — burnt umber, ••white.
Outermost tertials: white, •black, •raw umber. Edged with white, •raw umber.
Exposed middle and greater coverts: white, •raw umber.

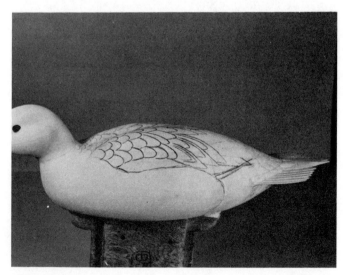

8-46 *Lay out the tertials, scapulars, and the location of the primaries.*

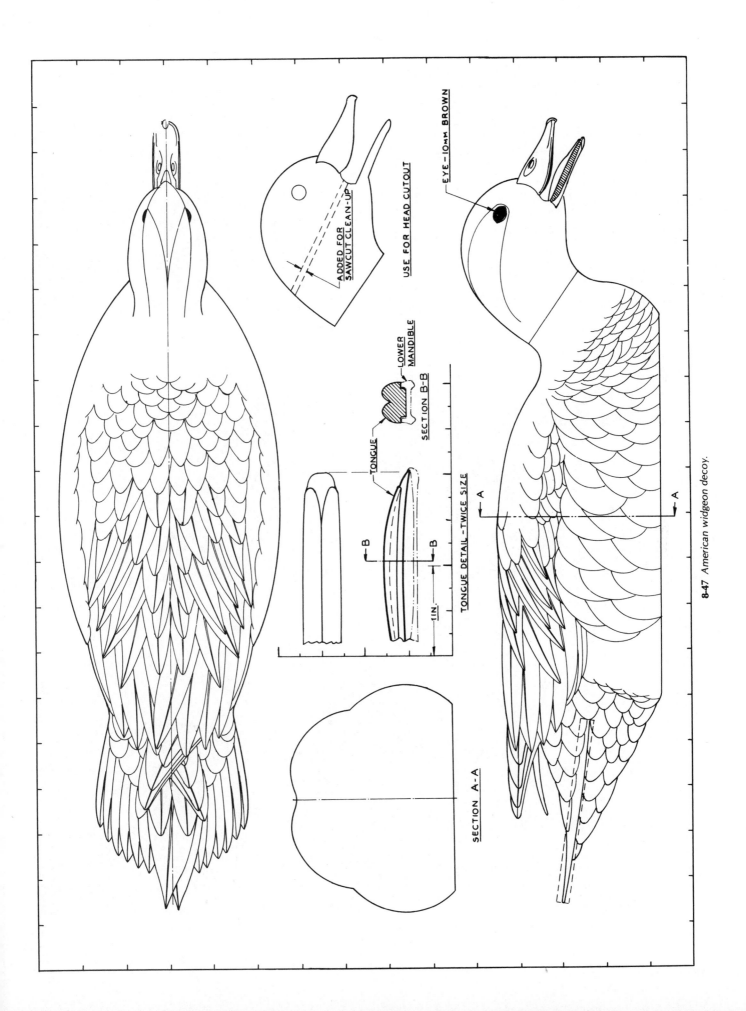

EYE-10mm BROWN

USE FOR HEAD CUTOUT

ADDED FOR SAWCUT CLEAN-UP

LOWER MANDIBLE

SECTION B-B

TONGUE

TONGUE DETAIL-TWICE SIZE

1 IN.

B

B

A

A

SECTION A-A

8-47 American widgeon decoy.

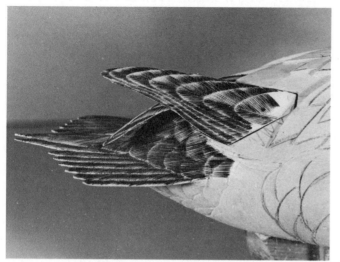

8-48 Carved primaries attached to the body.

8-50 Inserted and carved feathers have been painted.

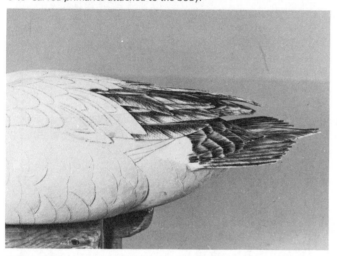

8-49 Individual tertial and some scapular feathers have been inserted.

8-51 Rear view of finished widgeon drake decoy.

8-52 Finished American widgeon decorative decoy (Collection of Doug Miller, Colorado.)

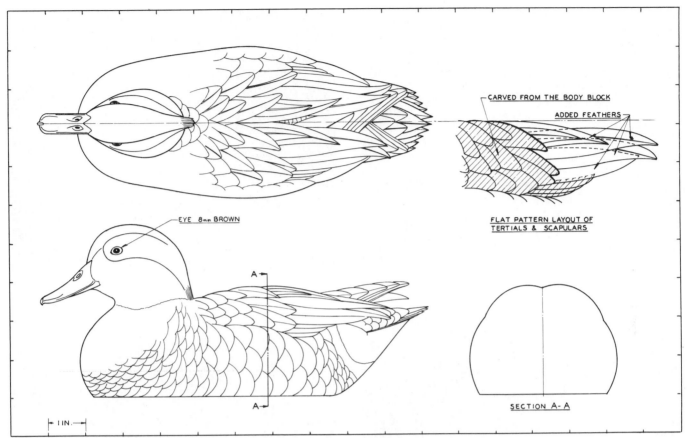

8-53 *Green-winged teal drake decoy.*

GREEN-WINGED TEAL DRAKE

The lovely, little green-winged teal drake, with his musical, chirp-like mating call, is one of the author's favorite ducks. In terms of beauty, he is second only to the gorgeous wood duck drake.

Here, as before, the primaries, tertials, and some of the scapulars may be inserted individually. This procedure is described and illustrated in Chapter 6 using a green-winged teal drake as an example (see Figures 6-153 through 6-156).

Head

Cheeks, sides of neck, throat, and crown: burnt sienna, raw sienna, white, ••raw umber.

Chin: add black to the above mixture.

Forehead and around base of bill: darker (add small amount of black to the head mixture).

Eye patch: cadmium yellow (medium), ••Thalo blue. Shades into black beneath and behind eyes. Edged on lower and front sides with white, •raw sienna.

Crest: Head color going into black, ••burnt umber, •Thalo blue on the rear, longer feathers.

Bill: black, ••burnt umber.

Body

Back, scapulars, and sides: white, •black. Vermiculated with burnt umber, ••black. Some outer scapulars marked with black, ••burnt umber, •Thalo blue on outer webs. Inner webs – white, •raw sienna; vermiculated with burnt umber, ••black.

Rump: Forward feathers – burnt umber. Feathers broadly edged with raw umber, white. Long, rear feathers – burnt umber, •black. Edged with white, •raw umber.

Upper tail coverts: black, ••burnt umber, •Thalo blue. Inner webs edged with raw umber, ••white.

Lower tail coverts: white, •raw sienna. Central feathers – black, ••burnt umber, •Thalo blue.

Chest: white, ••raw sienna. Spotted with black, ••burnt umber. Shading into breast with a lighter color (add white).

Breast: white, •raw umber.

Flanks: similar to sides, but lighter (add white).

Tail

Upper side: burnt umber, white, ••raw umber. Edged with white, •raw umber.

Lower side: white, •black. Edged with white, •burnt umber.

Wing

Primaries: burnt umber, ••white. Edged faintly with white, •burnt umber.

Tertials: burnt umber, white, raw sienna, raw umber. Lighter on inner webs (add more white). Outermost tertials edged broadly with black, ••burnt umber, •Thalo blue.

Secondaries: Outer – black, ••burnt umber, •Thalo blue. Tipped with white, •raw umber. Inner – cadmium yellow (medium), ••Thalo blue.

8-54, 55 *Little green-winged teal drake, two views.*

8-56 *The primaries and tertials have been inserted and the carving partially burned.*

8-57 *The carving is now ready to paint.*

8-58 *Finished green-winged teal drake decorative decoy (Collection of Lea Hall, Louisiana).*

8-59 *Western Canada goose.*

COMMON CANADA GOOSE DECOY
(See Figure C-2, page 99)

The Canada goose is without a doubt the most widely known of all the waterfowl and perhaps more American than the bald eagle. Their intelligence, strength, and fidelity are probably unsurpassed by any other bird. Although they vary from 2½ pounds (cackling goose) to over 20 pounds (giant Canada goose), their general physical characteristics, markings, and coloration are quite similar. The common Canada goose is next only to the giant Canada in size and is one of several strains that weigh on the average approximately 9 pounds. A block 7 x 9½ x 22 inches long is required for the body of a life-size carving.

Head
Bill: black, ••burnt umber (black Hyplar works well).
Cheek patch: white, •raw umber.
Rest of head and neck: black, ••burnt umber, •Thalo blue.

Body
Back and scapulars: burnt umber, raw sienna, white; feathers edged with white, •raw sienna, •burnt umber.

Sides: burnt umber, raw sienna, white; feathers shading to a lighter color towards the rear; feathers edged with white, •raw sienna, •burnt umber. Feathers become progressively smaller going forward. Lighter edges become closer together, producing a lighter over-all effect.
Rump: black, ••burnt umber, •Thalo blue.
Upper and lower tail coverts, flanks, and belly: white, •raw umber.
Breast: raw umber, white, ••raw sienna; feathers edged with white, •raw sienna, •burnt umber.
Chest: same as breast.

Tail
Upper side: black, ••burnt umber, •Thalo blue.
Lower side: burnt umber, white, •black.

Wing
Primaries: burnt umber. Slightly lighter (•white) near inner edges of feathers. Shafts — black.
Tertials: white, ••raw umber, •burnt umber. Inner webs and area near shaft — white, ••raw umber, ••burnt umber.
Tertial shafts: black.
Secondaries and wing coverts: same as back and scapulars.

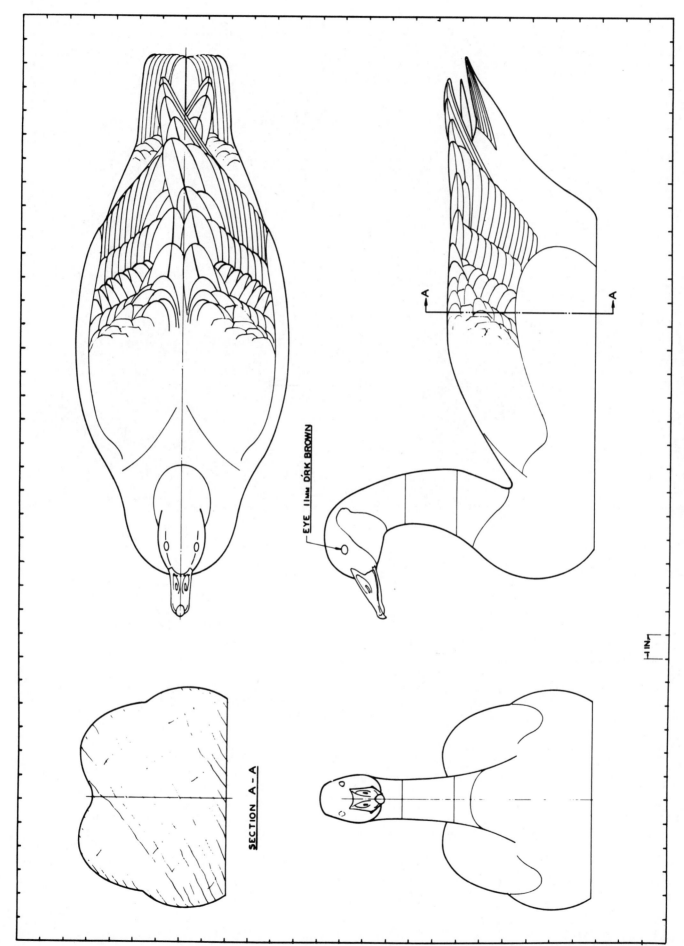

SECTION A – A

EYE 11mm DRK BROWN

A

A

⊢ IN ⌐

8-60 *Common Canada goose decoy.*

8-61 *Common Canada goose.*

8-62 *This view is most helpful in determining the cross-sectional shape.*

8-63 *Competitive Canada goose decoy (Collection of Donal O'Brien, Connecticut).*

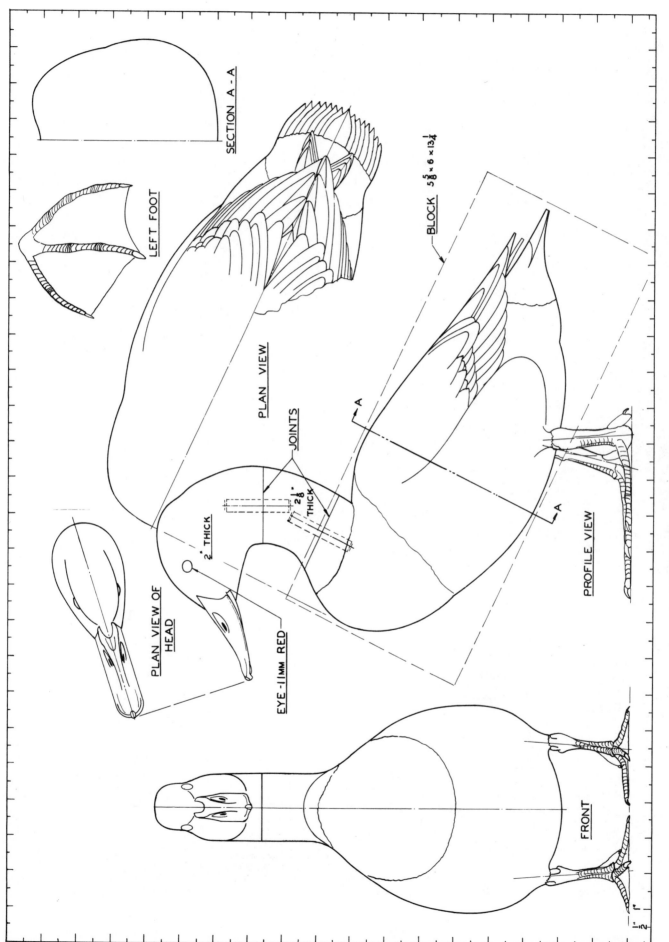

SECTION A - A

LEFT FOOT

PLAN VIEW

BLOCK 5⅝ × 6 × 13¼

JOINTS

PLAN VIEW OF HEAD

2" THICK

2⅛" THICK

EYE - 11MM RED

A

A

PROFILE VIEW

FRONT

½" = 1"

8-64 *Standing canvasback drake.*

STANDING CANVASBACK
(See Figure J-1, page 234)

The canvasback has been chosen for the first standing bird carving project. With the exceptions of extended wing carving and duplicating iridescence, everything covered thus far can be put to use in the carving of the standing canvasback.

Step-by-step pictures of the carving of the standing canvasback have been used to illustrate many points in Chapter 6. The reader may wish to refer to the sections on "Carving the Body" (page 110), "Feather Carving" (page 114), "Head Carving" (page 119), and "Carving Legs and Feet" (page 127) for detailed instructions and photographs.

Mixing colors for the canvasback drake (except for the legs and tarsi) was described in Chapter 2 (see pages 47-50, Figs. 2-32 through 2-49).

Tarsi and feet
Tarsi and toes: white, •black, •raw umber. Toe joints — darker (add •raw umber).
Webs: white, black, raw umber. Web near toes — same color as toes.
Claws: black, •burnt umber; use glossy medium.

8-65 *Painting the canvasback drake.*

8-66 *Standing canvasback drake carving, three views (Collection of Bill Toth, California).*

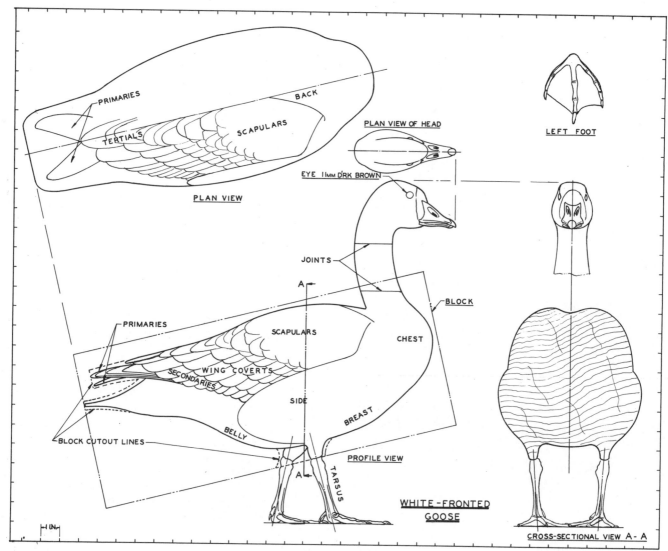

8-67 *Standing white-fronted goose.*

In the diagram: PRIMARIES, TERTIALS, SCAPULARS, BACK, PLAN VIEW OF HEAD, LEFT FOOT, PLAN VIEW, EYE 11MM DRK BROWN, JOINTS, BLOCK, PRIMARIES, SCAPULARS, CHEST, WING COVERTS, SECONDARIES, SIDE, BREAST, BLOCK CUTOUT LINES, BELLY, PROFILE VIEW, TARSUS, WHITE-FRONTED GOOSE, CROSS-SECTIONAL VIEW A-A, 1 IN.

8-68 *Adult white-fronted goose, two views.*

STANDING WHITE-FRONTED GOOSE

(See Figure B-2, page 98, and Figure O-2, page 239)

Although rare in the eastern half of the continent, the white-fronted goose is fairly common in the West. The adult birds, with their reddish bills, white area at the front of their heads, strikingly marked breasts, and yellowish feet, are beautiful, medium-size geese.

A block 7 ¾ × 8 × 19 inches is required for the body of a life-size carving. In almost all cases, it will be necessary to make not only the body block but also the head and neck from more than one piece of wood (see Chapter 6, "Gluing up the Block," page 95). Special attention should be paid to the shaping of the body cross section and the exposed part of the tibia.

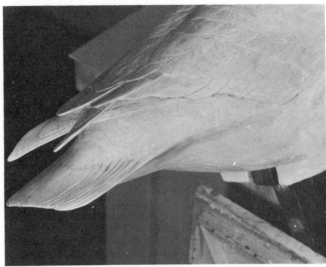

8-71 *Carve the crossed primaries as shown.*

8-69 *Rough carve the head and body.*

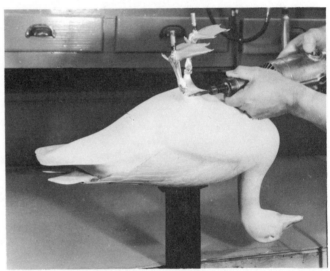

8-72 *Shaping the lower part of the tibia with a rotary file.*

8-70 *Carve the tertials and then lay out the wing coverts, secondaries, and primaries.*

8-73 *Painting the white-fronted goose carving.*

Head

Bill base: white, •Thalo blue, •cadmium red (deep).

Bill culmen and sides: white, cadmium red (deep). Blend into base.

Bill, area around nostrils: cadmium red (light), ••black.

Bill nail: white, •cadmium red (medium).

Bill, bottom of lower mandible: cadmium red (light), •black.

Forehead, front of cheeks, around base of lower mandible: white, •raw umber.

Rest of head and neck: raw sienna, raw umber, •white. Areas just behind white on head — add more raw umber.

Body

Back and scapulars: raw sienna, raw umber. Feathers edged with raw sienna, raw umber, ••white.

Sides: raw sienna, raw umber. Feathers edged with raw sienna, raw umber, ••white. Upper edges of large feathers broadly bordered with white, •raw umber, forming a white line along the side.

Rump: raw sienna, raw umber.

Upper tail coverts: white, •raw sienna. Shafts — white, •raw umber, •burnt umber.

Lower tail coverts: white, •raw umber.

Flanks and belly: white, •raw umber.

Breast: white, raw umber. Irregularly splashed with black, ••burnt umber and with raw sienna, raw umber, •white.

Chest, lower: raw umber, white. Feathers edged with white, •raw umber.

Chest, upper: raw sienna, ••raw umber, ••white. Feathers edged with white, ••raw umber.

Tail

Upper side: raw sienna, raw umber. Feathers edged with white, •raw umber. Shafts — burnt umber, black, white.

Lower side: raw umber, white. Feathers edged with white, •raw umber. Shafts — white, •burnt umber.

Wing

Primaries: burnt umber. Shafts — white, •raw sienna.

Secondaries: burnt umber.

Tertials: raw sienna, raw umber. Feathers edged with white, •raw sienna, •raw umber. Shafts — burnt umber.

Coverts, greater: white, ••burnt umber, •raw sienna, •black. Feathers broadly edged with white, •raw umber.

Coverts, primary: white, ••burnt umber, •raw sienna, •black.

Other coverts: same as tertials; inner coverts edged with white, •raw umber.

Tarsi and feet

Tarsi and toes: cadmium orange, ••cadmium yellow (medium), •raw umber. Toe joints — lighter (add more cadmium yellow (medium)).

Webs: cadmium yellow (medium), •raw umber.

Claws: white, ••alizarin crimson, •Thalo blue; use glossy medium.

8-74 *Finished white-fronted goose carving (Collection of Lea Hall, Louisiana).*

STANDING BRANT

The brant are true sea geese and seldom found away from salt water. Two species are native to North America: the black brant of the Pacific and the American brant of the Atlantic. These two species are slightly larger than a mallard duck and are very similar except for the extent of their white neck collars and coloration differences in their side and breast feathers.

Black brant

Head
Bill: black, ••burnt umber (black Hyplar works well).
Entire head and neck, except for neck collar: black, ••burnt umber.
Neck collar, incomplete behind: white, •raw umber; neck delicately barred with black, ••burnt umber on upper part of collar.

Body
Back and scapulars: burnt umber, white, ••black; feathers edged with white, raw sienna, •burnt umber, •black.
Sides: burnt umber, raw sienna, ••white, •black, shading lighter towards rear of feather; feathers edged with white, •raw umber; edging becoming broader on upper edges of long side feathers.
Rump: burnt umber, black.
Flanks, upper and lower tail coverts, and rear part of belly: white, •raw umber.
Breast: burnt umber, black, white; feathers broadly edged with white, ••burnt umber, ••black.
Chest: black, ••burnt umber; feathers near breast edged with burnt umber, ••black, ••white. Edging becomes smaller, feathers blend into black of neck.

Tail
Upper and lower surfaces: black, ••burnt umber.

Wing
Primaries and tertials: black, ••burnt umber.
Coverts: black, ••burnt umber; feathers faintly edged with black, burnt umber, ••white.

Tarsi and feet: black, ••burnt umber. Claws — same as feet; use glossy medium.

American brant (Same as black brant except as noted.)

Head: same as black brant, except neck collar is incomplete at front and back of neck.

Body
Back and scapulars: burnt umber, ••raw sienna, •black, ••white; feathers edged with white, •burnt umber, •raw sienna.
Sides: burnt umber, raw sienna, white, shading lighter towards rear of feather; feathers edged with white, •raw umber.
Flanks, upper and lower tail coverts, and belly: white, •raw umber.

Breast: white, ••raw sienna, ••burnt umber, •black; feathers edged with white, •raw umber, •raw sienna.
Chest: burnt umber, black.

Wing
Tertials: black, burnt umber; feathers tipped with white, •raw umber.
Coverts: black, burnt umber; feathers edged with white, raw umber.

8-75 *Black brant.*

8-76 *Black brant.*

8-77 *American brant.*

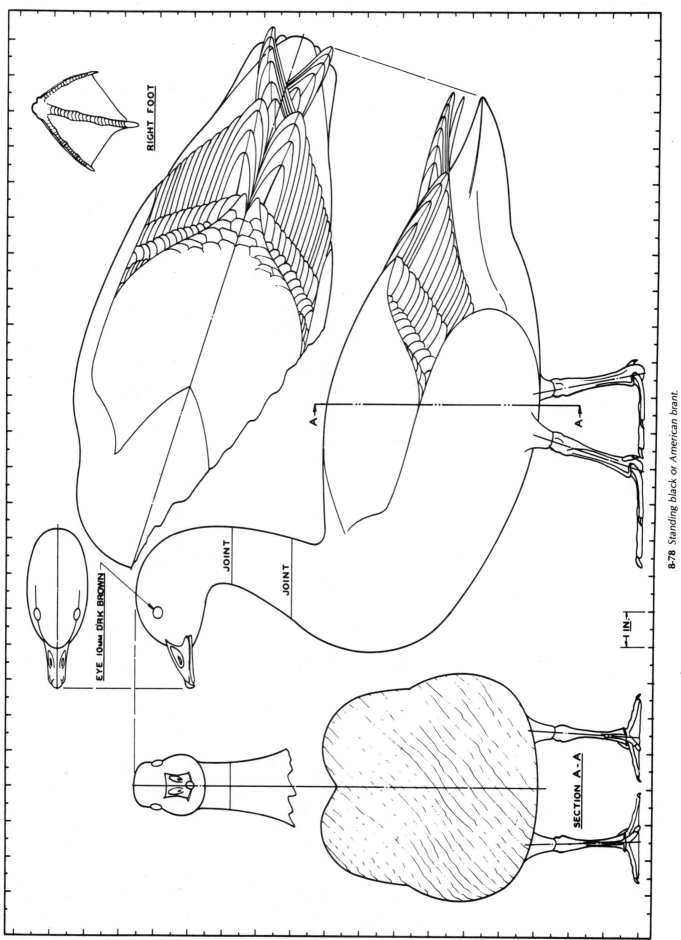

RIGHT FOOT

EYE 10mm D'RK BROWN

JOINT

JOINT

A

A

SECTION A-A

1 IN.

8-78 Standing black or American brant.

8-79 *Finished black brant carving (Collection of Dave Hagerbaumer, Oregon).*

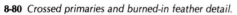

8-80 *Crossed primaries and burned-in feather detail.*

8-81 *Unpainted head of a brant carving.*

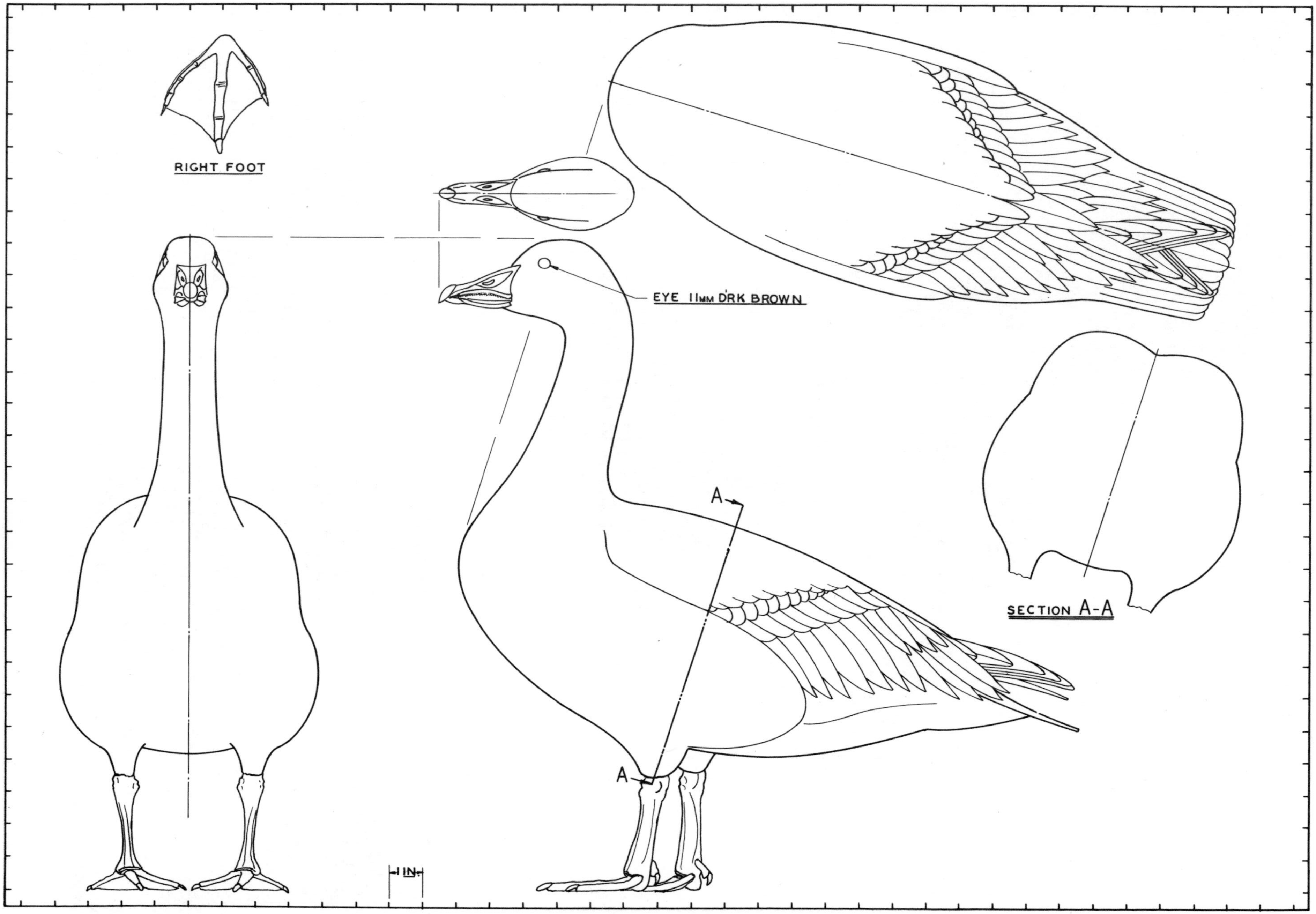

SECTION A-A

EYE 11MM DRK BROWN

RIGHT FOOT

1 IN.

8-82 Standing snow or blue goose.

8-83 *Adult blue goose.*

8-86 *Snow goose, profile view.*

8-84 *A pair of blue geese.*

8-87 *Adult snow goose.*

STANDING SNOW OR BLUE GOOSE
(See Figure F-1, page 102)

Except for coloration, the snow goose is identical with the blue goose; in fact, some ornithologists believe they may be color phases of the same species. Whether different species or the white or colored phase, these geese make most interesting carving subjects.

Snow Goose

Head
Bill, except for tip and "grinning patch": white, ••cadmium red (medium).
Bill tip: white, •raw umber.
Edges of upper and lower mandibles: black, ••burnt umber. Serrated edges of mandibles — white, •raw umber.
Entire head and neck: white, •raw umber; forehead and forward cheeks often stained with white, •cadmium red (light), •burnt umber.

8-85 *Blue goose in an interesting, resting pose.*

Body: entire body, tail coverts, and tail: white, •raw umber.

Wing
Primaries: black, ••burnt umber.
Greater coverts: white, black.
Rest of wing: white, •raw umber.

Tarsi and feet: white, cadmium red (deep), •raw umber. Claws – black, ••burnt umber; use glossy medium.

Blue Goose

Head and upper neck: same as snow goose.

Lower foreneck: burnt umber, white, ••raw sienna, ••black.

Body
Back, scapulars, and chest: burnt umber, white, ••raw sienna, ••black; feathers edged with white, •raw sienna, •burnt sienna.
Sides: white, ••burnt umber, ••raw sienna, ••black; feathers edged with white, •raw sienna, •burnt sienna.

Rump: white, •black, •cobalt blue.
Flanks: white, •raw umber.
Breast and belly: variable in coloration, some birds white, other birds same as side feathers.
Upper and lower tail coverts: white, •raw umber; mottled with white, •black, •cobalt blue.

Wing
Primaries: black, ••burnt umber. Forward webs near base – white, •black, •cobalt blue.
Secondaries: black, ••burnt umber; sometimes edged with white, ••black.
Tertials: burnt umber, black, •white. Feathers have broad edgings of white, •raw sienna. Edgings near base – white, black.
Coverts: white, •black, •cobalt blue. Some inner lesser coverts have black, ••burnt umber streak. Middle and greater coverts edged with white, •raw umber. Long, inner greater coverts – black, ••burnt umber with white, •black, •raw sienna edgings.

Tarsi and feet: same as snow goose.

8-88 *Snow goose carving (Collection of Jon Chaney).*

MOUNTAIN QUAIL

The mountain quail, a western game bird, is the largest and most beautiful of all the quail. With the exception of the long topknot feather, there are no unusual problems connected with carving this bird. For strength it is necessary to carve the long crest feather from metal.

Head
Bill: burnt umber, black, lighter at the tip.
Forehead: white, •raw umber.
Crown: white, ••black, ••burnt umber, •cobalt blue.
Forward part of cheeks and chin: white, •raw umber.
Back of head: same as crown but highlighted with raw sienna, white, ••burnt umber, •black.
Topknot feather: black, ••burnt umber, •Thalo blue.

8-91 *Sketch in the scapulars, tertials, and primary feather groups.*

8-89 *The head of this mountain quail carving was made of alder.*

8-92 *Carve the scapulars and tertials until they stand out from the body.*

8-90 *Rough carve the head and body in the normal manner.*

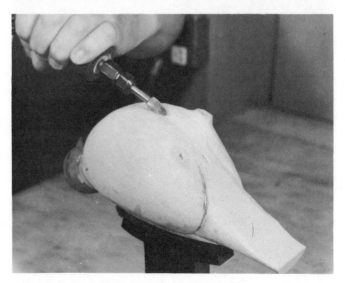

8-93 *The breast and belly areas may be shaped with a rotary file.*

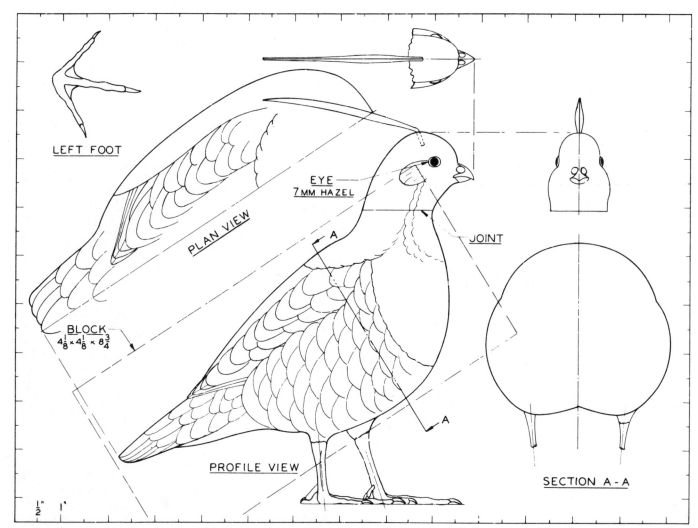

LEFT FOOT

PLAN VIEW

EYE
7 MM HAZEL

JOINT

BLOCK
$4\frac{1}{8} \times 4\frac{1}{8} \times 8\frac{3}{4}$

A

A

PROFILE VIEW

SECTION A - A

$\frac{1}{2}"$ 1"

8-94 *Mountain quail.*

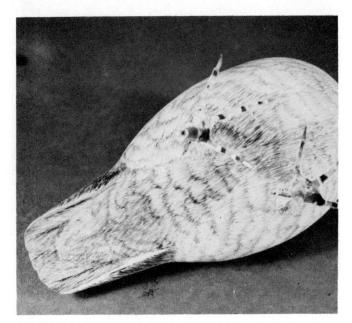

8-95 *Underside of the mountain quail carving.*

Neck
Hindneck: same as back of head.
Sides: same as back of head.
Foreneck and throat: burnt sienna, yellow ochre, cadmium red (deep), ••black; outlined on sides with white, •raw umber.

Body
Back and scapulars: raw sienna, white, ••burnt umber, •black.
Upper tail coverts: same as scapulars.
Sides: burnt sienna, yellow ochre, cadmium red (deep), •black; feathers barred and edged on upper parts with white, •raw umber.
Rump: yellow ochre (light), •burnt sienna.
Lower tail coverts: black, ••burnt umber, •Thalo blue; rear covert feathers striped and forward covert feathers striped and edged with yellow ochre, •burnt sienna.
Belly: white, •raw umber.
Forward breast and chest: white, ••black, •cobalt blue.
Rear part of chest: burnt sienna, yellow ochre (light), cadmium red (deep), ••black; feathers finely edged with white, •raw umber.

8-96, 97 *Mountain quail carving (Collection of Doug Miller, Colorado).*

8-98 *Construction details of the legs and feet.*

8-99 *Carving of a mountain quail in a feeding position.*

Tail
Upper and lower sides: burnt umber, raw sienna, white.

Wing
Primaries, inner webs: burnt umber, raw sienna, •white.
Primaries, outer webs: white, •burnt umber, •black. Shafts — burnt umber.

Secondaries, inner webs: same as primaries.
Secondaries, outer webs: same as scapulars.
Tertials: same as scapulars but broadly edged with white, •raw umber on inner webs.

Tarsi and feet: burnt umber, raw sienna, •white. Claws — burnt umber, raw sienna; use glossy medium.

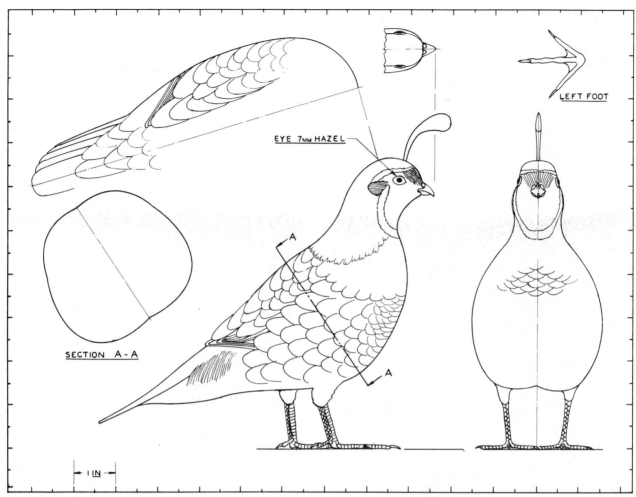

EYE 7MM HAZEL

LEFT FOOT

SECTION A-A

1 IN

8-100 *Gambel's quail or California quail.*

GAMBEL'S AND CALIFORNIA QUAIL
(See Figure A-1, page 97, and Figure P-3, page 240)

The beautiful and jaunty California quail and Gambel's quail are quite similar except for some differences in coloration and marking. Gambel's quail are found in the more arid southwestern part of the United States, while California quail, or valley quail as they are often called, are widely distributed in the valleys and low mountains of the western states.

Gambel's quail

Head

Bill: black, burnt umber, •white.

Forehead: black, ••burnt umber; feathers edged with white, •raw umber.

Crown: yellow ochre (light), burnt sienna; crown outlined on sides with white, •raw umber.

Chin and throat: black, ••burnt umber.

Back of head and neck: white, black, raw umber, •cobalt blue; feathers striped with burnt umber, black, •white.

Cheeks: black, ••burnt umber; black area outlined with white, •raw umber.

Ear coverts: white, burnt umber.

Body

Back and scapulars: same as neck; feathers highlighted slightly with raw sienna, white, ••burnt umber, •black.

Sides: cadmium yellow (medium), burnt sienna, cadmium red (deep), ••black; feathers striped with white, •raw umber.

Rump: same as back.

Upper tail coverts: white, ••black, ••cobalt blue, •raw umber. Shafts — black.

Lower tail coverts: white, •raw sienna; feathers broadly striped with white, raw umber.

Flanks: same as lower tail coverts.

Belly: white, •raw sienna.

Breast: black, ••burnt umber.

Chest: same as back of head and neck. Area between chest and breast — white, ••yellow ochre.

Tail

Upper and lower sides: same as upper tail coverts.

Wing

Primaries, rear web: white, raw sienna, ••burnt umber, •black.

8-101, 102 *Gambel's quail carving (Collection of Milt Weiler, New York).*

8-103 *California quail carving (Collection of Diane Byrnes, California).*

Primaries, front web: white, •black, •cobalt blue; Shaft — raw sienna.

Secondaries: same as back; outer webs edged with white, •raw sienna, •raw umber.

Tertials: same as secondaries; inner webs broadly edged with white, •raw sienna, •raw umber.

Tarsi and feet: burnt umber, black, ••white. Claws — darker; use glossy medium.

California quail

Head

Bill: black, burnt umber, •white.

Forehead: white, •raw umber; streaked with white, •yellow ochre and black.

Crown, forward and sides: black, ••burnt umber.

Crown, rear: black, ••burnt umber; highlighted with burnt umber, •yellow ochre, •white.

Chin, throat, and forward cheeks: black, ••burnt umber. Black area outlined with white, •raw umber.

Back of head and back and sides of neck: white, black, cobalt blue; feathers striped and edged with black, ••burnt umber; double tips of smaller feathers edged with white, •raw umber.

Ear coverts: black, ••burnt umber.

Body

Back, scapulars, and rump: white, black, raw sienna, cobalt blue.

Upper tail coverts and upper and lower tail: white, black, cobalt blue.

Lower tail coverts, flanks, and belly: white, ••raw sienna, •raw umber; feathers striped with white, •raw umber, •raw sienna, •burnt umber.

Breast: burnt sienna, cadmium yellow (medium), •black, shading forward to white, ••yellow ochre. Feathers outlined and delicately striped with black, ••burnt umber.

Chest: same as upper tail coverts.

Wing

Primaries: burnt umber, •white.

Secondaries: same as scapulars; outer webs lightly edged with white, •raw sienna.

Tertials: same as scapulars; inner webs broadly edged with white, •raw sienna, •yellow ochre (light).

Tarsi and feet: black, burnt umber, •white. Claws — black, •burnt umber; use glossy medium.

8-104 *A beautiful pair of California quail.*

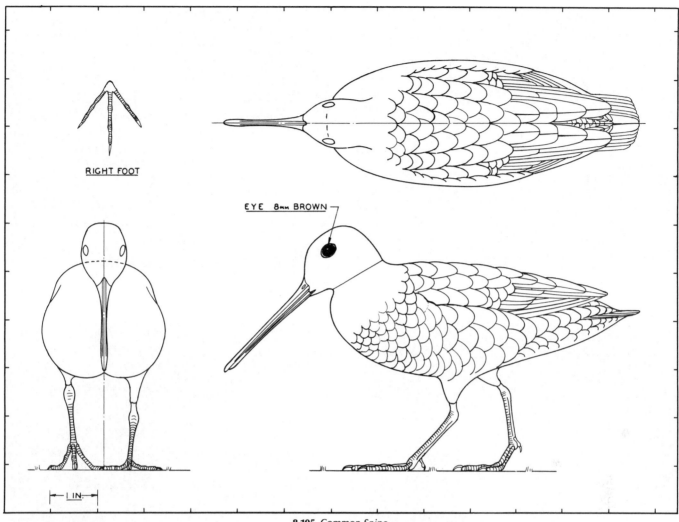

RIGHT FOOT

EYE 8mm BROWN

1 IN.

8-105 *Common Snipe.*

COMMON SNIPE
(See Figure E-2, page 101)

The common snipe is the smallest of our game birds. Its beautiful coloring and markings make it a most interesting carving subject. In the example illustrated in Figures 8-106 through 8-111, the primaries were carved as an integral part of the body block, and the tertials were inserted individually.

Head
Upper mandible: Culmen — white, ••burnt umber, ••burnt sienna. Sides — white, ••black, •burnt sienna. Nail — black, burnt umber.
Lower mandible: Sides and bottom — yellow ochre, •raw umber.
Throat: white, •raw sienna, •raw umber.
Head and neck (except for stripes): white, ••raw sienna, •raw umber.
Stripes: burnt umber, ••black.

Body
Back: black, burnt umber. Outer edges of feathers — white, ••raw sienna, •raw umber. Inner markings — raw sienna, •burnt sienna, •raw umber, •white

Scapulars: same as back.
Rump and upper tail coverts: black, burnt umber. Feathers edged with white, ••raw sienna, •raw umber.
Lower tail coverts: same as upper but lighter (add white).
Flanks: same as rump.
Sides: white, •raw umber, •black. Barred with raw umber, white.
Breast and chest: similar to flanks.
Belly: white, •raw umber.

Tail
Upper side: white, ••burnt sienna, •raw umber. Marked with black, ••burnt umber. Tips — white, raw sienna.
Lower side: similar to upper side but lighter (add more white).

Wing
Primaries: black, ••burnt umber, •white.
Coverts: burnt umber, ••black. Edged with white, •raw sienna, •raw umber.

Tarsi and feet: white, ••yellow ochre, •raw sienna, *very small* amount of Thalo blue. Claws — black, burnt umber, •white; use glossy medium.

8-106 *Carve the folded primaries from the body block.*

8-108 *The first tertial has been inserted.*

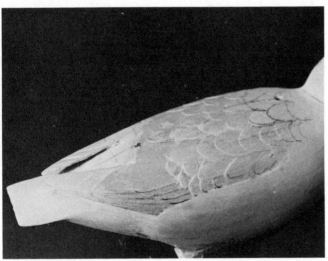

8-107 *Continue by carving the scapulars.*

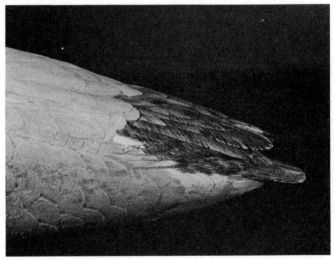

8-109 *The insertion of the tertials has been completed.*

8-110, 111 *Common snipe carving, two views (Collection of Mary Halbert, California).*

CHUKAR PARTRIDGE
(See Figure G-3, page 103)

Although not native to this country, chukar partridge, or chukar as they are commonly called, are well established in the semiarid high deserts and mountains of the western states. They are most often found in lonely, rugged, and inaccessible terrain and are a fine game bird.

Head

Bill: white, ••cadmium red (light), •cadmium red (deep).
Forehead stripe: black, ••burnt umber.
Forehead above stripe: white, •raw umber, •cobalt blue.
Crown top: white, ••raw umber, ••burnt sienna.
Crown sides: lighter than forehead (add white).
Chin and throat: white, ••raw sienna, •raw umber. Vestlike marking – black, ••burnt umber.
Back of head: same as top of crown.
Cheeks, lower: same as throat.
Ear coverts: yellow ochre (light), ••burnt sienna.
Eyelid: cadmium red (light), •raw umber.

Neck

Hindneck and sides: white, ••raw umber, ••burnt sienna, •cobalt blue.

Body

Back: same as hindneck and sides of neck.

Scapulars: same as back; feathers highlighted with same color as sides of chest. Add some blue highlights which are the same color as the front and lower chest.
Sides: white, ••raw sienna, barred with black, ••burnt umber, followed with crescent-shaped edging of cadmium yellow (medium), burnt sienna, ••raw umber.
Rump, upper tail coverts, and flanks: white, ••raw umber, ••cobalt blue, •burnt sienna.
Lower tail coverts: white, raw sienna, •burnt sienna, •black.
Belly: white, ••raw sienna, •burnt sienna, •black.
Chest sides: white, ••raw sienna, ••burnt sienna, •cobalt blue.
Chest front and lower chest: white, •raw umber, •cobalt blue, blending into sides of chest.
Breast: same as front and lower chest.

Tail

Upper and lower sides: yellow ochre, burnt sienna, ••white, •raw umber.

Wing

Primaries: burnt umber, white, ••raw umber. Shafts – white, ••burnt umber, •burnt sienna. Outer web of the outer primaries marked near tip with white, ••raw sienna.
Secondaries: same as rump and upper tail coverts.

Tarsi and feet: same as bill. Claws – burnt umber, black; use glossy medium.

8-112 *Chukar partridge.*

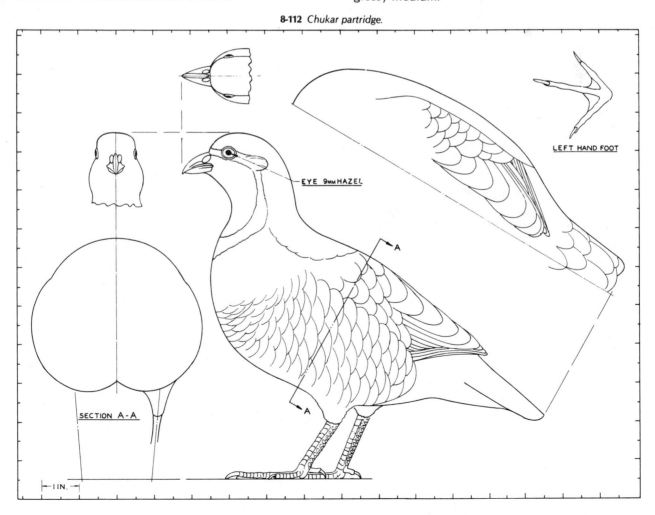

EYE 9mm HAZEL

LEFT HAND FOOT

SECTION A-A

A

A

1 IN.

8-113, 114 Chukar partridge carving (Collection of Jon Chaney).

8-115, 116 Chukar partridge.

8-117 *A pair of male wood ducks.*

PREENING WOOD DUCK
(See Figure B-1, page 98, and Figure K-2, page 235)

This preening wood duck project gives the amateur an opportunity to practice everything he has learned. In addition to doing his first wing carving, he will gain experience in carving the head and neck in a fairly extreme position.

Three hardwood inserts were used on the body and head of this carving: one for the long crest feathers of the head, another for the fanned-out tail (this insert should be made from two separate pieces), and the third for the primaries of the right wing. A hardwood insert for the primaries is not absolutely mandatory, as this feather group could be carved from the body block, provided that the feathers are made sufficiently thick.

It is rather difficult to work out accurately extreme head positions on the drawing. It is usually easier to roughly carve the body and head and to finish carving the bill prior to assembling these parts. In this way, the neck block can be altered to give a head angle that "looks right," and the head can be moved fore and aft and laterally until the desired position is obtained.

The mixing of colors for the wood duck (except for tarsi and feet) was covered above on page 176.

Tarsi and feet
Tarsi and toes: cadmium yellow (medium), •black. Toe joints — darker (add black).
Webs: black, white, raw umber. Web near toes — same color as toes.
Claws: black, ••burnt umber; use glossy medium.

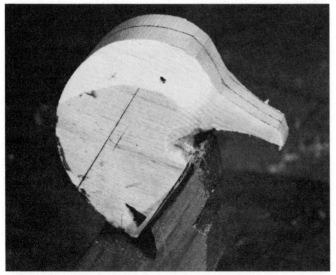

8-118 *Glue the head to a scrap piece of wood for support while carving.*

8-119 *Rough carve the body but leave plenty of wood in the neck area.*

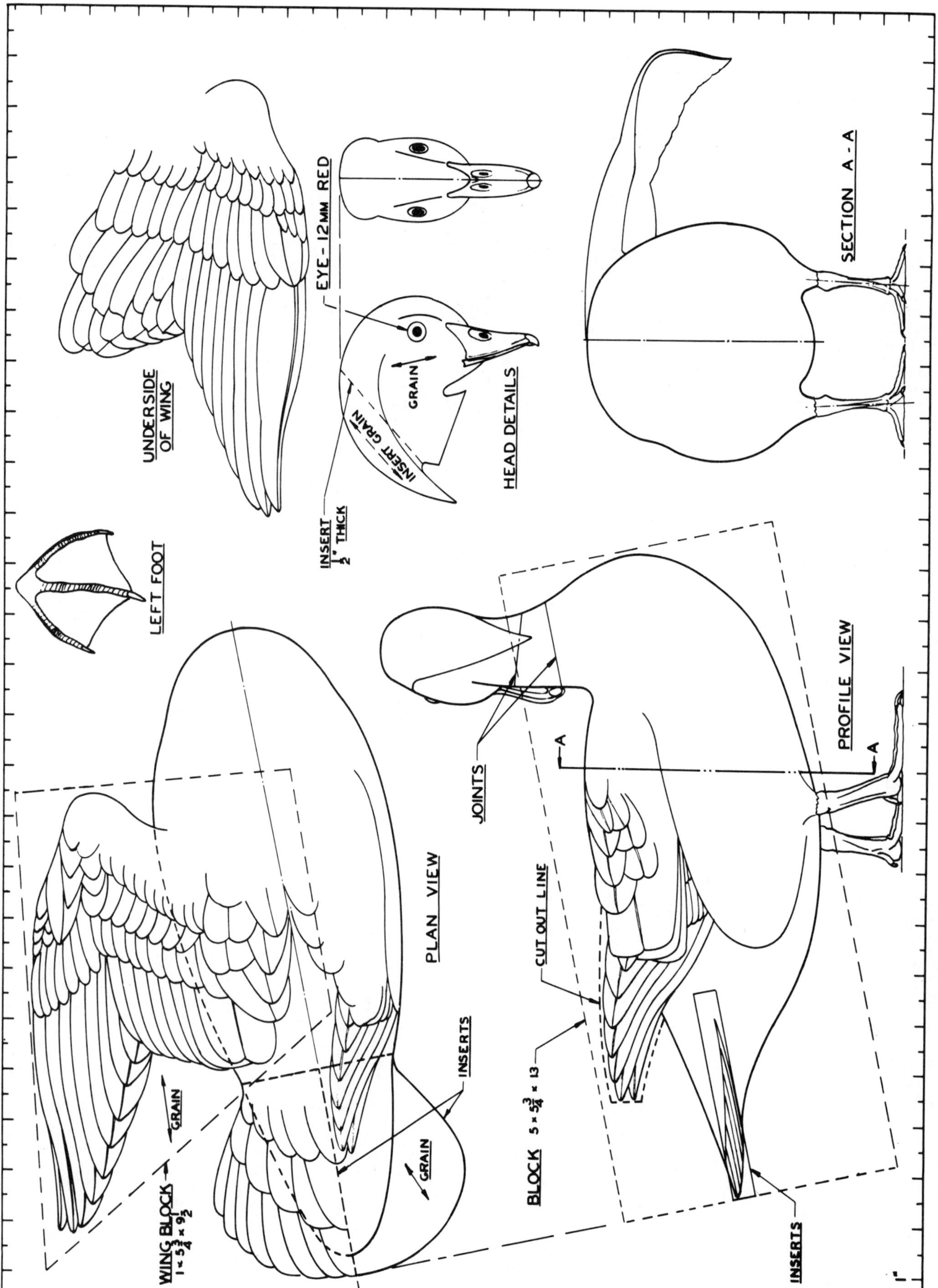

UNDERSIDE
OF WING

EYE - 12 MM RED

HEAD DETAILS

GRAIN

INSERT GRAIN

INSERT
$\frac{1}{2}$" THICK

SECTION A - A

LEFT FOOT

PLAN VIEW

JOINTS

CUT OUT LINE

BLOCK 5 × 5$\frac{3}{4}$ × 13

PROFILE VIEW

A

A

INSERTS

WING BLOCK
1 × 5$\frac{3}{4}$ × 9$\frac{1}{2}$

GRAIN

GRAIN

INSERTS

8-120 *Preening wood duck.*

8-121 *Alter neck block if necessary, position head, and assemble with epoxy.*

8-122 *Finish carving the neck and chest.*

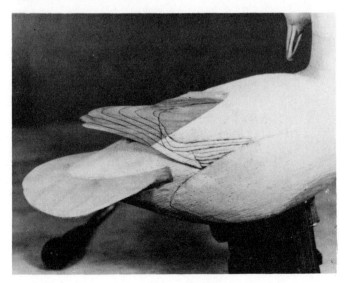

8-123 *Individually carve the primaries, secondaries, and tertials.*

8-124 *Lay out the tail coverts and tail feathers. Carve them individually.*

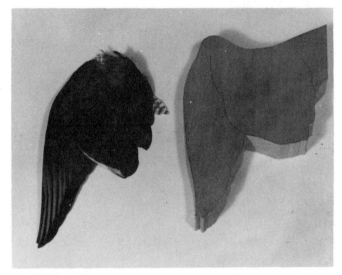

8-125 *The wing block may be made from one piece.*

8-126 *Shape the upper side of the wing with Surform rasps.*

8-127 *Rotary files are useful for removing wood from the underside of the wing.*

8-128 *Lay out and carve the individual feathers, both the upper and lower surfaces.*

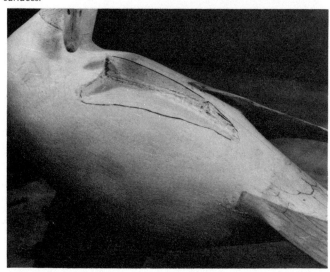

8-129 *Gouge out the body to receive the wing stub.*

8-130 *Attach the wing with epoxy. Use nails to hold the wing in position.*

8-131 *The legs were carved from brass rod and the feet from alder.*

8-132 *Add feather detail by burning over the entire surface of the carving.*

8-133, 134 *Preening wood duck carving (Collection of Dial Dunkin, Texas).*

8-135 *A later preening wood duck (Collection of author).*

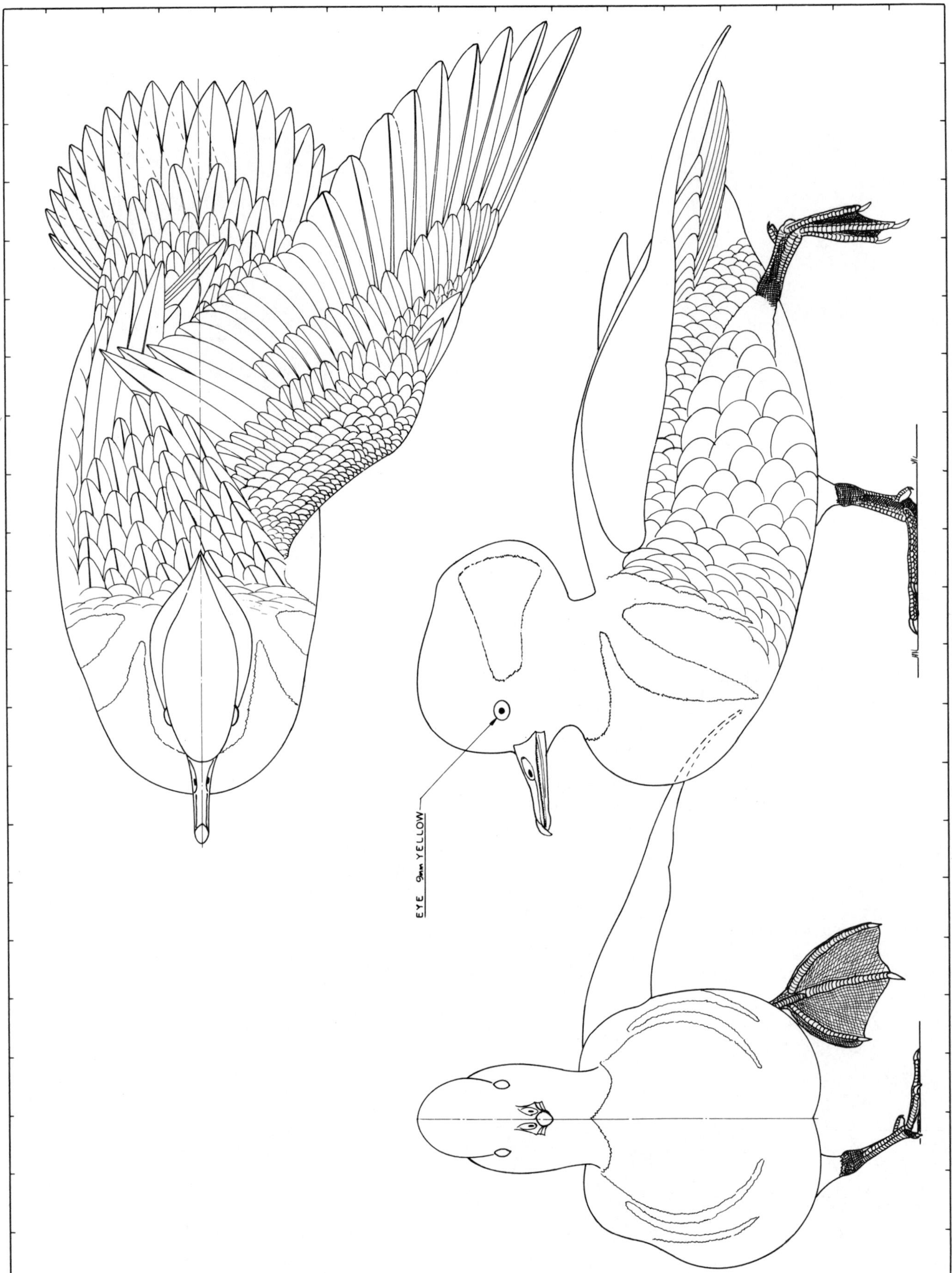

8-136 *Stretching hooded merganser drake.*

EYE 9mm YELLOW

8-137, 138 *Hooded merganser drake, two views.*

STRETCHING HOODED MERGANSER DRAKE
(See Figure E-1, page 101, and Figure M-2, page 237)

The strikingly marked hooded merganser drake, in a wing and leg stretching pose, is a good example of the extensive use of the individual feathering technique described in Chapter 6. In the carving illustrated, the tail feathers were inserted (see Figures 6-141 through 6-146) and the wing was constructed using inserted feathers (see Figures 6-159 through 6-178).

Head
Forehead: burnt umber, white, •black.
Crest: white, •raw umber. Edged with black, ••burnt umber, •Thalo blue.
Rest of head and neck: black, ••burnt umber, •Thalo blue.
Bill: black, ••burnt umber.

Body
Sides: raw sienna, ••yellow ochre.
Back, scapulars, and crescent-shaped markings on chest: black, ••burnt umber, •Thalo blue.
Rump and upper tail coverts: burnt umber. Feathers edged with raw sienna, •burnt umber.
Chest, breast, and belly: white, •raw umber.
Undertail coverts: white, ••raw sienna, •raw umber. Vermiculated with raw umber, white.

Tail
Upper side: black, burnt umber, •white. Tips edged with white, ••raw umber.
Lower side: white, •black, •burnt umber.

Wing
Primaries: black, burnt umber, •white. Inner webs – lighter (add white).
Secondaries: Inner webs – black, ••burnt umber. Edged broadly on outer sides, forward almost to the greater coverts, with white, •raw umber.
Tertials: black, ••burnt umber, •Thalo blue. Striped down shaft area with white, •raw umber.
Greater coverts: black, ••burnt umber, •Thalo blue forward, with most of exposed feathers white, •raw umber.
Lesser coverts: burnt umber. Edged faintly with white, ••raw umber.
Middle coverts: white, •raw sienna, •raw umber.
Lining: white, •raw umber. Lesser coverts – burnt umber, ••white. Some middle coverts – white, •raw umber.

Feet
Tarsi and toes: yellow ochre, •raw umber.
Webs and joints: raw umber, •yellow ochre.
Claws: black, ••burnt umber; use glossy medium.

8-139 *Mortise the body for the primaries.*

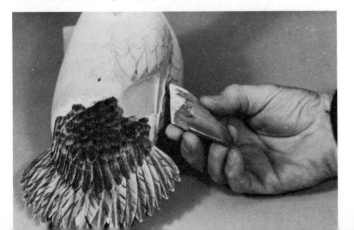

8-140 *Showing inserted tertials.*

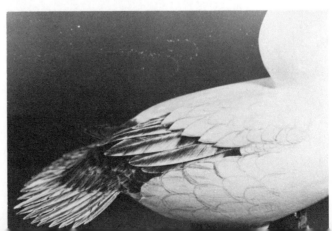

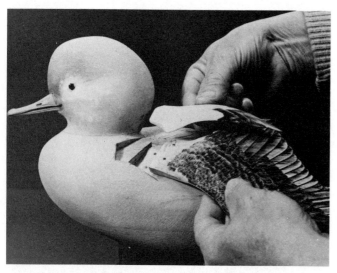

8-141 *Mortise the body for the wing stub and carve the scapulars from a separate piece.*

8-142 *Showing wing and scapulars attached to the body.*

8-143, 144, 145, 146 *Stretching hooded merganser drake carving (Collection of Dr. and Mrs. J. L. Silagi, Texas).*

8-147 *Greater prairie chicken carving (Collection of author).*

PRAIRIE CHICKEN
(See Figure D-1, page 100)

Although once very plentiful over much of the United States, the prairie chickens' range now is limited and their numbers are quite low. The lesser prairie chicken is quite similar to the greater except that it is smaller and lighter in coloration. The air sacs on the greater male are yellowish, while those on the lesser male are reddish. The published overall length and weight of the greater male is 18 inches, 2 pounds and 3 ounces; of the lesser male, 16 inches, 1 pound and 12 ounces. See Figures 6-139 and 6-140 for insertion of crest feathers and Figures 6-157 and 6-158 for insertion of wing primaries.

Head

Forehead, crown, back of head, and neck: burnt umber, raw sienna, white. Broadly edged with raw sienna, white, •raw umber.

Chin, cheeks, and throat: white, •raw sienna. Mark above and below eyes, auricular (ear coverts), and lower cheek with burnt umber.

Pinnates (stiff, narrow neck feathers): white, •raw sienna. Marked on outer edges with burnt umber. Inner webs of smaller feathers — burnt sienna, raw umber, white. Edged with burnt umber.

Air sacs (bare spots on neck): Greater — cadmium yellow (medium), ••cadmium orange, •raw umber. Lesser — cadmium red (light), cadmium orange, •raw umber.

Comb (above eye): cadmium yellow (medium), •raw umber.

Bill: raw sienna, ••burnt umber, •white.

Body

Scapulars, exposed wing coverts, rump, and upper tail coverts: burnt sienna, raw sienna, white. H-shaped markings — burnt umber, •black. Broadly tipped with white, •raw sienna, •raw umber.

Back: burnt sienna, raw sienna, white. Barred with burnt umber, •black. Feathers broadly tipped with white, •raw umber.

Sides, chest, breast, and belly: white, ••raw sienna, •raw umber. Feathers barred with burnt umber, •white. Bars finely barred with burnt sienna, raw sienna, white. Broadly tipped with white, •raw sienna, •raw umber.

Under tail coverts: white, •raw sienna, •raw umber. V-shaped markings — burnt umber.

Tail

Upper side: burnt umber, ••raw sienna, •white. Edged with burnt umber, ••raw sienna, ••white. Tipped with white, •raw sienna, •raw umber.

Lower side: burnt umber, ••raw sienna, •white. Tipped with white, •raw umber.

Wing

Primaries: white, ••burnt umber. Barred on outer webs with white, •raw sienna, •raw umber.

Secondaries: white, •raw sienna, •raw umber. Some triangular-shaped markings — burnt umber. Other triangular-shaped markings — burnt sienna, raw sienna, white.

Coverts: See scapulars.

Tarsi and feet

Tarsi covert feathers: white, •raw sienna, •raw umber. Barred with white, •burnt umber.

Toes: cadmium yellow (medium), •raw umber.

Claws: raw sienna, ••burnt umber, •white; use glossy medium.

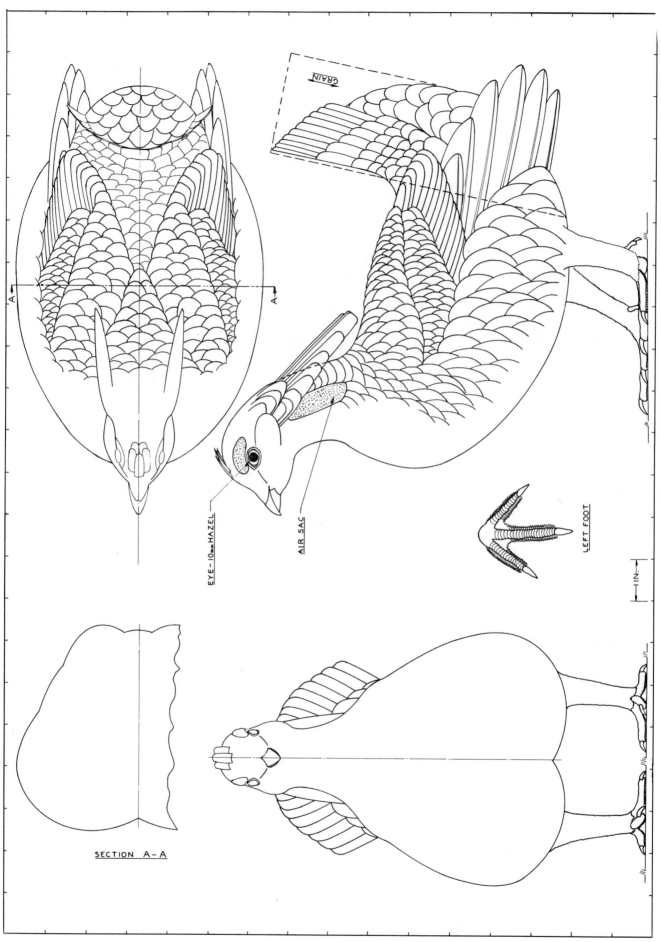

EYE-10mm HAZEL

AIR SAC

GRAIN

LEFT FOOT

1 IN.

SECTION A-A

A

A

8-148 *Greater prairie chicken (male).*

8-149 *After the bird is roughly carved to shape, lay out the scapulars and secondary feathers.*

8-150 *Carefully carve the underside of the tail.*

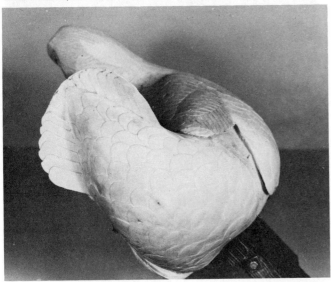

8-151 *The underside of the tail and the lower tail coverts have been carved. Relieve side feathers to receive primaries.*

8-152, 153, 154 *Male lesser prairie chicken carving (Collection of Dr. Ray Zeigler, Texas).*

8-155, 156 *Common Canada goose.*

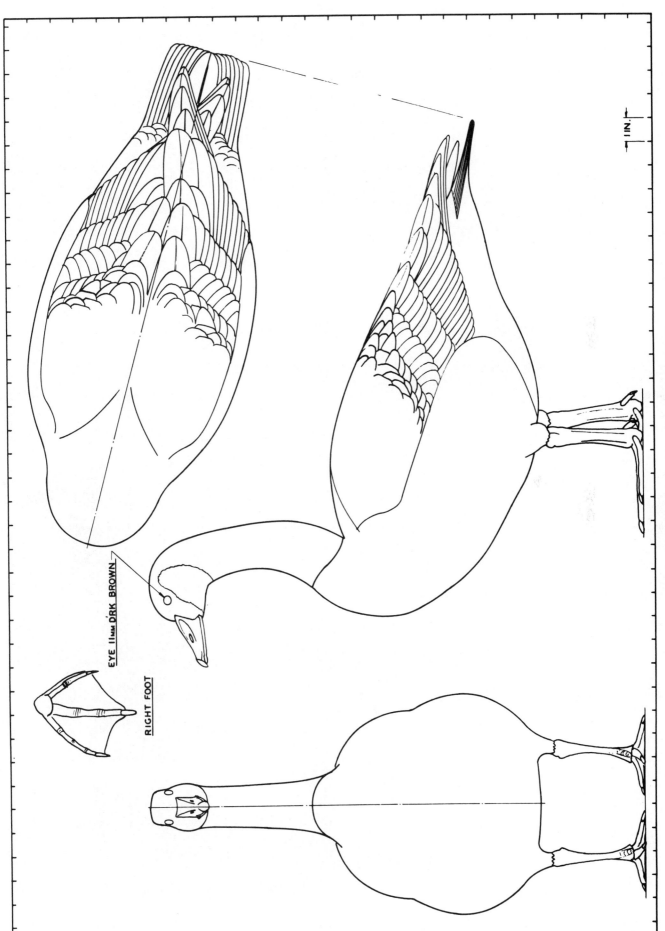

EYE 11mm DRK BROWN

RIGHT FOOT

8-157 Common Canada goose. An interesting advanced project.

⊤1IN.⊦

8-158 *Life-size Canada goose (Collection of Paul F. O'Brien, Jr., Louisiana).*

8-159 *Life-size Taverner's Canada geese (Collection of Doug Miller, Colorado).*

8-160, 161 *Feeding Canada goose.*

CHAPTER

9

Displaying the Carving

As stated in Part II, the success of a realistic bird carving primarily depends on four factors, the last – but by no means the least important – being the artistry shown in selecting the mount or support to display the finished carving. To the casual observer, it may seem that some carvers have an inherent artistic sense in designing or picking out a mount for a particular carving, while others, although capable of turning out top-quality carvings, lack the ability to display their work effectively. A certain amount of visual sense is necessary, of course, but this writer maintains that tasteful display of a carving results more from study, planning, and concerted effort than from innate artistic ability. When mounts made from natural materials enhance the aesthetic quality of a carving, it is not by happy accident. Undoubtedly, a great deal of patient, diligent searching had to be done before material of the size, shape, and color to complement the carving was found.

It is important to consider the method of mounting and displaying while the carving is in the planning stage. Furthermore, it is usually desirable to select the actual mount at this time. The pose of the carving can then be altered if necessary to conform with the mount, and the chances of obtaining unity between carving and mount will be greatly enhanced.

In some instances, an interesting piece of driftwood or similar material may inspire the creation of a carving or alter not only the species but also the pose of one already conceived. Seeing a certain natural form, the carver may immediately envision a particular bird perched upon its surface in a specific pose.

For instance, the author visualized and planned a carving of a single band-tailed pigeon alighting. Searching for a suitable mount, he came across the one shown in Figure 4-5, which struck his eye and altered his original concept; in order to use the root that attracted him, it was necessary to add the second, standing band-tailed pigeon to achieve a balanced composition.

Although these inspirations do occur, more often the carver first visualizes the bird and pose, and then happens upon a mount that seems formed by nature especially for his carving.

It is difficult, if not impossible, to set down any hard-and-fast rules for selecting the mount for a carving. Some of the more obvious generalizations include the following:
1. The mount should reflect, if possible, the natural habitat of the bird.
2. The base or mount should be proportionate to the carving. It should not be so large as to overpower the carving, nor so small that the carving is inadequately or precariously supported.
3. Avoid selecting mounts that appear unstable. For example, it is possible to mount a carving on a branch extending from a piece of driftwood that has sufficient weight so that it will not tip over under normal conditions; however, the undesirable feeling of top-heaviness and instability can still persist.
4. Any fresh-appearing, man-made alterations to mounts made from natural materials should be avoided whenever possible. If it becomes necessary to cut or rework the natural surface, the cuts should be artificially aged by burning, wire-brushing, staining, or other means. The more formal bases described later in this chapter are exceptions.

SHADOW BOXES, PLAQUES, AND DIORAMAS

Half-body decoy carvings, such as those covered in Chapter 1, are usually mounted on a fabric-covered surface and displayed in a frame or shadow box. The mounting surface is normally made from ¼-inch plywood cut to fit the frame. Locate the carving on the board and drill holes to accommodate two mounting screws. Cut a piece of linen fabric or similar material somewhat larger than the board and iron smooth. Brush white glue, thinned with water, evenly but sparingly on the board. Lay the fabric on a smooth surface and place the board on top of it, holding it in place with weights. After the glue has dried, cut off the excess fabric with a sharp knife or razor blade.

Another effective means of displaying half-body decoys is to mount them directly on a weathered or antiqued board.

9-1 *Cinnamon teal plaque (Collection of Tom Knuckles, California).*

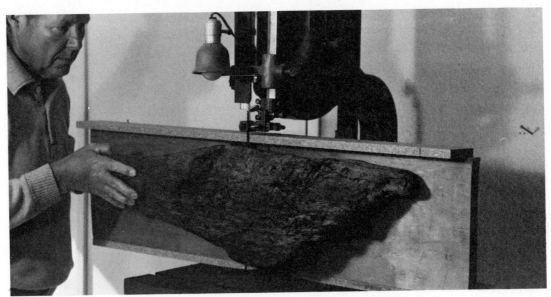

9-2 *One method of making straight cuts on an irregular piece of driftwood. Driftwood is attached to jig with wood screws. Movable upper board serves as a cutting guide.*

Flying carvings can also be attractively mounted within a frame or shadow box, although a great deal of skill and artistry is required, both in the carving and the mounting, to produce a realistic and pleasing effect. For a mount of this type, a painted natural habitat scene is generally used as the background. The background can also include three-dimensional objects such as branches and leaves, cattails, or others. These props can be natural materials or can be carvings made to depict natural materials.

Miniature carvings can be effectively displayed by creating a three-dimensional scene or diorama. Here again, considerable skill is needed, especially in realistically blending the three-dimensional foreground with the curved, painted background. A great deal of ingenuity is also involved in faithfully duplicating plants, trees, and other natural objects, so necessary for completing a true-to-life scene.

DRIFTWOOD

The most popular way of displaying a realistic bird carving is to mount the bird on an attractive piece of driftwood (Fig. 9-3). The term driftwood is very loosely applied to almost any piece of wood, usually (but not always) in its natural form, that has been weathered and sometimes shaped by the elements. Interesting pieces of weathered wood, in an infinite number of shapes and sizes, can be found almost anywhere: on the seashore, along streams or lakes, on the desert, in the mountains, under the ground (roots of dead trees can make very attractive mounts), or sometimes in the backyard.

In most instances, driftwood, after dirt and other extraneous materials are removed, is used in its natural state; however, some carvers prefer to coat the exposed surface with flat or low-luster varnish or similar finish. Quite often, especially when the driftwood has been in contact with the ground over an extended period, the wood is infested with termites or other wood-eating insects. These insect holes usually add to the rustic charm of the piece, but when it becomes a mount, any further wood eating must be prevented. The surest way to kill all of the wood-eating insects is to have the piece of driftwood fumigated by an authorized termite-control service. Another satisfactory method is to soak the piece in chlordane.

Whenever possible, the driftwood selected should be self-standing or able to be made self-standing in the desired position by a flat saw cut. In some cases, it may be necessary to attach the driftwood piece to a separate base in order to make it stand. This should be avoided whenever possible, according to some collectors. Other collectors prefer the piece of driftwood to be mounted on a more formal base. Burls, sliced from the trunks of dead trees, make excellent mounts, especially for the smaller bird carvings. The saw cut should be trued so that the base will rest accurately against a flat surface. In all cases, the support surfaces should be covered with felt or another soft material to prevent the possible scratching of fine furniture.

A piece of driftwood often can be cut in many different ways, creating just as many different effects. Before making any cuts, the carver should study the piece carefully, bearing in mind how he intends to mount the carving and determining how it will appear relative to the base. It is often necessary to remove certain parts of the piece, leaving an exposed, fresh-appearing cut. If the undesirable protuberances are small, it may be better to break them off rather than to cut them. In either event, the exposed, unweathered wood should be made to match the rest of the mount as closely as possible. Various methods can be used to accomplish this. Some of the more common ways are burning, wire brushing, gouging, staining or some other antiquing means, or a combination of two or more of these methods.

SEMIFORMAL BASES

Some carvers prefer to mount at least some of their carvings on bases a little less rustic than driftwood. In the past, the author has mounted quite a few of his standing birds on semiformal bases composed of a single cross-sectional slice cut from the trunk, burl, or roots of beautifully grained trees. The sides of the base are left in their natural state but the top is given a furniture finish. Almost any thoroughly cured, beautifully textured and colored wood can be used for a base of this kind. Burls — walnut, redwood, and others — are especially desirable.

In making this type of base, slice the wood to the approximate thickness desired on a band saw. Machine both the upper and lower surfaces of the slice with a planer-type cutter in conjunction with a drill press (Fig. 9-5). Fill all checks and other defects with casting resin, dyed opaque black (Fig. 9-6). After the casting resin has completely cured, sand smooth the top side of the base – do final sanding with 6/0 paper. Remove all loose matter such as dirt

9-3 *Coot mounted on driftwood with a walnut base (Collection of Steve Gothard).*

9-4 *Horned grebe mounted on a small burl (Collection of Steve Gothard).*

9-5 *Machine the slice flat with a drill press-driven planer.*

9-6 *Fill all checks and imperfections with casting resin dyed black.*

The base is now ready to be finished. A fine finish can be obtained by filling the minute low spots and sanding down the high spots until the finished surface is uniformly smooth. The author uses lacquer sanding sealer applied with a spray gun, although brushing lacquer (such as Deft) can be used with good results. After the first coat is applied and thoroughly dry, sand down the surface almost to the bare wood, using 400 wet or dry sandpaper, and smooth further with 3/0 steel wool. This sanding removes the high spots and prevents the sealer from building up. Apply another coat of sealer. Repeat this procedure until the desired finish is obtained. Sanding sealer produces a satin finish. If a glossy finish is desired, a coat or two of high-gloss finish lacquer, thinned about 50 per cent with lacquer thinner, is applied with a spray gun.

and bark from the sides of the base with a rotary wire brush powered by an electric drill motor. If it becomes necessary to shape the base on the back side, make all cuts on a bevel and sand smooth. Then, texture these cuts by vigorous wire brushing and stain, if necessary, to match the natural surfaces.

9-8 *Carvings can be used to decorate desk sets.*

9-7 *Typical functional mount — lesser Canada goose lamp.*

Other semiformal bases can be cut from boards of different wood species, carved and sanded, or gouge carved to the desired shape, finished with a coat or two of lacquer sanding sealer, and rubbed smooth with 3/0 steel wool. Bases of this type, and those molded from clay or plaster, can be effectively painted with oil or acrylics to represent natural materials such as sand, mud, or rock.

FUNCTIONAL MOUNTS

Game bird carvings are often attractively used to decorate functional objects. Some of the more popular decorative items include table lamps, wall lamps, desk sets, paperweights, and bookends (Figs. 9-7, 8, 9).

9-9 *Half-body decoys can be displayed on attractive wall lamps.*

9-10 *Pair of California quail (Collection of Ward Bros. Foundation Museum, Salisbury, Maryland).*

Very unusual and beautiful lamp bases can be made from cross-sectional pieces made as described in the preceding section. Decoy carvings are normally used to decorate lamps of this type, although standing and flying bird carvings can be used just as effectively.

Designs for handsome functional mounts are limited only by the imagination and ingenuity of the carver.

FORMAL BASES

During the past ten years or so, when fine, realistic bird carving came into its own as a legitimate American art form, mounting bases have become more elaborate and formal. Many top artists now go to extremes in attempting to create aesthetic bases that reflect the natural habitat of the bird being depicted.

The bases on most fine carvings are made from beautifully grained hardwoods, black walnut being probably the most popular. Some bases are assembled using molding stock; however, most are made from solid material with the edge detail either added by means of a router/shaper or, in the case of round bases, turned on a wood lathe.

The easiest way to add edge detail is with the router using a piloted cutter. During recent years, routers have become

less expensive, and there now are many differently shaped cutters from which to choose. The base is first cut to shape and sanded smooth. The router is then moved around the periphery of the base with the pilot riding against the outside edge. The cutting of the final edge should not be attempted in one pass — three or more passes, increasing the depth of cut each time, produces smoother results. After the final cut has been made, the edge must be sanded perfectly smooth. The base can then be finished with a brushing lacquer sealer, such as Deft, or regular lacquer sanding sealer can be sprayed on to attain a more professional appearance. A number of applications of the lacquer sealer, sanded or steel-wooled between coats, is required to obtain a good finish.

If a simulated ground effect is desired, the top of the base should be undercut before cutting it out from the flat stock. This can be done by making an inside template from ¼-inch plywood approximately ¼ inch smaller (around the periphery) than the finished top detail of the base. The top can then be undercut using a straight cutter in conjunction with a template guide on the router.

Ground can be simulated with water putty. First, fill the undercut area with putty mixed with sufficient water so that it will pour. Then, mix more putty with very little water, permitting the formation of lumps or small clods, and add this lumpy material while the putty on the base is still wet (Figure 9-12). Spray water on the lumps, which makes them adhere to the wet putty. After the putty has thoroughly dried, paint it the desired color with either acrylics or oils.

Elliptically shaped bases are often more pleasing to the eye and blend with the carving better than round ones. Figure 9-15 shows a simple way of laying out a true ellipse. First, the length and width of the ellipse must be determined. It is much simpler, and cheaper, to determine the desired size by making trial bases from scrap, such as plywood or heavy corrugated paper. The carving can then be placed on these makeshift bases and the overall effect appraised. When the final dimensions have been chosen, lay out two lines at right angles to each other, representing the major and minor axes of the ellipse, on paper or cardboard. Next, make two marks on the edge of a strip of cardboard or thin wood whose distance between is equal to exactly one half of the length of the ellipse. Add a third mark at a distance equal to one half of the width of the ellipse as measured from the mark on the right-hand end of the strip. By keeping the mark at the extreme left-hand end of the strip on the minor axis and the mark just to the right on the major axis, as many points on the ellipse as desired can be marked off.

The use of natural materials, such as leaves, plants, grass, or other actual plant or animal life (and those commercially made) on carving bases, is generally considered taboo, especially on carvings that are entered into competition. The duplication of these natural materials with wood, paper, metal, plastics, etc., is limited only by the imagination, ingenuity, and resourcefulness of the individual carver.

The leaves on the bases shown in Figures 9-13 and 9-17 were made from thin lead sheet and the twigs from brass rod, soft soldered to the lead. The acorns, which are hard to discern, were turned from wood on a lathe. The lichen in the foreground of the snipe base shown in Figure 9-14 was made from end-grain jelutong. The individual shoots were formed with a tool similar to a nail set. The grass was cut from thin brass sheet, inserted in styrofoam, and epoxied in place.

9-11 *Protect edge of base with masking tape.*

9-12 *After water putty is poured, lumpy putty is added to the wet surface.*

9-13 *Finished base for stretching hooded merganser (see Figure 8-143).*

9-14 *Base for snipe (see Figure 8-111) is ready for the water putty simulated ground.*

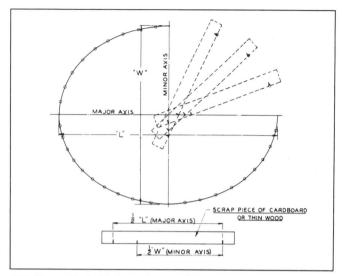

9-15 One method of laying out a true ellipse.

9-18 The bracket fungi added to this piece of driftwood were made from thin lead sheets.

9-16 Base for a quail carving is being turned on a wood lathe.

9-19 Base for Canada goose carving (see Figure 8-158). The corn stalks were carved from wood, the leaves were made from lead sheet.

9-17 Finished base for quail carving (see Figure 9-10).

9-20 Base for California quail carving (see Figure 8-103). The ivy leaves were made from thin brass sheet.

PART IV

Game Bird Carving Data

One of the greatest difficulties the realistic bird carver faces is obtaining accurate structural information on a particular bird. This scarcity of published information was one of the factors that prompted the writing of this book. Ideally, each carver should have access to actual specimens; since this is not possible for many, the author incorporated structural information on a number of game bird species in drawings presented in earlier chapters. In addition, photographs of those parts of most game birds pertinent to the carver and important dimensional information on all the game birds have been included in the remaining chapters.

CHAPTER

10
Classification and General Description

The game birds of the United States can be classified into five main groups: waterfowl; upland game birds; pigeons and doves; shorebirds; and marsh dwellers.

Each of these groups is divided into families and subfamilies, and some of their more important physical characteristics are described and illustrated below.

WATERFOWL

This group of game birds is of one family, the Anatidae, which is further divided into seven subfamilies. One subfamily, the swans, although hunted extensively in the early years, are now protected.

Geese

General characteristics of geese are intermediate between ducks and swans. Sexes are alike in coloration and markings. Neck is longer than on ducks but shorter than body. Bill is high near base, narrow in the middle, and tapers toward tip. General posture on land – body parallel to ground; on water – buoyant with tail high and body at an angle to the surface. Tarsi near center of body.

River or puddle ducks

Generally smaller than geese. Neck shorter than body. Sexes unlike in coloration and markings. Bill usually broad and flattened, but varies considerably among the various species. General posture on land – body parallel to ground; on water – buoyant with tail high and body at an angle to the surface. Tarsi near center of body. Speculum generally brightly colored, often iridescent. Hind toe without lobe. Feed in shallow water by tipping; dive only to escape danger.

10-1 *Blue goose.*

10-2 *Common Canada goose.*

10-3 *Common mallard male, a river or puddle duck.*

10-5 *Female redhead, a typical diving duck.*

Sea or diving ducks

Similar to puddle ducks, except for the following characteristics. General posture on land — body more erect; on water — profile low with body parallel to water and tail near or touching water. Tarsi farther back. Feet larger. Hind toe with lobe. Speculum less brightly colored and usually not iridescent. Dives to feed.

10-6 *Female redhead.*

10-4 *Pair of American widgeons, typical river or puddle ducks.*

Mergansers

Similar to diving ducks except that bill is long, narrow and tapered, and is round in cross section.

Ruddy ducks

Similar to diving ducks, except that bill is broad, short, and strongly hooked downward at tip; tarsi located even farther back; tail feathers stiff and spikelike with very short tail coverts; neck thick and short.

10-7 *Male ruddy duck in breeding plumage.*

I-1 *Common mallard drake.*

I-2 *Mallard hen.*

I-3 *Mallard drake.*

J-1 *Canvasback drake.*

J-2 *Canvasback hen.*

K-1 *Bufflehead drake.*

K-2 *Wood duck drake.*

L-1 *Pintail drake.*

L-2 *Pintail hen.*

M-1 *American widgeon drake.*

M-2 *Hooded merganser drake.*

N-1 *Cinnamon teal drake.*

N-2 *Cinnamon teal pair.*

O-1 *Blue-winged teal drake.*

O-2 *White-fronted geese.*

P-1 *Shoveler drake.*

P-3 *California quail (male).*

P-2 *Shoveler hen.*

P-4 *California quail (female).*

10-8 *Standing fulvous tree duck.*

10-9 *Fulvous tree duck.*

10-10 *Bobwhite quail.*

Tree ducks

Seem to be connecting link between true ducks and geese. Long neck. Tarsi and feet long, located near center of body. Body posture on land – more erect than puddle ducks; on water – buoyant and tail fairly high. Hind toe without lobe.

UPLAND GAME BIRDS

The upland game birds of the United States comprise three families. Although these birds vary greatly in size (6-ounce quail to 20-pound-and-over turkeys), they all have plump bodies, large pectoral muscles, and short, thick bills. Their legs are heavily muscled and are well adapted for scratching, walking, and running. Their wings are short and broad, capable of strong, fast flight, but only for short distances.

Quails (Phasianidae)

Small, chicken-like birds. Sexes unlike in coloration and markings. Tarsi and feet bare. Male has no spurs. Posture of body variable from parallel to the ground to almost vertical, depending on activity.

10-11 *Chukar partridge.*

Partridges (Phasianidae)

Medium-size birds not native to this country. Sexes alike in coloration and markings. Tarsi and feet bare. Males have blunt spurs. Body posture similar to quail.

Pheasants (Phasianidae)

Birds not native to this country. Male, large and exotically colored and marked; female, slightly smaller and drab. Long arched tail. Tarsi and feet bare. Males have large, sharp spurs. Posture of body usually not quite as erect as quail and partridge.

10-12 *Ring-necked pheasant.*

10-13 *Female ruffed grouse (beautiful taxidermy work by Wendell Gilley).*

10-14 *Male turkey.*

Grouse (Tetraonidae)

Medium-to-large-size birds with short, down-curved bills and feathered nostrils. Tarsi and feet partly or completely covered with feathers. Sexes generally similar in coloration and markings. Males of some species have inflatable air sacs on neck. Body posture similar to quail.

Turkeys (Meleagrididae)

Males much larger than females. Sexes generally similar in coloration and markings. Bill short. Skin on head and neck bare, brightly colored on males. Tarsi and feet bare. Males have spurs. General body posture similar to pheasants. Males have a beard of black bristles hanging from chest.

10-15 *White-winged dove.*

PIGEONS AND DOVES

This group of small-to-medium-size migratory birds (family Columbidae) has only three important game-bird species: mourning dove, white-winged dove, and band-tailed pigeon. Although slimmer than quail, they have large pectoral muscles, fairly long and narrow wings, and are capable of fast, strong flight over considerable distances. Their tails are long, but their heads are small, with short, slim bills. Tarsi and feet are bare with a well-developed hind toe for walking and perching. Body posture is generally at a small angle to the ground.

SHOREBIRDS

This group is composed of one family (Scolopacidae) with two game birds: woodcock and Wilson's, or common, snipe. Many other shorebirds, while no longer legally hunted, are very popular subjects with many bird-carvers.

10-16 *Common snipe (Photo by Paul Johnsgard).*

Wilson's snipe

Plump body, short tail, and long, pointed wings. Tarsi and feet bare. Tarsi fairly long. Small head with long, narrow, and tapered bill. General posture – body parallel to ground.

Woodcock

Chunky body with short tail, short and heavy neck, and long, tapered bill. Eyes set high and far back on head. Wings short and rounded, unlike other shorebirds. Tarsi and feet bare. General posture – body parallel to ground.

MARSH DWELLERS

The small-to-medium-size birds in this group are of one family (Rallidae) and include the rails, gallinules, and coots. Although the least popular from the sportman's standpoint, they can be very interesting subjects for carvings. Bodies are rather short and chunky. Three of the rails (king, Virginia, and clapper) have small heads with long, slender bills. The other game birds in this group have short, thick bills. While the coots and gallinules fly fairly well, the rails are weak flyers. The tarsi and large feet are bare. Coots have flaps on both sides of their toes to aid in swimming. General posture on land – bodies parallel to the ground; on water – bodies buoyant and parallel to the surface.

10-17 *Coot.*

10-18 *King rail.*

CHAPTER

11
Dimensional Data

The following dimensional information has been assembled as an aid to the carver without access to actual specimens. This information, at the very best, must be considered an approximate average. Scientific dimensional data for birds are normally limited to wingspan, overall length, and weight; they do not include the information most necessary to the carver — body length, width, and height; head and bill dimensions; and foot and tarsus dimensions. Whenever possible, these dimensions were obtained from actual specimens. In some cases, however, dimensions were approximated from photographs; in other cases, dimensions were ratioed from other similar species, using their overall lengths as the basis for comparison.

It must be remembered that the bird's dimensions vary for a particular species; also, some dimenions on an individual bird vary considerably due to muscular feather control. Check the dimensions included in this chapter when-

ever you have the opportunity and, if there are differences, note them. Also, collect additional information whenever a specimen is available. Some of the useful information that can be obtained from a fresh specimen include the following:

1. Color of bill, tarsi, and feet. These parts lose their color when they are dry, therefore accurate color sketches are invaluable.
2. Plan-view drawing of the bird with wings and tail outstretched. A plan-view drawing of the wing and tail in an intermediate position is also useful for preening and other poses.
3. Distance from tip of tail to rearmost side feather.
4. Location of primaries and tertials relative to tip of tail, when the wings are folded.
5. Size and color of the live bird's eyes.
6. Actual shape of foot in the standing position.

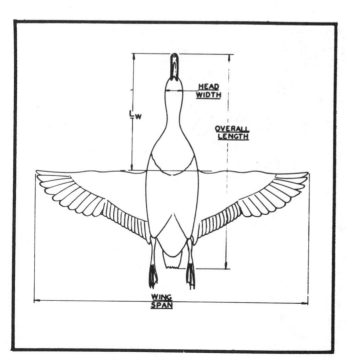

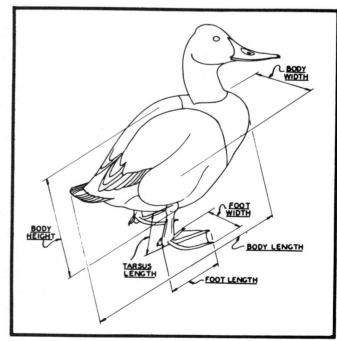

WATERFOWL

SPECIES	SEX	OVERALL LENGTH	WING-SPAN	WEIGHT (lb./oz.)	BODY LENGTH	BODY WIDTH	BODY HEIGHT	HEAD WIDTH	FOOT LENGTH	FOOT WIDTH	TARSUS LENGTH	L_w
Geese												
Common Canada goose	M	37.0	69.0	9/4	21.5	9.0	7.8	2.3	4.2	3.75	3.75	17.25
	F	35.0	64.0	7/14	20.0	8.5	7.25	2.1	4.0	3.6	3.7	16.5
Lesser Canada goose	M	29.0	58.0	6/0	18.0	8.0	6.75	1.9	3.25	3.0	3.5	13.25
	F	27.0	55.0	4/8	16.75	7.75	6.5	1.8	3.0	2.9	3.3	12.3
Cackling and Richardson's geese	M	25.0	52.0	3/8	16.0	6.4	5.8	1.7	2.75	2.5	3.0	10.75
	F	23.0	48.5	2/14	14.75	6.2	5.6	1.65	2.7	2.4	2.9	10.0
White-fronted goose	M	29.0	59.0	5/0	18.75	7.5	6.6	1.9	3.25	3.12	3.25	13.5
	F	26.75	55.5	4/13	17.12	6.9	6.45	1.85	3.12	3.0	3.2	12.5
Lesser snow and blue geese	M	29.0	58.0	5/5	19.0	7.5	6.75	1.9	3.25	3.12	3.75	13.5
	F	27.6	56.5	4/11	18.0	7.12	6.3	1.85	3.1	3.0	3.7	12.9
Ross's goose	M	24.5	51.0	2/15	16.0	6.5	6.0	1.8	2.75	2.5	3.12	10.5
	F	23.0	49.5	2/11	15.0	6.1	5.7	1.75	2.65	2.25	3.06	10.0
Black and American brant	M	25.0	47.0	3/5	16.0	6.6	6.0	1.7	2.75	2.5	3.0	10.75
	F	23.0	45.5	3/2	14.75	6.1	5.5	1.65	2.65	2.4	2.9	10.0
Barnacle goose	M	26.5	53.0	4/0	17.0	6.5	6.0	1.7	2.8	2.75	2.8	11.3
	F	23.5	52.0	3/9	15.37	6.0	5.6	1.65	2.7	2.65	2.75	10.3
Emperor goose	M	27.0	52.0	6/2	17.5	7.5	6.5	1.8	3.0	2.8	3.0	11.6
	F	26.5	51.0	6/0	17.12	7.25	6.37	1.8	3.0	2.8	3.0	11.4
River or Puddle Ducks												
Mallard and black	M	23.0	36.0	2/13	14.25	6.0	5.2	1.9	2.75	2.75	2.2	12.0
	F	21.5	35.0	2/6	13.25	5.8	5.0	1.8	2.7	2.7	2.1	10.0
Gadwall	M	21.0	35.0	2/0	13.25	5.6	4.9	1.8	2.4	2.3	1.75	9.7
	F	19.5	33.0	1/14	12.75	5.4	4.7	1.75	2.4	2.3	1.75	9.0
American widgeon	M	19.75	33.25	1/11	13.0	5.4	4.7	1.7	2.3	2.0	1.6	9.3
	F	18.5	31.0	1/9	12.0	5.2	4.5	1.6	2.3	2.0	1.6	8.7
Pintail	M	*26.0	35.0	2/2	*17.25	5.5	5.37	1.87	2.5	2.4	1.87	12.0
	F	20.75	32.0	1/13	13.0	5.2	5.0	1.8	2.4	2.3	1.87	10.0
Green-winged teal	M	15.8	24.6	0/13	9.5	3.87	3.7	1.7	1.6	1.6	1.37	7.6
	F	14.5	23.75	0/12	9.37	3.6	3.5	1.4	1.5	1.5	1.25	7.0
Blue-winged teal	M	15.8	24.6	0/13.5	10.0	4.3	4.0	1.4	1.75	1.75	1.37	7.8
	F	15.2	23.6	0/13.5	9.75	4.2	3.8	1.4	1.75	1.75	1.37	7.5
Cinnamon teal	M	16.0	25.0	0/13	10.0	4.3	4.0	1.4	1.75	1.75	1.37	8.0
	F	15.5	24.0	0/12	9.75	4.2	3.8	1.4	1.75	1.75	1.37	7.8
Shoveler	M	20.0	32.5	1/9	12.5	5.0	4.6	1.7	2.37	2.3	1.75	10.0
	F	18.6	29.8	1/4	11.6	4.6	4.2	1.6	2.25	2.2	1.75	9.75
Wood duck	M	19.0	29.25	1/4	12.5	4.75	4.5	1.65	2.25	2.1	1.70	9.5
	F	17.0	27.0	1/0	11.5	4.25	4.0	1.6	2.2	2.0	1.6	8.5

*Includes the 2.75-inch-long tail feathers.

Sea or Diving Ducks

SPECIES	SEX	OVERALL LENGTH	WING-SPAN	WEIGHT (lb./oz.)	BODY LENGTH	BODY WIDTH	BODY HEIGHT	HEAD WIDTH	FOOT LENGTH	FOOT WIDTH	TARSUS LENGTH	L_w
Redhead	M	19.75	32.5	2/7	12.0	5.25	4.6	2.0	3.0	3.6	1.87	9.7
	F	19.0	31.0	2/4	12.0	5.1	4.5	2.0	3.0	3.6	1.87	9.37
Canvasback	M	22.0	32.0	2/14	13.0	6.0	5.25	2.0	3.1	3.5	2.0	12.0
	F	20.9	30.5	2/12	12.6	6.0	5.2	2.0	3.1	3.5	2.0	11.3
Greater scaup	M	18.5	31.0	2/0	11.5	5.25	5.2	1.9	2.8	3.2	1.8	9.75
	F	17.5	30.0	1/15	11.5	5.25	5.0	1.9	2.8	3.2	1.8	9.0
Lesser scaup	M	17.0	28.75	1/14	10.25	5.0	4.75	1.75	2.7	3.18	1.75	8.75
	F	16.25	26.5	1/12	10.0	5.0	4.62	1.62	2.7	3.0	1.62	8.5
American golden-eye	M	19.0	30.5	2/1	12.5	5.4	5.2	2.0	3.0	3.3	1.75	10.0
	F	17.5	28.0	1/12	11.5	5.0	4.75	1.75	3.0	3.3	1.75	9.25
Barrow's golden-eye	M	20.0	31.4	2/6	13.0	5.5	5.25	2.0	3.0	3.25	1.75	10.75
	F	17.5	28.0	1/12	11.5	5.0	4.75	1.8	3.0	3.25	1.75	9.25
Ring-necked duck	M	17.0	28.75	1/11	10.5	5.0	4.75	1.7	2.75	3.0	1.6	9.75
	F	16.5	27.0	1/8	10.25	4.75	4.50	1.65	2.75	3.0	1.6	9.5
Bufflehead	M	14.75	23.5	1/0	10.0	4.37	4.0	2.0	2.25	2.5	1.37	6.37
	F	13.5	21.9	0/12	9.12	4.12	3.6	1.6	2.0	2.12	1.37	5.6
Old Squaw	M	*21.12	29.0	1/13	*16.37	5.0	4.75	1.75	2.4	2.6	1.56	9.5
	F	15.7	27.5	1/11	11.0	4.75	4.5	1.6	2.37	2.5	1.5	8.87
Harlequin	M	17.5	26.5	1/8	11.8	4.8	4.5	1.75	2.6	2.8	1.5	10.0
	F	15.9	24.0	1/3	10.75	4.5	4.1	1.6	2.5	2.6	1.5	9.0
Steller's eider	M	18.0	29.0	1/15	12.25	5.25	5.1	1.75	2.56	2.7	1.6	10.25
	F	17.5	28.75	1/13	11.87	5.12	5.1	1.6	2.5	2.68	1.6	10.0
American eider	M	24.0	40.0	4/6	16.2	6.8	6.56	1.6	3.35	3.54	2.37	11.7
	F	22.75	38.75	3/6	15.4	6.5	6.25	2.25	3.12	3.25	2.0	11.0
Pacific eider	M	25.75	43.0	5/12	17.37	7.3	7.0	2.0	3.6	3.7	2.4	12.56
	F	23.75	40.5	5/7	16.0	7.0	6.7	2.3	3.37	3.5	2.25	11.6
King eider	M	22.75	36.5	4/0	15.3	6.5	6.25	2.3	3.15	3.25	2.28	11.0
	F	21.0	36.4	3/10	14.25	6.3	6.0	2.25	2.84	3.09	2.12	10.25
Spectacled eider	M	21.75	36.25	3/10	14.5	6.2	5.95	2.25	2.75	2.83	1.8	10.6
	F	21.0	34.5	3/8	14.0	6.0	5.75	2.1	2.5	2.7	1.68	10.25
Hooded merganser	M	18.0	26.0	1/8	11.68	4.5	4.25	1.8	2.4	2.5	1.62	8.87
	F	17.0	24.5	1/4	11.0	4.25	4.0	1.6	2.37	2.4	1.5	8.37
American merganser	M	25.5	36.75	3/7	16.0	6.4	6.0	1.75	3.12	3.37	2.3	13.62
	F	23.5	35.5	2/6	14.75	5.4	4.8	1.6	3.0	3.0	2.12	12.5
Red-breasted merganser	M	23.0	33.25	2/10	14.37	5.5	5.2	1.75	3.0	3.25	2.25	12.25
	F	21.0	30.75	1/13	13.5	5.37	5.12	1.6	2.75	2.9	1.9	11.0
Ruddy duck	M	14.75	21.5	1/4	9.87	4.5	4.2	1.8	2.4	2.75	1.5	7.1
	F	14.0	21.0	1/2	9.37	4.0	3.8	1.7	2.4	2.75	1.5	6.75
White-winged scoter	M	21.5	38.0	3/7	14.5	6.12	5.9	2.0	3.54	3.75	2.5	10.5
	F	20.5	37.0	2/10	13.87	6.0	5.8	1.9	3.25	3.5	2.3	10.0
Surf scoter	M	19.6	32.0	2/3	13.6	5.6	5.4	2.0	3.25	3.5	2.0	9.4
	F	18.0	31.0	2/0	11.75	5.0	4.8	1.75	3.0	3.25	2.0	8.75
American scoter	M	19.75	33.0	2/8	13.0	6.0	5.8	2.0	3.25	3.5	2.0	9.5
	F	18.5	32.5	2/3	12.25	5.4	5.0	1.7	3.12	3.37	2.0	8.8

*Includes the 4.375-inch-long tail feathers.

UPLAND GAME BIRDS

SPECIES	SEX	OVERALL LENGTH	WING-SPAN	WEIGHT (lb./oz.)	BODY LENGTH	BODY WIDTH	BODY HEIGHT	HEAD WIDTH	FOOT LENGTH	FOOT WIDTH	TARSUS LENGTH	L_w
Ruffed grouse	M	18.0	24.0	1/6	13.1	4.5	3.9	1.62	2.36	2.5	2.1	6.8
	F	17.0	22.8	1/3.5	12.4	4.4	3.8	1.5	2.25	2.36	1.87	6.4
Sage grouse	M	30.0	36.0	5/5	21.9	8.5	7.35	1.87	2.87	2.8	2.4	11.5
	F	22.0	27.0	3/0	16.0	6.25	5.4	1.5	2.5	2.5	2.2	8.37
Sharp-tailed grouse	M	17.5	28.0	2/1	12.8	5.75	4.8	1.75	2.37	2.37	2.0	6.75
	F	17.5	28.0	1/13	12.8	5.5	4.5	1.56	2.37	2.37	2.0	6.75
Greater Prairie chicken	M	18.0	27.5	2/3	13.3	5.75	4.8	1.75	2.37	2.25	2.0	6.62
	F	18.0	27.5	1/13	13.3	5.62	4.7	1.56	2.25	2.25	1.9	6.62
Lesser Prairie chicken	M	16.0	24.4	1/15.5	11.8	5.7	4.7	1.5	2.25	2.25	1.9	5.9
	F	16.0	24.4	1/11.5	11.8	5.5	4.5	1.4	2.25	2.25	1.9	5.9
Blue grouse	M	22.0	31.0	2/13	15.37	5.87	5.25	1.4	2.5	2.31	2.2	7.8
	F	18.5	27.75	1/14	13.5	5.25	4.62	1.37	2.37	2.25	2.12	7.0
Spruce grouse	M	15.75	21.75	1/6	11.5	4.5	3.87	1.4	2.16	2.09	1.7	5.9
	F	15.5	21.0	1/5	11.3	4.4	3.8	1.3	2.16	2.89	1.7	5.87
Willow ptarmigan	M	17.0	26.5	1/12	11.25	5.0	4.6	1.5	2.04	1.9	1.5	6.4
	F	16.0	26.0	1/10	10.75	4.75	4.25	1.4	2.04	1.9	1.5	6.0
Rock ptarmigan	M	14.5	24.5	1/5	9.62	4.5	4.0	1.4	1.87	1.87	1.4	5.5
	F	13.5	23.75	1/4	9.0	4.6	4.0	1.3	1.87	1.87	1.4	5.2
White-tailed ptarmigan	M	12.0	19.5	1/1.5	8.0	4.2	3.8	1.25	1.7	1.7	1.2	4.5
	F	11.5	19.0	0/15	7.62	4.1	3.7	1.25	1.7	1.7	1.2	4.37
Bobwhite quail	M	10.0	15.0	0/9	7.5	3.5	3.25	1.25	1.56	1.56	1.5	3.0
	F	9.5	14.0	0/8.5	7.18	3.4	3.1	1.1	1.56	1.56	1.5	3.0
Scaled quail	M	11.0	15.0	0/8.7	8.25	3.5	3.25	1.25	1.5	1.5	1.4	3.1
	F	10.0	14.5	0/7.7	7.5	3.4	3.1	1.1	1.5	1.5	1.4	3.0
California quail	M	10.5	15.0	0/6.6	8.25	3.5	3.25	1.25	1.5	1.5	1.4	3.1
	F	9.5	14.0	0/6.5	7.5	3.25	3.0	1.1	1.5	1.5	1.4	3.0
Gambel's quail	M	11.0	15.0	0/7.3	8.25	3.5	3.25	1.25	1.5	1.5	1.4	3.1
	F	10.0	14.5	0/7.3	7.5	3.25	3.0	1.1	1.5	1.5	1.4	3.0
Mountain quail	M	10.5	17.0	0/10.3	8.5	4.0	3.5	1.3	1.75	1.75	1.56	4.0
	F	10.25	16.5	0/10	8.37	3.8	3.25	1.2	1.75	1.75	1.56	3.9
Harlequin quail	M	9.0	17.0	0/7.9	6.0	3.5	3.25	1.25	1.5	1.5	1.4	2.8
	F	8.5	16.5	0/7.1	5.75	3.25	3.0	1.12	1.5	1.5	1.4	2.7
Ring-necked pheasant	M	35.0	30.5	2/11	29.0	6.25	5.62	1.7	2.6	2.6	3.25	8.0
	F	24.0	28.0	2/2	19.0	6.0	5.25	1.6	2.5	2.5	3.12	6.87
Turkey	M	49.0	68.0	16/5	36.0	12.5	10.5	2.0	4.5	4.25	6.5	16.5
	F	36.0	48.0	9/5	26.5	9.25	8.0	1.9	3.75	3.50	5.75	12.0
Chukar partridge	M	13.5	22.4	1/4	10.0	4.5	3.87	1.4	2.12	2.0	1.9	5.0
	F	13.0	21.5	1/2	9.56	4.4	3.75	1.3	2.12	2.0	1.9	4.8
Gray partridge	M	13.0	21.5	1/0	9.6	4.3	3.75	1.4	2.0	2.0	1.8	4.8
	F	12.0	20.0	0/15.3	8.87	4.2	3.6	1.3	2.0	2.0	1.8	4.62

SPECIES	SEX	OVERALL LENGTH	WING-SPAN	WEIGHT (lb./oz.)	BODY			HEAD WIDTH	FOOT		TARSUS LENGTH	L_w
					LENGTH	WIDTH	HEIGHT		LENGTH	WIDTH		
Pigeons and Doves												
Mourning dove	M & F	11.87	17.25	0/4.5	9.75	2.7	2.5	.81	1.18 / *1.68	1.18	1.0	3.82
White-winged dove	M & F	11.75	18.87	0/5.7	8.62	2.7	2.5	.81	1.37 / *2.06	1.37	1.12	3.8
Band-tailed pigeon	M & F	15.5	26.25	0/13	12.0	4.37	3.5	1.2	1.8 / *2.43	1.8	1.25	5.0
Shore Birds												
Wilson's snipe	M & F	10.5	16.75	0/4.2	6.5	2.62	2.37	1.0	1.65	1.56	1.35	5.5
Woodcock	M	10.5	16.5	0/6.2	6.37	3.25	2.75	1.12	1.75	1.6	1.3	5.5
	F	11.5	17.5	0/7.7	7.0	3.37	2.87	1.12	1.75	1.6	1.3	6.0
Marsh Dwellers												
King rail	M	16.0	22.5	0/11	9.6	3.7	3.5	1.25	2.8	3.2	2.6	8.87
	F	15.0	21.0	0/10	9.0	3.6	3.4	1.25	2.8	3.2	2.6	8.25
Virginia rail	M & F	10.5	14.25	0/3.6	6.3	2.4	2.6	1.0	1.8	1.7	1.62	5.75
Clapper rail	M	15.0	21.0	0/12	9.0	3.8	4.0	1.25	2.75	3.15	2.56	8.25
	F	14.0	19.0	0/11	8.4	3.7	3.9	1.2	2.67	2.95	2.4	7.75
Sora rail	M & F	9.75	14.0	0/2	5.62	2.12	2.25	.8	1.75	1.96	1.28	4.5
Common gallinule	M & F	14.0	23.5	1/0	10.0	4.12	3.5	1.25	3.37 / *4.75	4.0	2.56	6.3
Coot	M & F	15.25	26.25	1/6	10.25	4.75	4.75	1.37	3.37 / *4.5	3.75	2.5	7.0

*Including length of hind toe.

12
Game Bird
Feet and Tarsi

The proper location and position of the tarsi for a given pose or activity are very important considerations in planning a standing carving. Approximate tarsi locations, both profile and front view, for game birds in their normal, relaxed stance are given below. The bird's leg (tarsus) location in the profile view is extremely variable, inasmuch as its location and position are affected by three points of articulation. (The location of a man's leg relative to his body is affected by two points of articulation.) The location and position of the tarsus in the front view are not quite as variable since the femur (thigh) on a bird articulates fore and aft only. The carver should be thoroughly familiar with the bone structure and points of articulation of the bird's legs and tarsi. See Chapter 3, especially Figures 3-10 and 11.

Representative photographs (which can be scaled) of the tarsi and feet of the different game bird families are presented on the following pages. The tarsi and feet of birds in the same family (subfamily, in the case of waterfowl) are similar, except for size. Therefore, by using the dimensions given in Chapter 11 in conjunction with these pictures, the size and shape of the foot and tarsus for a particular game bird can be approximated with a fair amount of accuracy.

Family or Subfamily	H (%)	*W (%)
Waterfowl		
Geese	38-42	50
River or puddle ducks	45-50	54-58
Sea or diving ducks and mergansers	45-55	60-65
Ruddy duck	50	60-65
Tree duck	50	55
Upland game birds		
Quails	30-35	40-45
Partridges	35-45	40-45
Pheasant	25	40-45
Grouse	35-40	40-45
Turkey	35	40-45
Pigeons and doves	35	45
Shore birds	45	40-45
Marsh dwellers	35-40	40-45

*Considerably less when bird is striding, especially upland game birds.

Approximate Tarsi Location

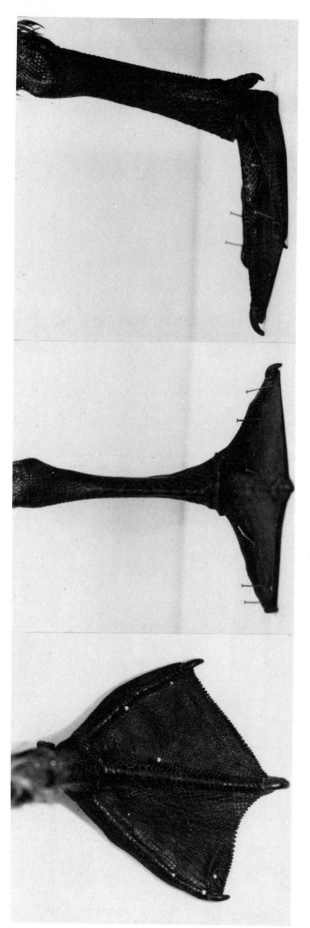

Lesser Canada goose, right foot (13/16 life-size).

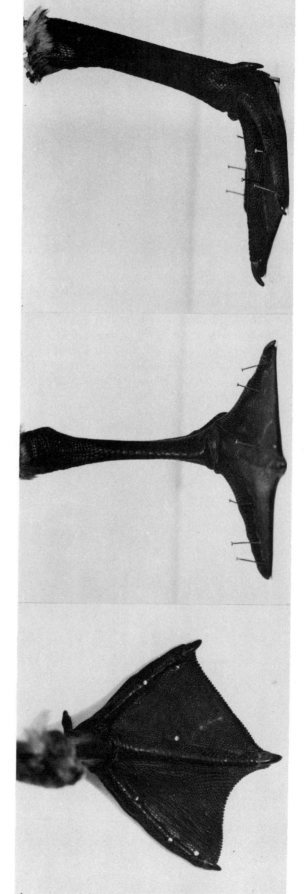

Cackling Canada goose, right foot (13/16 life-size).

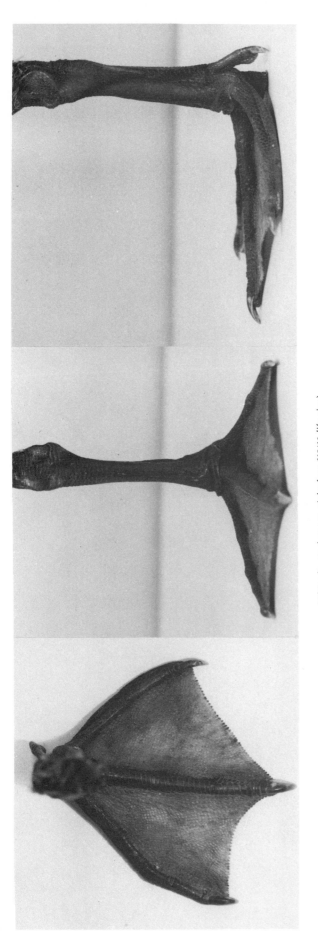

White-fronted goose, right foot (13/16 life-size).

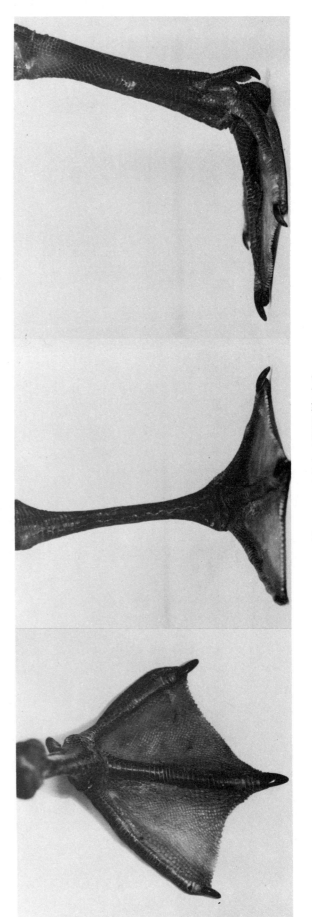

Lesser snow or blue goose, right foot (13/16 life-size).

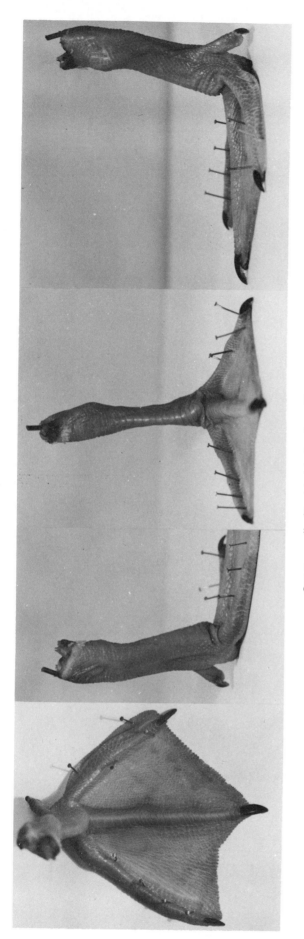

Common mallard (male), right foot (13/16 life-size).

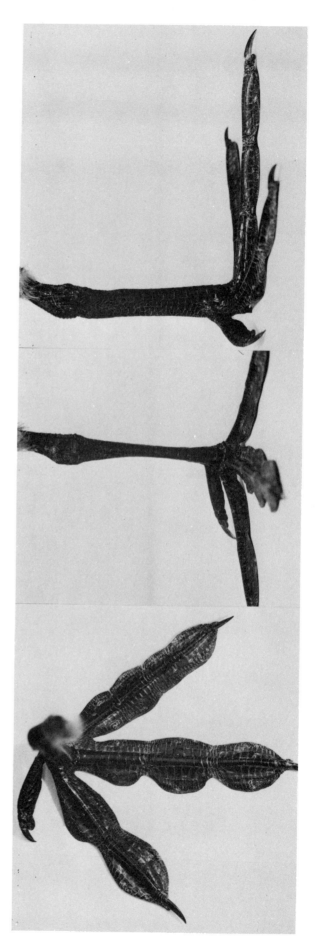

Coot, left foot (13/16 life-size).

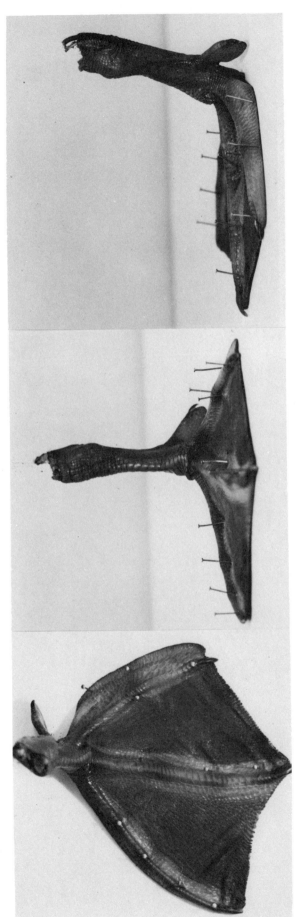

Canvasback (female), right foot (13/16 life-size).

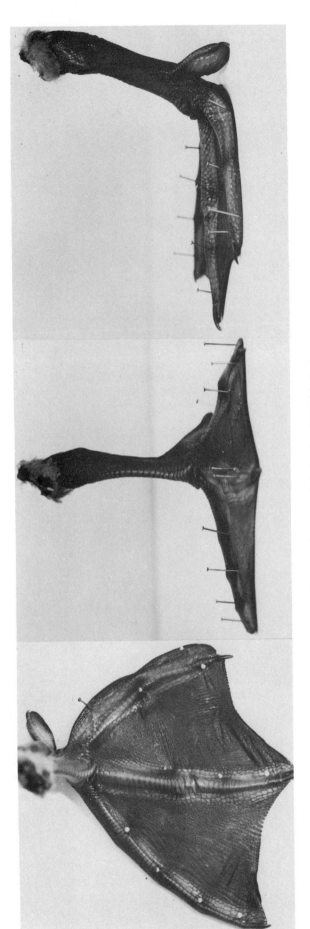

White-winged scoter (male), right foot (13/16 life-size).

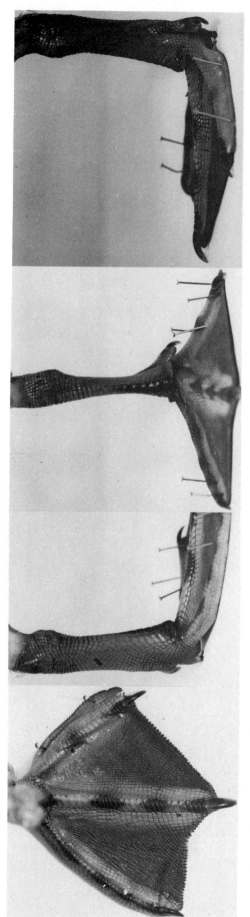
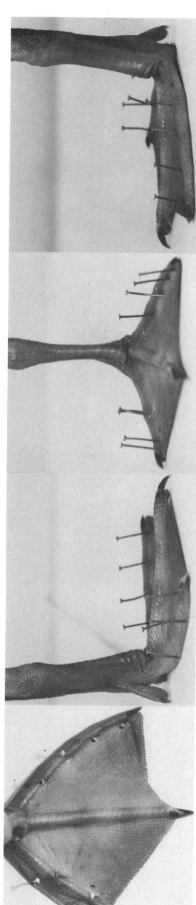
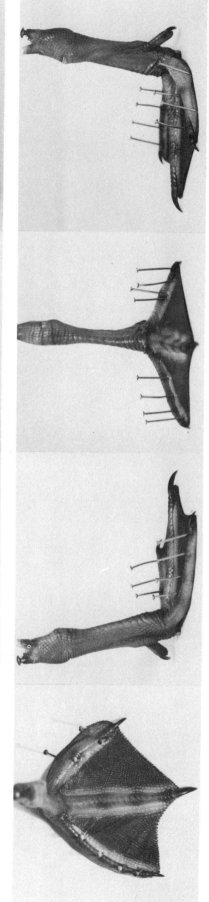

Top row: Pintail (male), right foot (life-size).

Center row: Shoveler (male), left foot (life-size).

Bottom row: Green-winged teal (male), right foot (life-size).

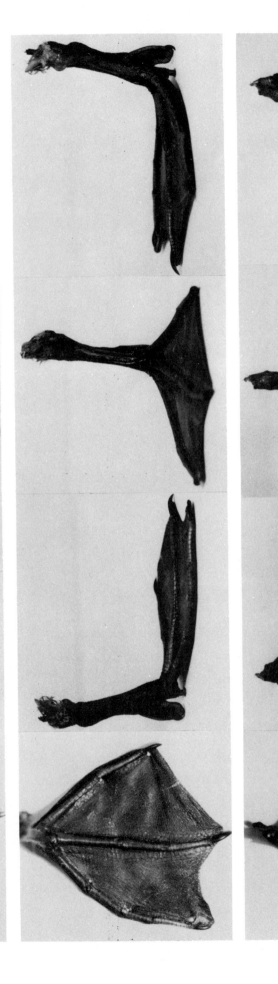

Top row: Ruddy duck (male), right foot (life-size).

Center row: Bufflehead (male), right foot (life-size).

Bottom row: Wilson's snipe (male), right foot (life-size).

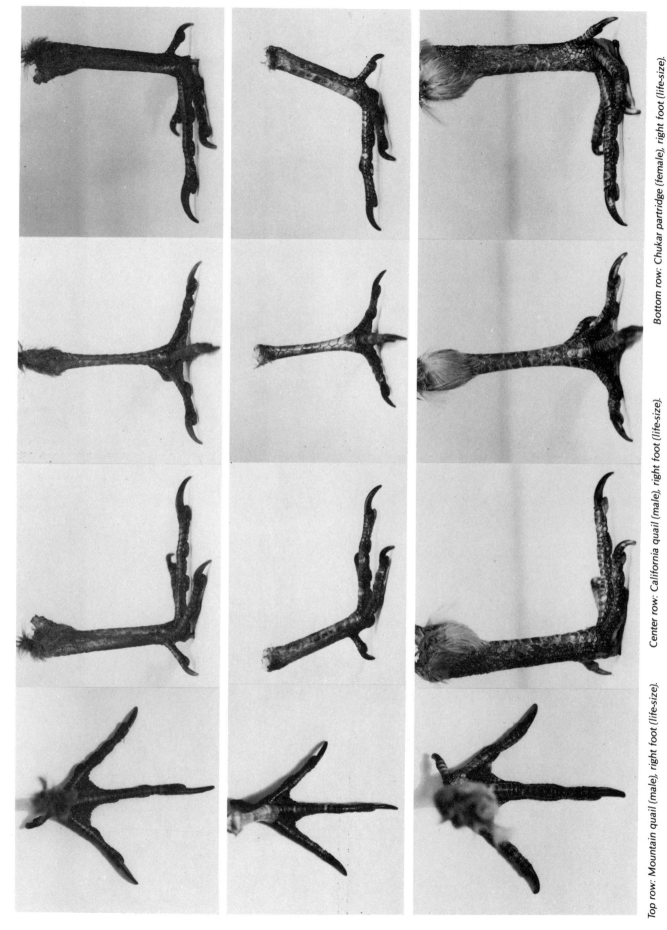

Top row: Mountain quail (male), right foot (life-size).   Center row: California quail (male), right foot (life-size).   Bottom row: Chukar partridge (female), right foot (life-size).

Ring-necked pheasant (male), right foot (13/16 life-size).

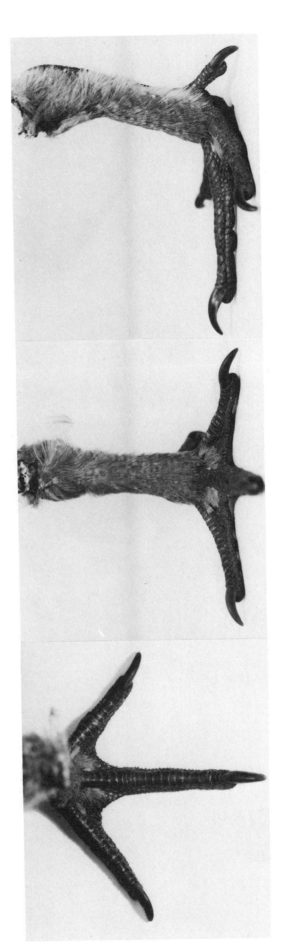

Blue grouse (male), right foot (life-size).

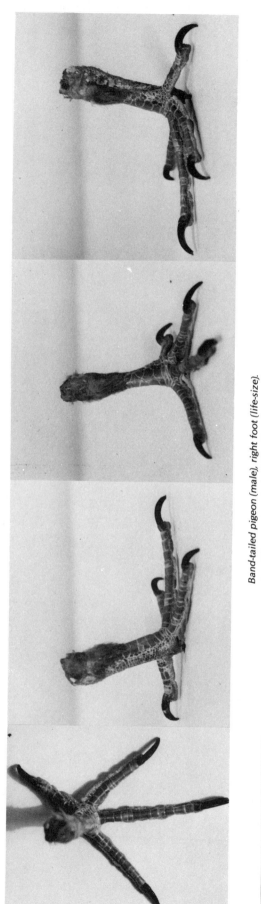

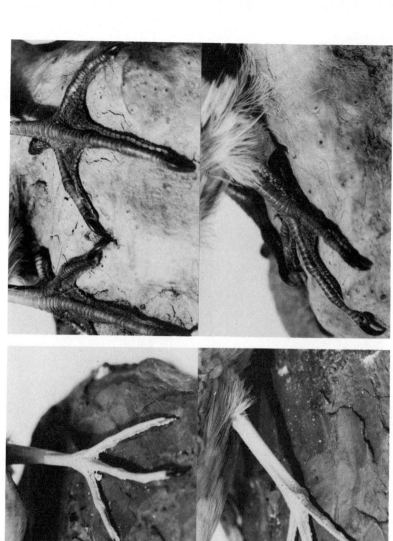

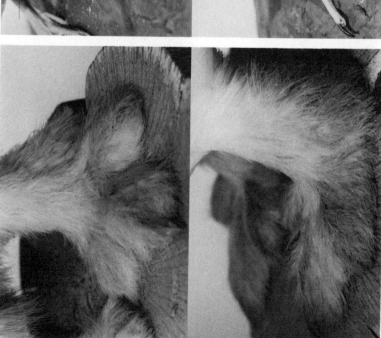

Band-tailed pigeon (male), right foot (life-size).

Ruffed grouse, left foot (life-size).

Woodcock, left foot (life-size).

Willow ptarmigan, left foot (life-size).

CHAPTER 13

Game Bird Bills

The size and shape of the bill on a particular game bird is fixed and must be accurately duplicated to achieve an advanced or professional carving. Obviously, having an actual three-dimensional specimen from which to work is ideal. For those carvers who do not have access to game bird specimens, life-size photographs of the profile, top, and bottom views of the bills of all the game birds are included in this chapter.

INDEX TO SPECIES

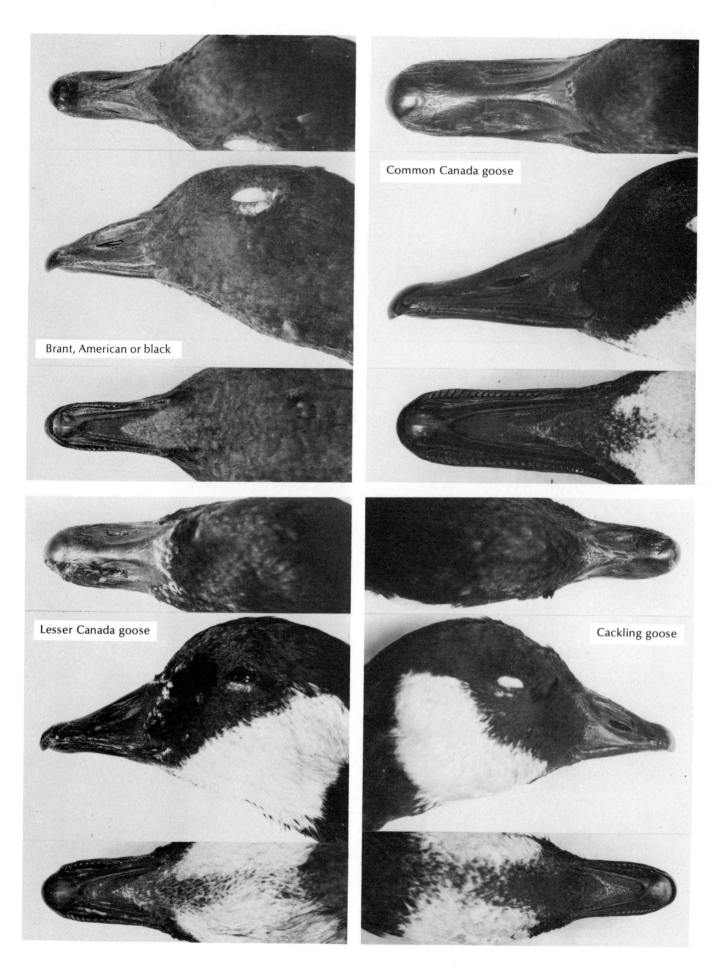

Common Canada goose

Brant, American or black

Lesser Canada goose

Cackling goose

Emperor goose

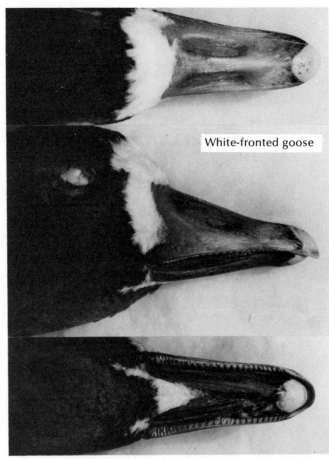

White-fronted goose

Ross's goose

Snow or blue goose

American widgeon (male)

American widgeon (female)

Gadwall (male)

Gadwall (female)

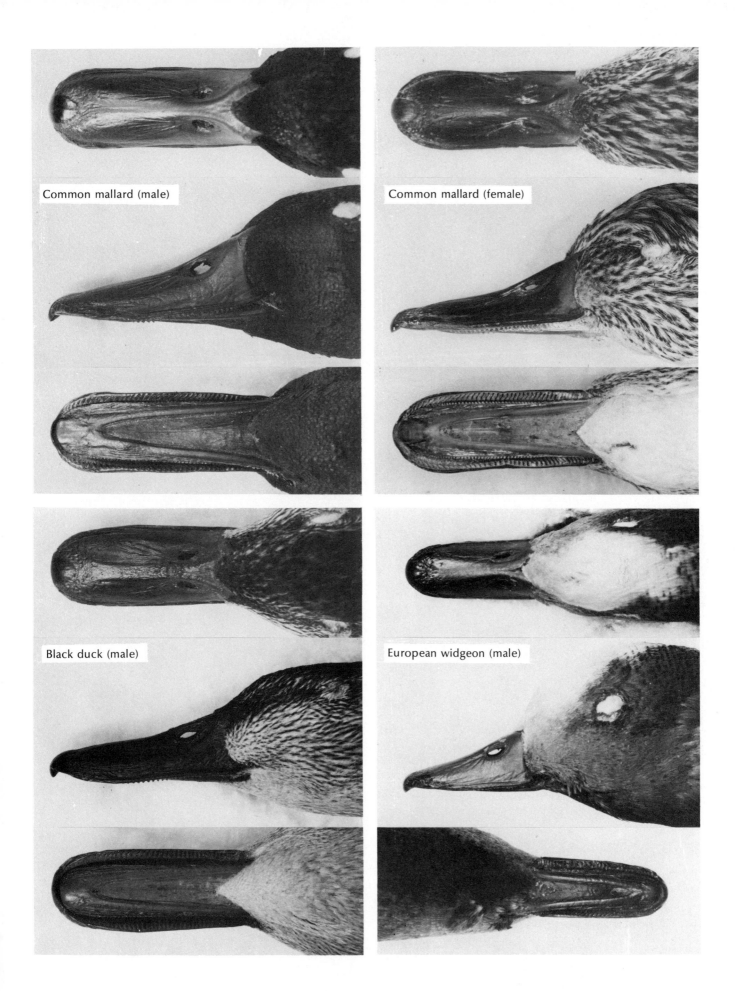

Common mallard (male)

Common mallard (female)

Black duck (male)

European widgeon (male)

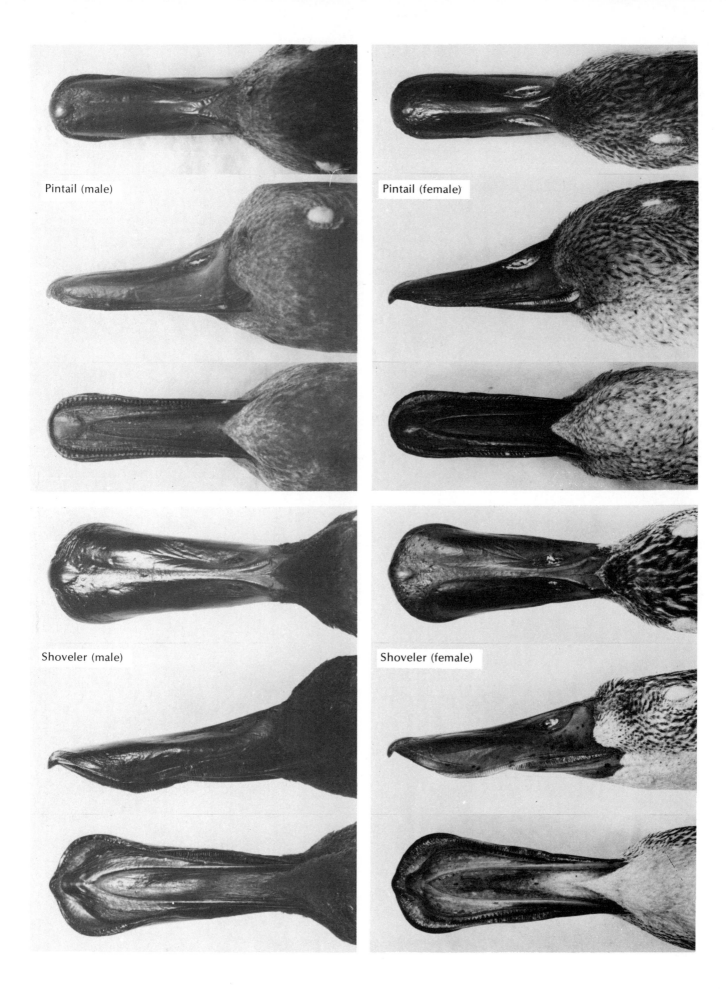

Pintail (male)

Pintail (female)

Shoveler (male)

Shoveler (female)

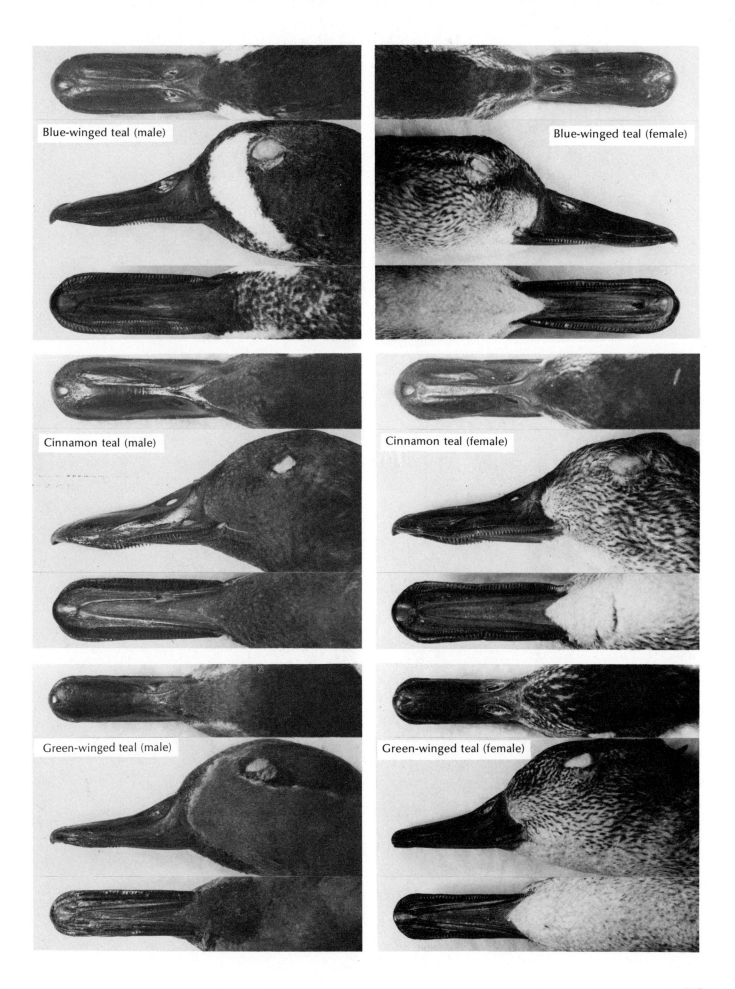

Blue-winged teal (male)

Blue-winged teal (female)

Cinnamon teal (male)

Cinnamon teal (female)

Green-winged teal (male)

Green-winged teal (female)

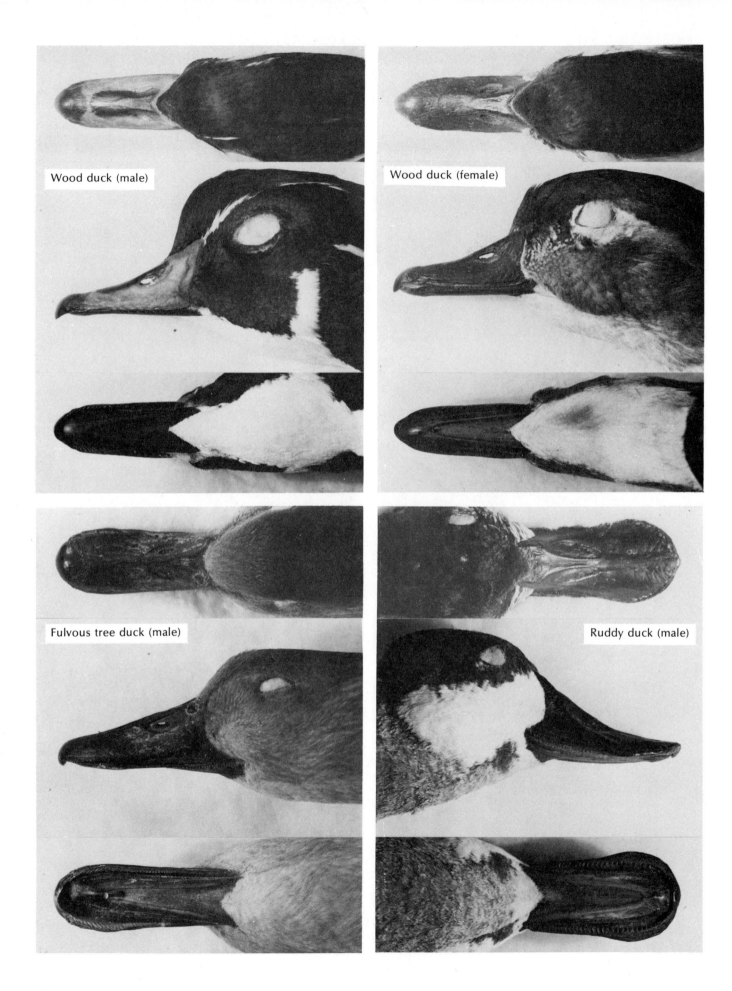

Wood duck (male)

Wood duck (female)

Fulvous tree duck (male)

Ruddy duck (male)

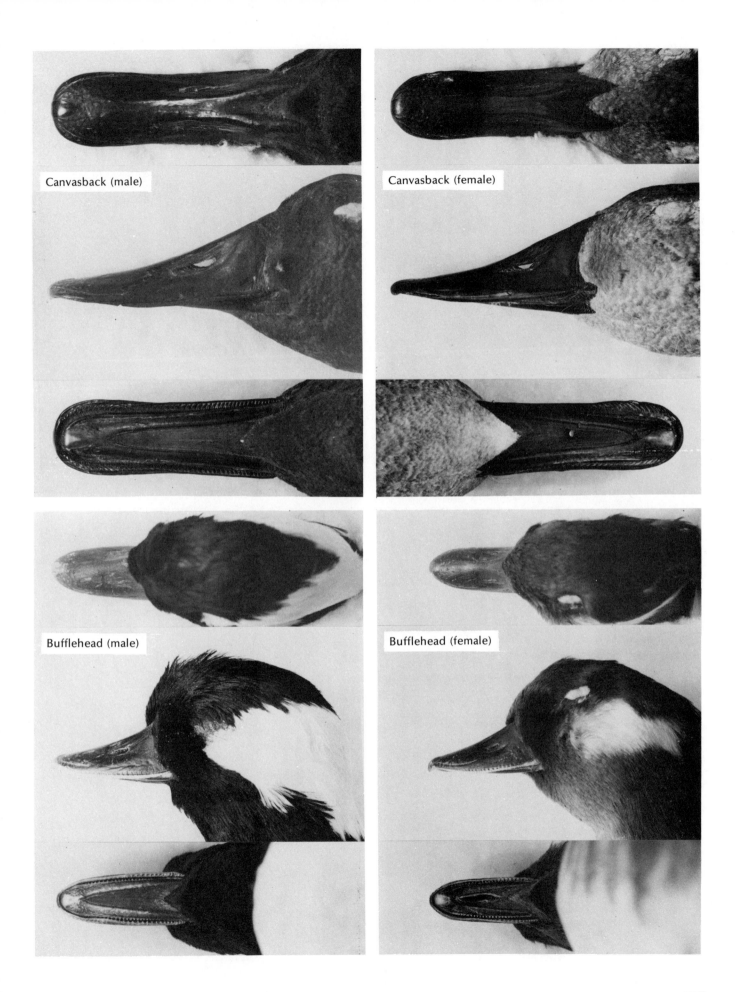

Canvasback (male)

Canvasback (female)

Bufflehead (male)

Bufflehead (female)

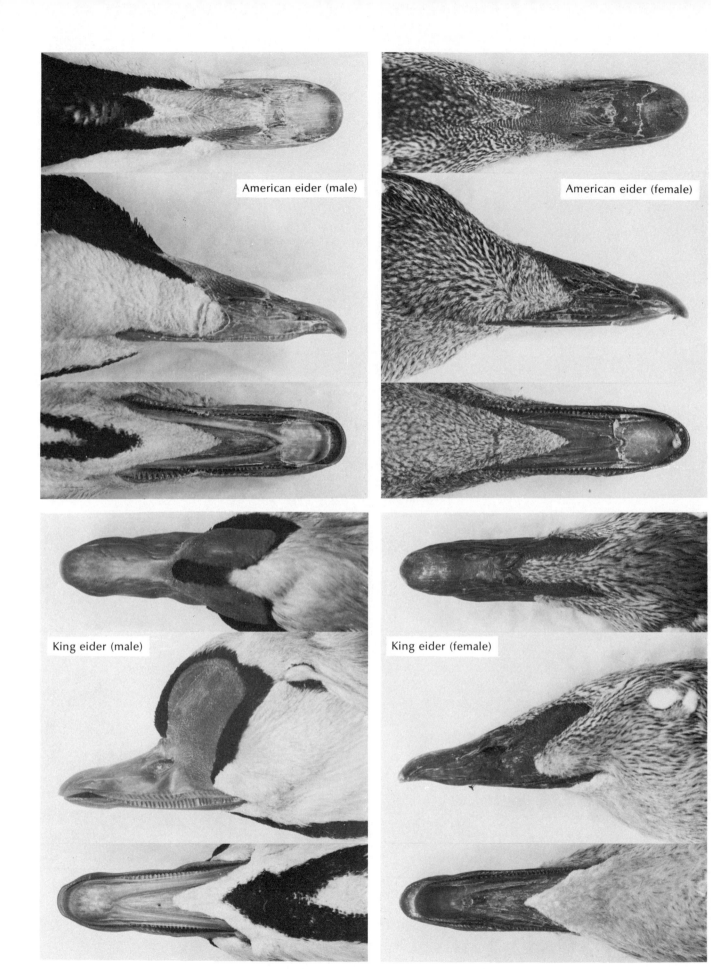

American eider (male)

American eider (female)

King eider (male)

King eider (female)

Spectacled eider (male)

Spectacled eider (female)

Steller's eider (male)

Steller's eider (female)

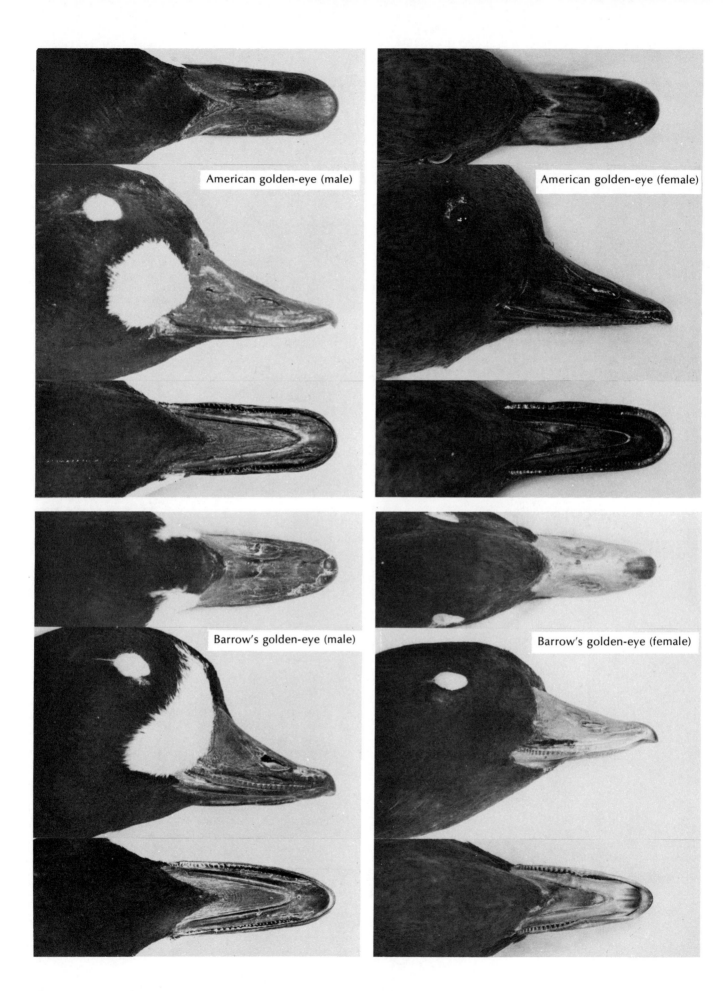

American golden-eye (male)

American golden-eye (female)

Barrow's golden-eye (male)

Barrow's golden-eye (female)

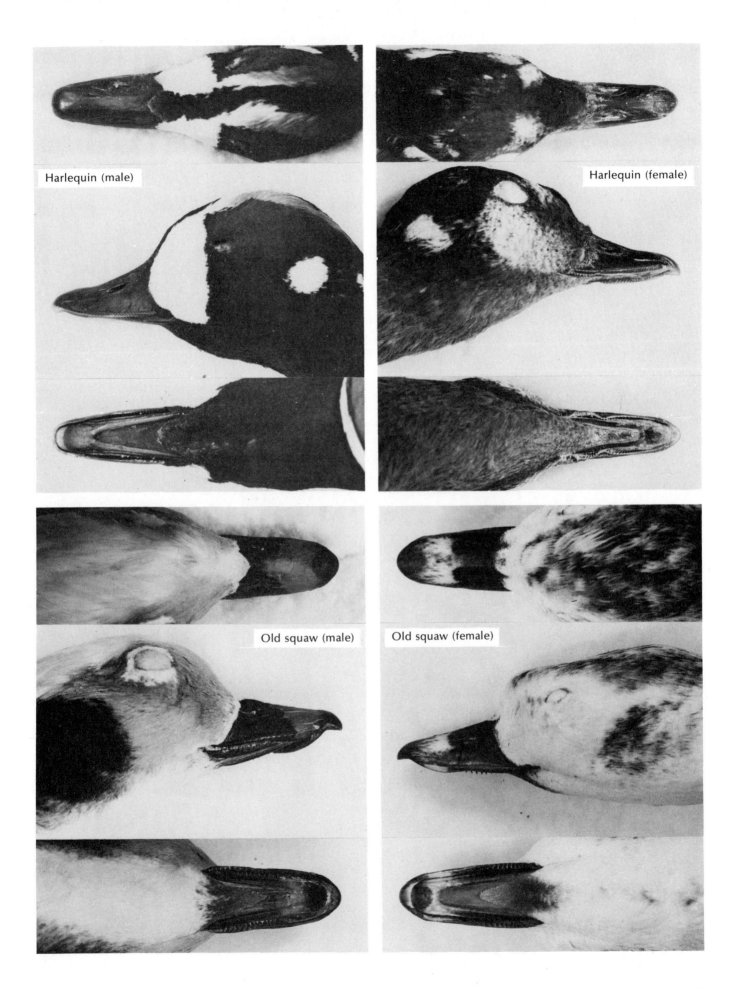

Harlequin (male)

Harlequin (female)

Old squaw (male)

Old squaw (female)

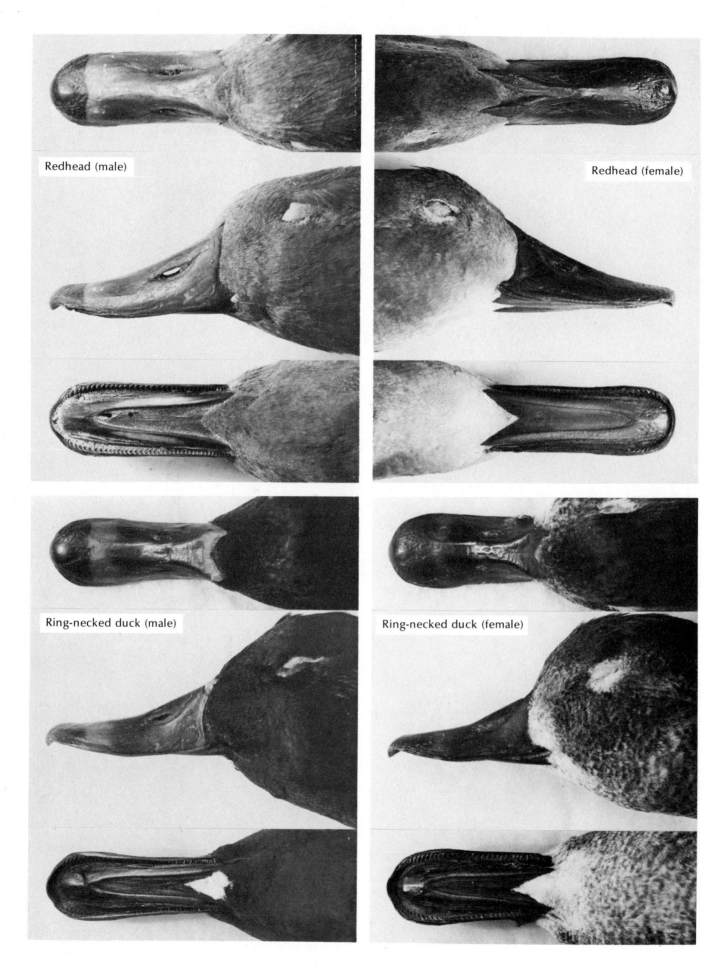

Redhead (male)

Redhead (female)

Ring-necked duck (male)

Ring-necked duck (female)

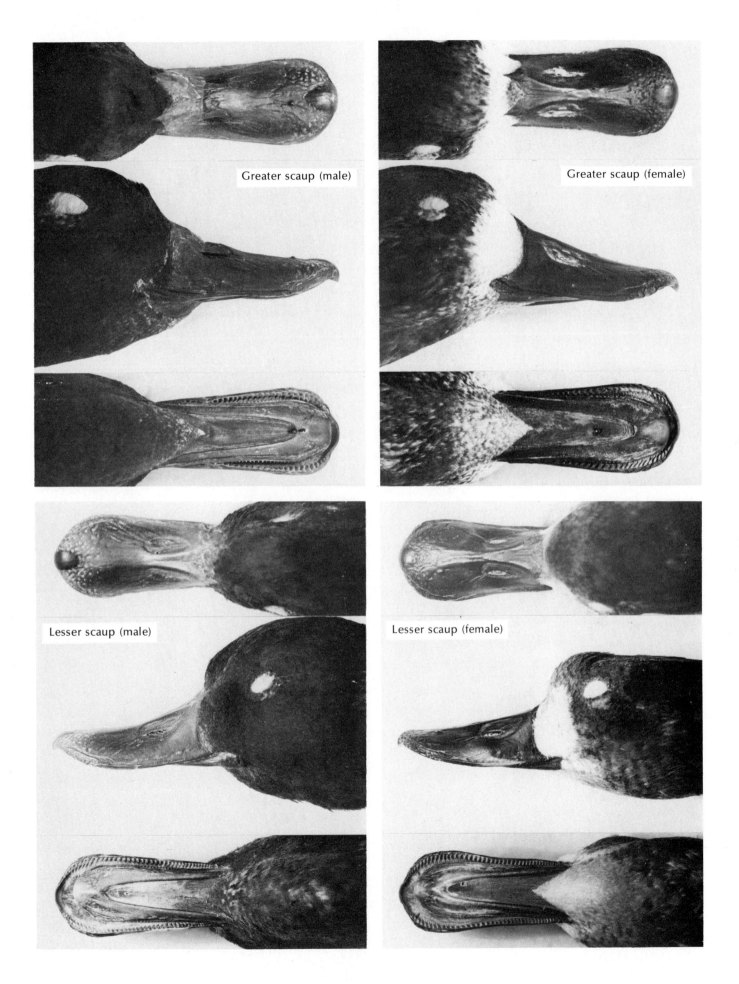

Greater scaup (male)

Greater scaup (female)

Lesser scaup (male)

Lesser scaup (female)

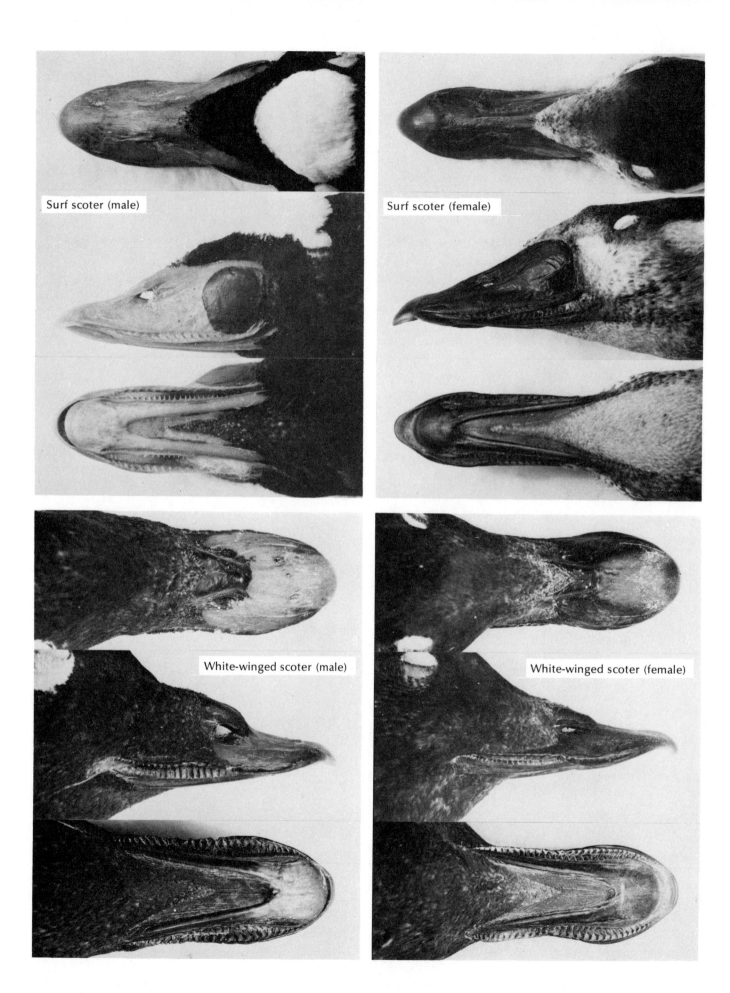

Surf scoter (male)

Surf scoter (female)

White-winged scoter (male)

White-winged scoter (female)

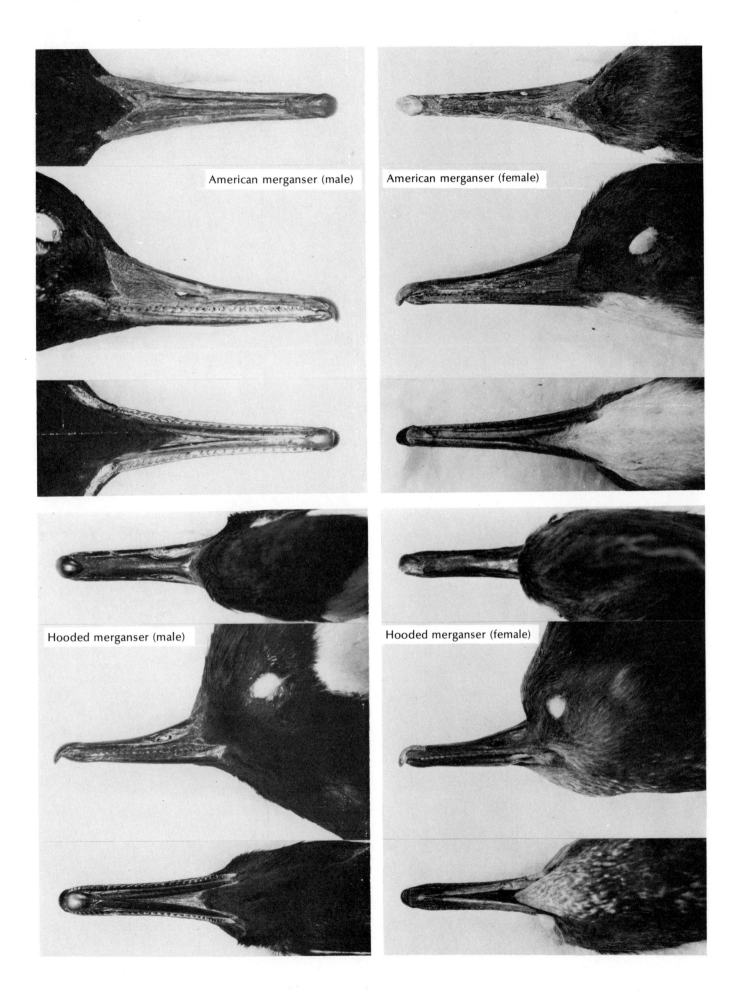

American merganser (male)

American merganser (female)

Hooded merganser (male)

Hooded merganser (female)

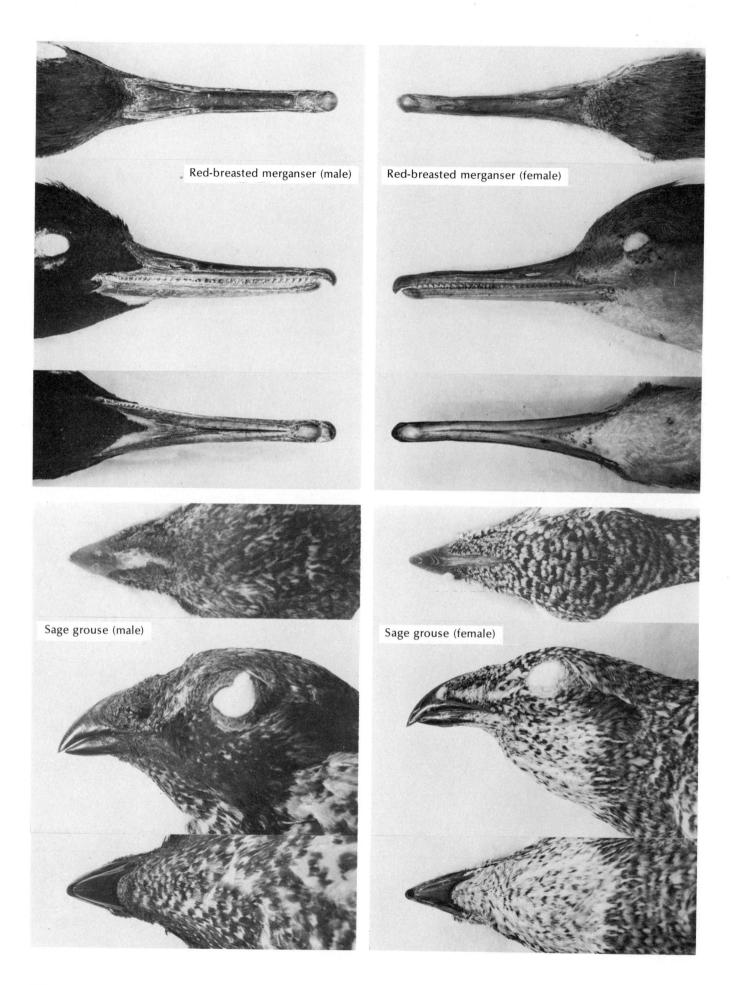

Red-breasted merganser (male)

Red-breasted merganser (female)

Sage grouse (male)

Sage grouse (female)

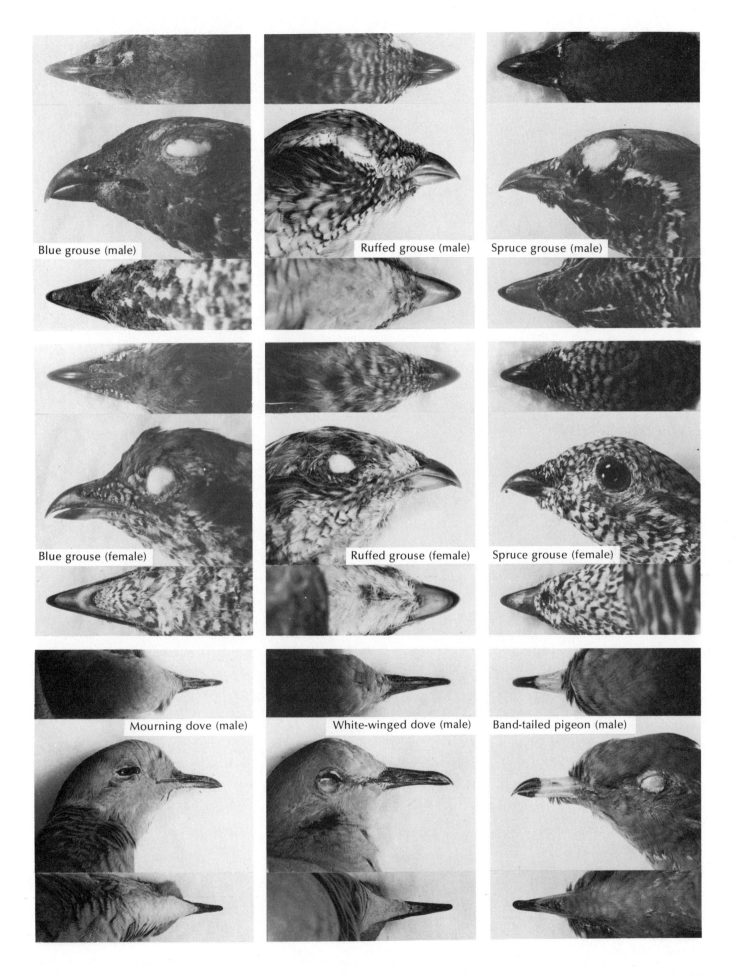

Blue grouse (male)

Ruffed grouse (male)

Spruce grouse (male)

Blue grouse (female)

Ruffed grouse (female)

Spruce grouse (female)

Mourning dove (male)

White-winged dove (male)

Band-tailed pigeon (male)

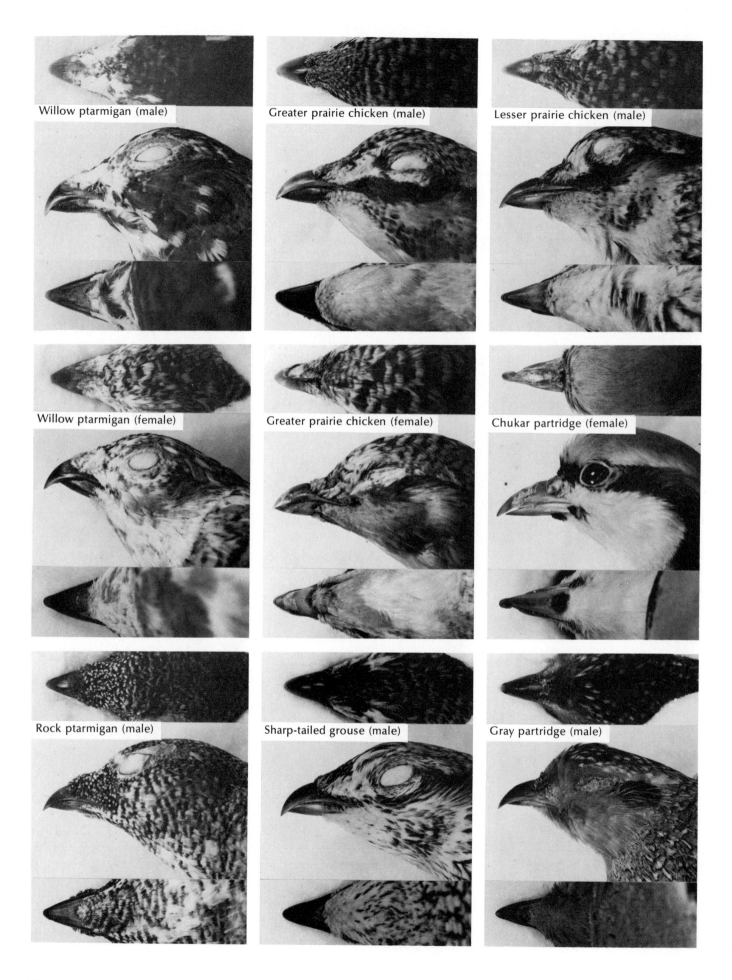

Willow ptarmigan (male)

Greater prairie chicken (male)

Lesser prairie chicken (male)

Willow ptarmigan (female)

Greater prairie chicken (female)

Chukar partridge (female)

Rock ptarmigan (male)

Sharp-tailed grouse (male)

Gray partridge (male)

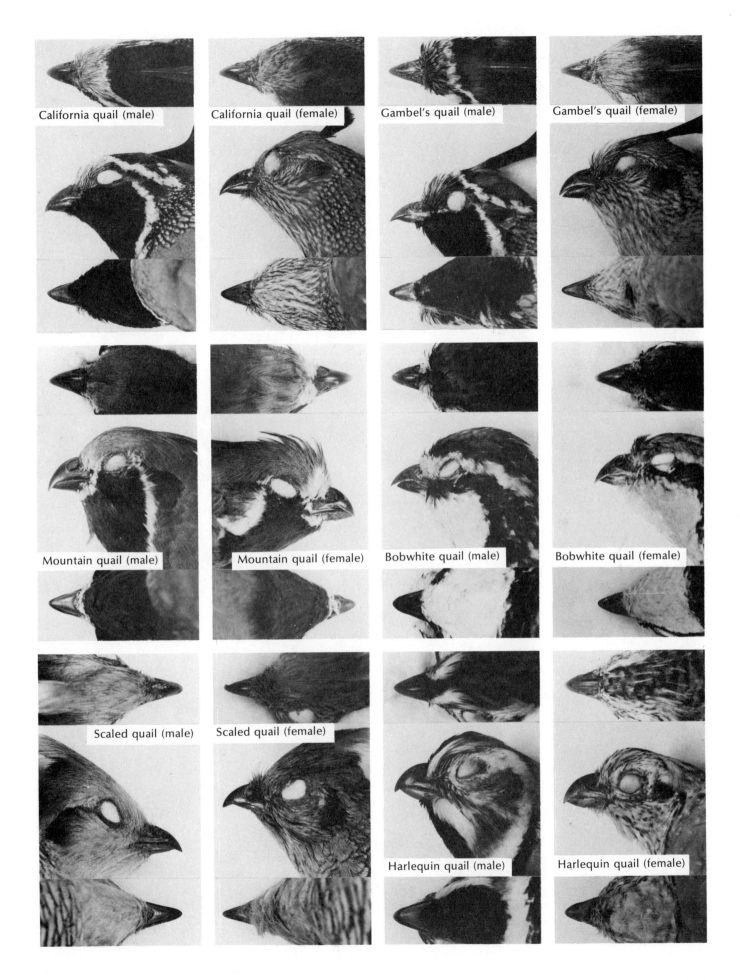

California quail (male)

California quail (female)

Gambel's quail (male)

Gambel's quail (female)

Mountain quail (male)

Mountain quail (female)

Bobwhite quail (male)

Bobwhite quail (female)

Scaled quail (male)

Scaled quail (female)

Harlequin quail (male)

Harlequin quail (female)

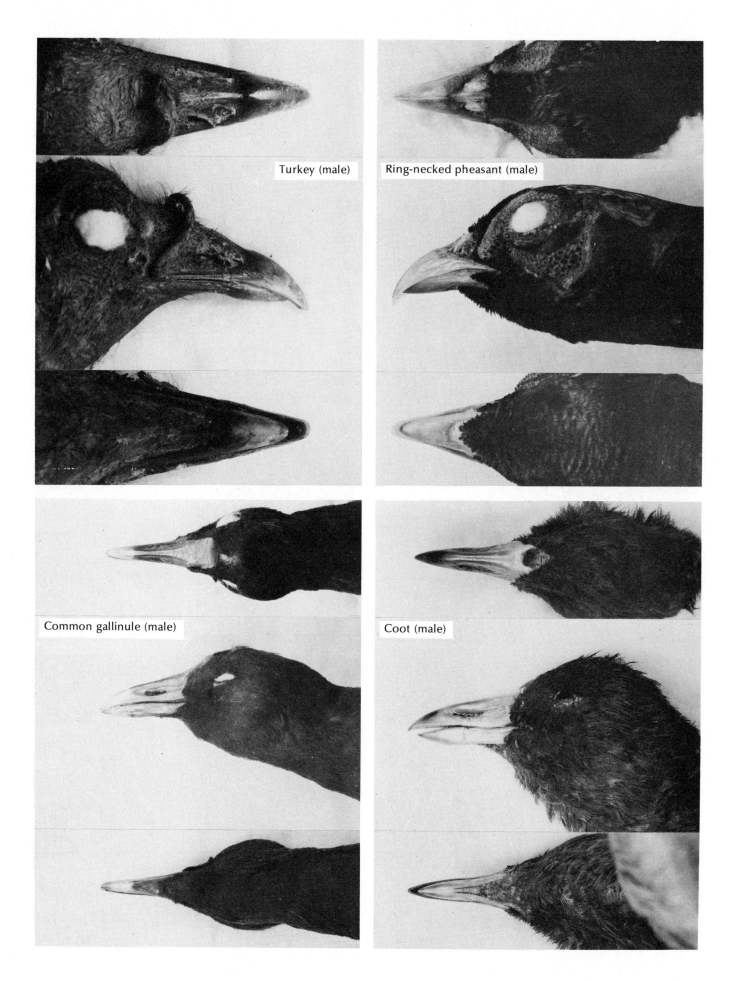

Turkey (male)

Ring-necked pheasant (male)

Common gallinule (male)

Coot (male)

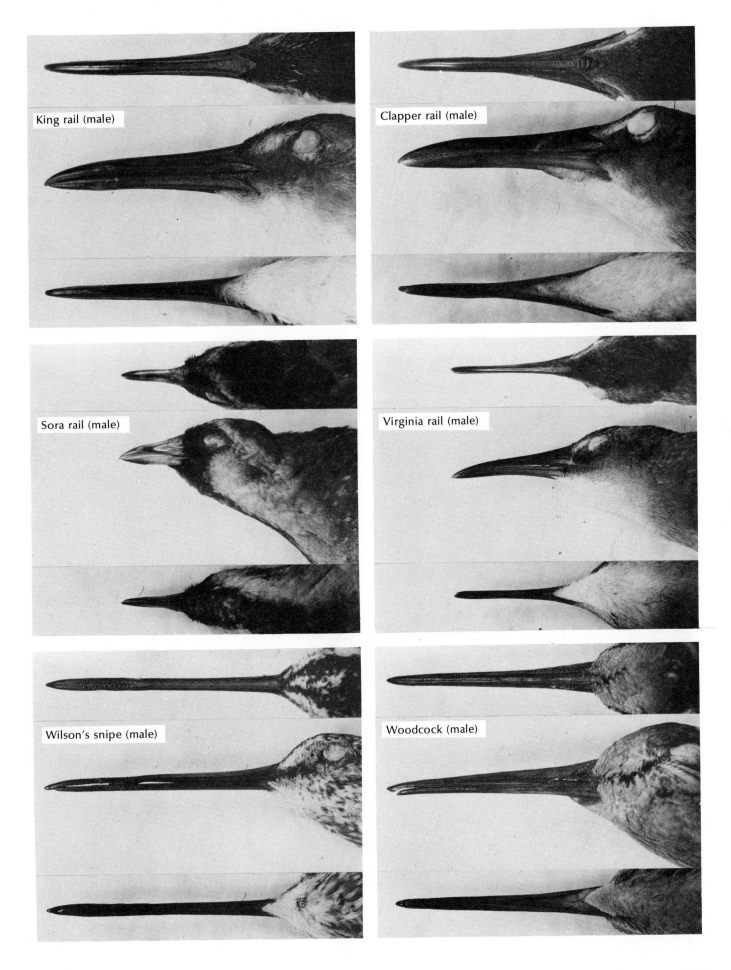

King rail (male)

Clapper rail (male)

Sora rail (male)

Virginia rail (male)

Wilson's snipe (male)

Woodcock (male)

Appendix

SOURCES OF INFORMATION

Game Bird Pictures

Allan, Arthur A. *Stalking Birds with a Color Camera*. National Geographic Society, (out of print).

——. "Duck Hunting with a Color Camera." *National Geographic*, October 1951.

Audubon Magazine. National Audubon Society, 950 Third Ave., New York, N.Y. 10022.

Bauer, Erwin A. *Duck Hunter's Bible* (paperback). Doubleday, n.d.

Burk, Bruce. *Waterfowl Studies*. Winchester Press, 1976.

Butcher, Devereau. *Seeing America's Wildlife in Our National Refuges*. Devin-Adair, (out of print).

Clement, Roland C. *The Living World of Audubon*. Grosset and Dunlap, (out of print).

Hanson, Harold C. *The Giant Canada Goose*. Southern Illinois University Press, 1965.

Heintzelman, Donald S. *North American Ducks, Geese, and Swans*. Winchester Press, 1978.

Johnsgard, Paul A. *Grouse and Quails of North America*. University of Nebraska Press, 1973.

——. *Handbook of Waterfowl Behavior*. Comstock Pub. Assoc. (Cornell University Press), 1965.

——. *North American Game Birds of Upland and Shoreline*. University of Nebraska Press, 1975.

——. *Waterfowl of North America*. Indiana University Press, 1975.

——. *Waterfowl: Their Biology and Natural History*. University of Nebraska Press, 1968.

Kortright, F.H. *The Ducks, Geese, and Swans of North America* (rev. ed.). Stackpole, 1975.

Lansdowne, James F. *Birds of the Eastern Forest*. 2 vols. Houghton Mifflin, 1968.

——. *Birds of the Northern Forest*. Houghton Mifflin, 1966.

Linduska, Joseph P., ed. *Waterfowl Tomorrow*. Washington, D.C.: U.S. Government Printing Office.

Line, Les, and Russell, Franklin. *The Audubon Society Book of Wild Birds*. Harry N. Abrams, 1976.

National Wildlife Magazine. 1412 Sixteenth St., NW, Washington, D.C. 20036.

Queeny, Edgar M. *Prairie Wings* (reprint of 1946 ed.). Schiffer, 1979.

Rand, Austin L. *American Water and Game Birds*. Dutton, (out of print).

Spaulding, Edward S. *The Quails*. Macmillan, (out of print).

Terres, John K. *The Audubon Society Encyclopedia of North American Birds*. Alfred A. Knopf, 1980.

Todd, Frank S. *Waterfowl: Ducks, Geese, and Swans of the World*. Harcourt Brace Jovanovich, 1979.

Van Wormer, Joe. *The World of the Canada Goose*. Lippincott, 1968.

Water, Prey, and Game Birds of North America. National Geographic Society, n.d.

Williams, Cecil S. *Honker*. D. Van Nostrand, (out of print).

Zim, Herbert, and Sprunt, Alexander. *Game Birds*. Western, 1961.

Bird Anatomy

Aymar, Gordon. *Bird Flight*. Dodd, Mead, (out of print).

Beebe, C. William. *The Bird*. Dover, (out of print).

Darling, Lois and Louis. *Bird*. Houghton Mifflin, (out of print).

Pettingill, Olin Sewall, Jr. *Ornithology in Laboratory and Field*. Burgess, 1970.

Bird Carving

Chip Chats Magazine. National Woodcarvers' Association, 7424 Miami Ave., Cincinnati, Ohio 45243.

Decoy Collector's Guide Magazine. Harold D. Sorenson, 213 Franklin St., Burlington, Iowa 52601.

Gilley, Wendell. *The Art of Bird Carving*. Hillcrest Publications, 190 South 100 East, Spanish Fork, Utah 84660.

Lacey, John. *How to do Wood Carving*. Fawcett, (out of print).

Le Master, Richard. *Wildlife in Wood*. Chillicothe, Ill.: Modern Technology, Inc., 1978.

Murphy, Charles F. *Working Plans for Working Decoys*. Winchester Press, 1979.

North American Decoys Magazine. Hillcrest Publications, 190 South 100 East, Spanish Fork, Utah 84660.

Small, Anne. *Masters of Decorative Bird Carving*. Winchester Press, 1981.

Starr, Jr., George Ross. *How to Make Working Decoys*. Winchester Press, 1978.

Tawes, William I. *Creative Bird Carving*. Cornell Maritime, 1969.

Photography

Jacobs, Lou, Jr. *Amphoto Guide to Lighting*. Amphoto, 1979.

Oberrecht, Kenn. *The Outdoor Photographer's Handbook*. Winchester Press, 1979.

Studio Lighting for Product Photography. Kodak Professional Data Book No. 0-16.

Warham, John. *The Technique of Bird Photography*. Focal Press, 1973.

Taxidermy

Blake, Emmet R. *Preserving Birds for Study*. Chicago Natural History Museum, (out of print).

Elwood, J.W. *Lessons in Taxidermy*. Omaha, Neb.: Northwestern School of Taxidermy.

Herter, George Leonard, and Barrie, Myron E. *The Science of Modern Taxidermy*. Waseca, Minn.: Herter's Inc.

Moyer, John W. *Practical Taxidermy*. Ronald Press Co.

Pray, Leon L. *Taxidermy*. Macmillan, 1943.

——. *Bird Studies for the Taxidermist*. Greenfield Center, N.Y.: Modern Taxidermist Publication.

Cast Feet

Richard Delise, 920 Springwood Drive, West Chester, Penn. 19380.

Glass Eyes

Christian J. Hummul Co., P.O. Box 2877, Baltimore, Md., 21225.
Herter's Inc., Route 1, Waseca, Minn. 56093.
Robert J. Smith, 14900 West 31st Ave., Golden, Col. 80401.
Tohickon Glass Eyes, P.O. Box 15, Erwinna, Penn. 18920.
West Coast Taxidermy Supply Co., 648 San Mateo Ave., San Bruno, Calif. 94066.

Carving Tools

Brookstone Co., 127 Vose Farm Road, Peterborough, N.H. 03458.
Constantine's, 2050 Eastchester Rd., Bronx, N.Y. 10461.
Curtis Woodcraft Supply Co., 344 Grandview St., Memphis, Tenn. 38111.
Foredom Electric Co., Inc., Bethel, Conn. 06801.
Harmen Company, Inc., 34 Parkway, Little Falls, N.J. 07424.
Leichtung, Inc., 4944 Commerce Parkway, Cleveland, Ohio 44128.
Knott's Knives, 106 South Ford Ave., Wilmington, Del. 19805.
Nick Purdo, 27340 Jean, Warren, Mich. 48093. (Custom knives.)
Syracuse Woodcarving Supply, 2910 Erie Blvd., Syracuse, N.Y. 13224.
Wildlife Carving Supply Headquarters, 317 Holyoke Ave., Beach Haven, N.J. 08008.
Wood Carvers Supply Co., 3056 Excelsior Blvd., Minneapolis, Minn. 55416.
Woodcraft Supply Corp., 313 Montvale Ave., Woburn, Mass. 01801.

Burning Tools

Colwood Electronics, 715 Westwood Ave., Long Branch, N.J. 07740. (The Detailer.)
Hot Tools, Inc., P.O. Box 615, Marblehead, Mass. 01945.

Tool Sharpening

Frank Mittermeier, 3577 E. Tremont St., Bronx, N.Y. 10465. (Catalog.)
Craftsman Illustrated Sharpening Manual. Sears, Roebuck and Co. Mail Order Catalog No. 9K2924.

Carving Woods

Albert Constantine and Sons, 2050 Eastchester, Bronx, N.Y. 10461.
Beauty-Wood Industries, Apt. 2, 339 Lakeshore Rd. East, Mississauga, Ontario, Canada.
Craft Cove, 2315 W. Glen at Route 150, Peoria, Ill. 61611.
Gallup Hardwoods, 16 Cypress Ave., Sherwood Park, Alberta, Canada T8A 1J4
James E. Rowley, Lazy R, East Brooksfield, Vt. 05036.
James L. Wallis, 821 Columbia Ave., Palmyra, N.J. 08065.
Kent Courtney, Woodsman, 1413 Texas Ave., Alexandria, La. 71301.
Paxton Beautiful Woods, 2825 Hemphill, Fort Worth, Texas 76110.
Penberthy Lumber Co., 5800 S. Boyle Ave., Los Angeles, Calif. 90058.
Reel Lumber, 454 S. Anaheim Blvd., Anaheim, Calif. 92805.
Robert M. Albrecht, 18701 Parthenia St., Northridge, Calif. 91324.
The House of Hardwood, 532 W. Royalton Rd., Grafton, Ohio 44044.
Wood Carvers Supply Co., 3056 Excelsior Blvd., Minneapolis, Minn. 55416.
Wood-Crafter's Supply Center, 1715 N. Sherman Drive, Indianapolis, Ind. 46218.
Woodcraft Supply Co., 313 Montvale Ave., Woburn, Mass. 01801.
Trail o' Shavings Carving Shop, Floodwood, Minn. 55736.

Index

Boldface page numbers indicate color photographs of carvings or live birds.